The Internationalization of U.S. Markets

THE INTERNATIONALIZATION OF U.S. MARKETS

Edited by
David B. Audretsch and Michael P. Claudon

NEW YORK UNIVERSITY PRESS
New York and London

Library of Congress Cataloging-in-Publication Data

The Internationalization of U.S. markets / edited by David B. Audretsch and Michael P. Claudon
p. cm.
"Selection of the papers presented at the Tenth Annual Middlebury College Conference on Economic Issues, which took place April 7-9, 1988"—Foreword.
Includes bibliographies and index.
ISBN 0-8147-0594-4
1. United States—Foreign economic relations. 2. Investments, Foreign—United States. 3. United States—Commercial policy. 4. United States—Commerce—Japan. 5. Japan—Commerce—United States. I. Audretsch, David B. II. Claudon, Michael P. III. Middlebury College Conference on Economic Issues (10th : 1988) IV. Title: The Internationalization of United States markets.
HF1455.I65 1989
337.73—dc20 89-3435
CIP

New York University Press books are printed on acid-free paper, and their binding materials are chosen for strength and durability.

CONTENTS

ACKNOWLEDGMENTS

As recent events have demonstrated, alliances involving partners on both sides of the Atlantic are often not easy to implement. Our case proved to be no exception. Without the willingness of key people to go beyond the usual call of duty, neither the conference nor this resulting volume would have been possible. We are particularly grateful to Mrs. Sheila Cassin, who coordinated the conference arrangements. While this is never a simple task, with one organizer in Berlin and the other frequently in some distant city negotiating the establishment of an international economics institute, an unusual burden fell on Mrs. Cassin.

A similar challenge was presented to production editor Colleen Duncan, who with the assistance of Elizabeth Leeds prepared the manuscript for publication. Their careful attention to detail and considerable patience throughout several drafts of the volume is greatly appreciated.

Of course, none of this would have been possible without generous financial support from the Geonomics Institute and its founder, Robert A. Jones, to whom we are very grateful.

David B. Audretsch and Michael P. Claudon

FOREWORD

This volume contains a selection of the papers presented at the Tenth Annual Middlebury College Conference on Economic Issues, which took place April 7-9, 1988. Held under the auspices of the Geonomics Institute, the conference assembled leading scholars to discuss and present research on the recent phenomenon of the internationalization of U.S. markets. All of the papers presented at the conference were invited by the organizers. Following the presentation of each paper was a critique by a discussant and an open debate involving all participants, which frequently proved to be lively and stimulating.

In this foreword I am not going to discuss the internationalization of markets for either goods or financial assets. That task is left to the others in this volume. Rather, I propose to deal with highly specialized markets, in a way largely outside the traditional economic analysis of international trade and imperfect competition. Some of the ideas may possibly stimulate thought in the traditional areas. I propose to deal with the markets for food, language, sport, human capital embodied in intellectuals, and common labor. In addition, I will suggest what the recent trends imply for the accepted theory of the multinational corporation.

Let me open with the proposition that initially, before communication and demonstration effect, regions and countries are autarkic, letting their tastes conform to their resource endowments.

This foreword is a lightly edited version of the opening remarks delivered at the Middlebury Conference on Economic Issues, April 7, 1988. No effort has been made to conceal the informality of the oral presentation.

Waverly Root has expressed it that France is divided into three parts: those that cook with butter (Normandy and its neighboring departments), those with olive oil in Provence, and those in the eastern regions that use goose and other kinds of fat.

Another example is veal. Italy lacks grazing land and thus cannot raise beef cattle. To save the milk, young bullocks are slaughtered early for veal. It is a classic problem in capital theory, comparable to the question given—or at least that used to be given—to graduate students on their generals: When do you chop down the tree? When do you slaughter the calf? Francesco Forte once told me that the higher the regional rate of interest the whiter the veal. But while the Italian taste for veal started in autarky, it grew into a case of international trade based on differences in tastes. Today, or at least the last time I discussed the question in Italy, veal calves were imported into Italy from Argentina by airplane.

Start with different tastes developed in autarky. In due course, the demonstration effect has brought about such a homogenization of tastes that virtually every major city is populated with restaurants serving native, French, German, Greek, Chinese, Japanese, Polynesian, and Indian cooking. Mexican food is spicy because spices were needed to preserve meat in a hot climate without refrigeration. It spread in time across the border as Tex-Mex cuisine, and is probably now above the Arctic Circle. But Paris does not go in for exotic cooking the way Tokyo does, especially for French. Paris will have restaurants specializing in different regions, along with a few Russian places, but the French are different, much more parochial.

Mostly I have been discussing the internationalization of the U.S. market in food. It works the other way, too, as McDonald's, Burger King, Pizza Hut, and the like, go abroad. I hope I will be forgiven if I do not pursue this stressful subject. And the same goes for hotel-keeping, where Hiltons, Sheratons, and Intercontinentals spread around the world—except Paris to any great extent—to the detriment of hostelries with character, such as Browns or Dukes of London.

Let me move from the inner man to the market for language. Language, like money, is a medium of exchange, with great economies of scale internationally. There is a certain degree of specialization. In ecclesiastical matters in Christendom, for a long time it was Latin that was the *lingua franca*. Latin was also used in biology to permit cross-cultural discussion of genera and species. French was used for diplomacy and Dutch in the sixteenth and seventeenth centuries for business, along with the rixdollar, which superseded the Venetian ducat. English became the universal language in the nineteenth century, and American in the twentieth century. To those who believe in local culture, local initiative, and "small is beautiful," it is distressing to see Scandinavian, Swiss, Italian, German, and, to a still limited extent, French scientific journals appearing more and more in American. This is a case wherein the U.S. market was not internationalized, but the foreign market Americanized.

As American economic leadership and the dollar weaken, will there be a change in the world's international medium of exchange for words? There is an old joke (from the 1950s, I think) that when the optimists in this country were learning Russian, the pessimists were learning Chinese. I am impressed that David McClain is taking a couple of years off to learn Japanese. I suspect, however, that the language is too difficult to learn by enough people to serve adequately in intermediating communication.

The older of you will forgive me, I hope, if I turn to the younger to repeat one of my witticisms of the 1960s, comparing monetary reform with various proposals for dealing with international markets for language: Mundell-Kemp-type proposals for returning to the gold standard are the equivalent of attempting to restore Latin as the international medium of exchange; advocates of freely flexible exchange rates are analogous to those who say that no one need learn foreign languages except interpreters, who shall be present for all international dealings; and the SDR (Special Drawing Right) is the equivalent of Esperanto, while the continued use of a national money such as the dollar as the vehicle currency is the same as the unfair system under which the English and the Americans have no need to learn foreign languages, yet everyone else learns English.

In the market for sport, there has been a movement for a long time for the internationalization of the U.S. market—golf from Scotland, tennis and yacht racing from England, ice skating from Holland, skiing from Norway and Switzerland, and, in some fanciful accounts, baseball from an old English game called "rounders." Today, the movement has reversed. Baseball has been exported to Japan and the Caribbean, and it is thus anachronistic to think of the "World" Series as played between two American teams. Basketball has been exported to Europe, taking hold especially in the Soviet Union and Italy. Exhibition football games have recently drawn large crowds in England. Moreover, attempts to import the sports of other countries have either failed, as in the case of the professional soccer league, or have succeeded only within narrow confines, such as the Canadian sport of lacrosse, which does well primarily in Maryland.

Sport further exhibits interesting economies of scale, most evident perhaps in tennis, where first one country and then another dominates world play for years at a time. Nothing succeeds like success; winners attract new potential winners. In my youth, Yale had marvelous swimming teams year after year because potentially great swimmers were attracted to that university due to the success of Coach Kipfuth.

In professional football and basketball, an attempt to contain economies of scale and positive feedback by a draft system gives first choices in drafting entering players to the least successful teams. As with any good market, trading started in draft choices. Something like the draft system might be developed in international trade to dampen the momentum of nothing exceeding like excess, or the economies of scale that some believe constitutes a "new" theory of international trade, though it has been around at least since John Williams in 1929. I especially oppose generalized preferences as a step in this direction, as they foster higher tariffs from which preferences can be given—as the history of Empire or Commonwealth preference demonstrated—and as in practice they have been so qualified as to constitute a mess of pottage. What I have in mind is much more a double standard: free trade for developed countries, and tariff or quantitative restrictions for infants after they have tried to understand the traps and dangers. The distinction leaves the difficult problem of whether the drinking, driving, voting, and enlisting age should be established at sixteen, eighteen, or twenty-one, the so-called graduation problem. Japan, for example, should have graduated years ago. I think it is a close question, however, whether it is appropriate to threaten Brazil with full-scale retaliation over the software issue. I am reminded of the somewhat shameful tariff episode in the "chicken war" with Europe in the 1950s, which raised the issue of whether a one- or two-year advance of one country over another should be perpetuated by free trade forever.

I promote infant-industry restrictions from childhood to some stage in adolescence, but what about geriatric tariffs? My intellectual instinct is opposite to that of Lord Kaldor or Jaroslav Vanek. I say now, "Pull the plug." My opposition to geriatric tariffs is partly inspired by a line from a Swiss sociologist, Rudolf Braun, writing on the agony of the hand-loom weavers under competition from the factory. The strong swimmers, he wrote, meaning the most skilled of the hand-loom weavers, took a longer time to drown.

The international market for intellectuals has been around for a long time. It is largely one-way, attracting citizens of foreign countries to the United States, though the employment of David Audretsch and Frederic Scherer in industrial-organization research in Berlin may be a sign that the direction of the wind is changing. Let me stick to economists, though the recent recruiting of historian stars Paul Kennedy to Yale and Geoffrey Parker to Illinois from England is a sign of the times.

It should be noted that small countries in upper-income brackets are natural exporters of intellectuals because they can produce more than they need. The best economic staff ever put together, I dare say, was that of the Economic and Financial Department of the League of Nations under Alexander Loveday of Britain in the interwar period, with Condliffe of New Zealand, Haberler of Austria, Hill of Australia, Hilgerdt and Ohlin of Sweden, Meade of England, Nurkse of Estonia, Rasminsky of Canada, and Tinbergen of the Netherlands.

Harvard has prided itself during the twentieth century on hiring the best economists in the world, and in pursuit of this policy acquired Joseph Schumpeter, Wassily Leontief, Gottfried Haberler, and most recently Amartya Sen and János Kornai. Special circumstances brought many economists to this country, including persecution under Hitler or the opportunity to study at an American university, which leads naturally to taking a position here. Some Americans have gone abroad after marrying a native of a foreign country.

The one-way nature of the pull is particularly demonstrated by the record of Canadian economists who take jobs in the United States. If the two markets were fully integrated, and since the population of the United States is eleven times that of Canada, one would expect to find one Canadian economist working in the United States for every eleven Americans, but also eleven American economists working in Canada for every one Canadian economist. The first is true, and American economics has obtained from Canada many of its luminaries, notably John Kenneth Galbraith, Harry Johnson, Ronald McKinnon, Robert Mundell, L. G. Reynolds, and Lorie Tarshis (who returned to Canada after retiring from a post in this country). The reverse has not occurred because Canadians choose not to be fully integrated with the United States, despite the free trade treaty. As Albert Breton and Harry Johnson have underlined, nationalism is a Canadian public good for which the country is willing to pay.

The movement to the United States of economists from developing countries poses somewhat different issues. There are many stars, but there is also a large body of average talent that could be useful in their own countries if they were not discouraged working there by inadequate salary, complementary factors, and/or prestige. For many, it is better to take a run-of-the-mill job in the United States than one higher in the rank order at home. The impact on world welfare is problematic. The issue is more sharply drawn when one contemplates the case of physicians from the Philippines who work in third-rate hospitals in the United States. For the first few years, while they compare their position with the counterfactual of being back home, they are content. After a time, however, the point of reference shifts and they become unhappy again as they feel trapped in what is a limited position, judged by U.S. standards.

The unanswerable question in most of these cases is whether the movement arises from the pull or the push, the demand or the supply, the chicken or the egg. In the case of Great Britain lately, however, the push seems clear. Economists, as well as historians, are emigrating to the Antipodes, to Canada, to the United States, and, in one case I know, to Germany, despite the width of the cultural gap.

The limited extent of movement of American economists abroad is insufficient to lead to much Americanization of global markets. Many are hit-and-run missions, such as that undertaken by Edwin Kemmerer and H. P. Willis in the early 1920s, the teams of such groups as the Harvard Development Advisory Service, and members of staffs on teams from the IMF or the IBRD. To the extent that this makes an impact, it is internationalization of global intellectual markets, not Americanization.

The movement of common labor is too vast a topic to address in a brief foreword, but I will make one point: Such labor migrating to a country starts off as a noncompeting group, but over time is likely to become integrated into the wider labor market and compete. This does not always happen. The Italian Lombards who served as London bankers in the late Middle Ages went back to Italy to marry and again later to die. Vast numbers of the Greeks and Italians who came to this country at the end of the last century and the first years of this century stayed twenty-five years or so, but eventually returned to the old country to start a business with their stake in dollars or to retire. Some found it hard to reintegrate back home—they would stand around the village square in their blue serge suits and were called "Americanos."

Whether or not they integrate after time, shifting the reference group with which they compare themselves from those left behind to those with whom they now worked—and how rapidly (if integrated) this occurs—depends on many variables: laws regarding citizenship; size of the group of fellow immigrants and its cohesion; residential agglomeration; level of education; color; and difficulty of learning the language, a problem especially for Turks in Germany and for Japanese in English-speaking countries, but relatively easy for natives of countries with complex languages, such as Russian, Greek, or Hebrew (though accents may persist). But that integration is ultimately complete, possibly apart from race and gender, is hard to deny as one contemplates two major states with governors one generation down from immigrants.

I will wind up this foreword by addressing a theoretical question in the field of the multinational corporation, a field combining international economics and industrial organization. The massive movement of U.S. direct investment abroad leading to the Americanization of global markets has been followed by a surge of foreign investment in this country, which contributes to the internationalization of U.S. markets. But there is something of a reverse trend coming into evidence. It is partly cyclical: oil companies, for example, are less interested in owning their tankers when the tanker market is depressed. Vertical integration is to a considerable extent defensive, as Jürg Niehans made clear in a seminar paper in a book edited by Tamir Agmon and me, *Multinationals from Small Countries* (1977). Vertical integration takes place downstream if there is fear one might be cut off from markets—BP buying Standard Oil of Ohio when it discovered oil on the North Slope of Alaska, for example—and upstream when there is fear of being cut off from inputs, including transportation. In boom, the incentive to integrate in both directions picks up. In recession, the incentive to integrate upstream weakens. Part of the sale of their tankers by oil companies, and readiness to let go of mines, comes from the easing of inflation.

I have a greater interest in the theory we all bought about the internalization of external economies, another theory that goes way back, perhaps to the Rosenstein-Rodan *Economic Journal* article of June-September 1943. The multinational corporation on this showing was a bundle of synergy, one hand washing the other, coordinate planning that improved on atomistic competitive markets. The notions are explicit in Stephen Hymer's dissertation and are asserted somewhat stridently by later writers. But the wave of takeovers leading to the selling off of various constituent parts of multinational corporations poses a question as to how wide and deep this motive for foreign direct investment has been. Many companies seem to be worth more dead than alive, butchered rather than in live weight. I participated in a panel of the Academy of International Business in Chicago in November 1987 and developed this theme to some extent. It was not welcomed. The scrappy data I collected were from the press of September 1987, but showed company after company taking over others, both in hostile and friendly fashion, and then selling off bits and pieces—shoulders, hams, sides, steaks, whatever. These companies proved to be decomposable matrices rather than tightly woven integers.

Schlumberger sold Fairchild Semiconductor of California. The Belzbergs of Canada sold off parts of Scovill they had bought in February 1985 for $540 million for $714 million, as reported September 1, all the time retaining the fastener plant, some of which it sold to Britain and some to a French company. When the Beatrice Company, which produced everything from lingerie and luggage to chow mein, ketchup, and orange juice, broke up, some of its Australian subsidiaries were sold to Cadbury-Schweppes of Britain. Sarah Lee Corporation sold off its Electrolux division in one direction and its consumer products division to Akzo N.V. in the Netherlands. I.C.I. bought the basic chemical elements of Stauffer Chemical Company from Unilever in July, selling them to Rhône-Poulenc in September. Hercules Inc. of Delaware backed out of its joint venture with Montedison Sp. A., selling its interest to its partner. Pearson P.L.C., a media and financial services conglomerate in England that owned a grab-bag, including the *Financial Times, The Economist,* Madame Tussaud's, an amusement park, and Château Latour vineyards, was reported in the *Times* of September 28 to be worth 10 percent more in breakup value than the value of the shares when Rupert Murdoch started to acquire them. Takeovers and selling of bits and pieces seem to me to cast doubt on the generality of the internalization theory.

I hesitate in the remaining space to offer alternative explanations of the takeover-breakup pattern. The initial direct investment may have been a mistake of the follow-the-leader mania, bubble, or overtrading variety; the company may be in trouble and forced to amputate to save the rest; inflation may have raised the value of bits, especially those with real estate; there may be a cyclical aspect to investment and disinvestment in the vertical chain, as already noted; and there is a real possibility that some of the original acquisitions and subsequent reshuffling have been more concerned with simple-minded market share than with synergy.

In the papers that follow, the best scientific knowledge on the internationalization of U.S. markets is presented. The reader can expect to confront a phenomenon that challenges some of our most accepted and cherished theories in economics.

Charles P. Kindleberger

INTRODUCTION:
THE GLOBALIZATION OF AMERICAN MARKETS

One of the distinguishing features of the American economic landscape is the propensity for perceived problems and issues to emerge and enjoy the limelight, only to be replaced by a newer, more urgent issue several months or years later. That is, like its cultural equivalent, the U.S. economic scene seems to be given to trends and fads. While West Germany has had a singular economic problem over the last two decades, a chronically high rate of unemployment, and the inherent economic problem in Japan has been consistently recognized as a deficiency of natural resources, *the* economic problem in the United States evolved from unemployment in the early 1960s to poverty in the late 1960s, an energy shortage in the early 1970s, stagflation and high interest rates in the late 1970s, and unprecedented budget deficits in the early 1980s. Thus, when the issue of "international competitiveness" swept Washington in early 1987, it may have appeared to be just another economic fad on the horizon. Not only were there already eighteen reports undertaken by the U.S. government to describe international competitiveness in great detail by January 1987, but by the spring, "competitiveness was rolling off the lips of everyone in Washington."[1]

That an issue such as international competitiveness had in a remarkably short time ascended to a rank among the highest priorities in the nation's capital is not particularly unusual. As mentioned above, issues such as tax incentive policies, anti-inflation

1. "Can America Compete?" *Business Week*, April 27, 1987, pp. 41-3.

programs, and anti-poverty campaigns, among numerous others, had all enjoyed their shining moments of prestige in the limelight of American attention. What perhaps distinguishes the issue of international competitiveness from its predecessors is both the chronic nature of the problem and the consequences, which will surely bring about a restructuring of the U.S. economy.

At the heart of the battle for global markets are the manufacturing industries. While the annual percentage increase in real GNP was nearly 3.5 percent between 1950 and 1960, and nearly 4 percent between 1960 and 1970, it decreased considerably to about 2.8 percent between 1970 and 1980, and even further to around 2.5 percent between 1980 and 1986. What growth has been accomplished recently has mostly emanated from the service sector and not from the manufacturing sector. In fact, employment in the American manufacturing sector fell from 40 percent of the total workforce in 1959 to 27.7 percent of the workforce in 1984. At the same time, the share of workers in the service sector rose from 40 percent in 1959 to 72.3 percent in 1984. Subsequently, Lester Thurow (1985) observed: "Today it's very hard to find an industrial corporation in America that isn't in really serious trouble basically because of trade problems . . . . The systematic erosion of our competitiveness comes from having lower rates of growth of manufacturing productivity year after year, as compared with the rest of the world."

The advent of foreign competition in U.S. manufacturing markets is the result of the interaction of at least two factors: the gradual recovery from World War II by Western Europe and Japan, and the evolution of U.S. manufacturing industries toward the mature and declining stages of the product life cycle. Its postwar U.S. dominance is not surprising, because the United States emerged as the only nation that was economically stronger after the war than preceding it, and given the war's devastation of both allies and former enemies. Because both Japan and West Germany achieved their economic miracles through assimilating U.S. technology, American preeminence was rarely questioned. The capital intensity characterizing mass production, combined with the relative capital abundance in the United States, seemed to ensure continued American dominance. Even as the Marshall Plan and other U.S. assistance contributed to the restoration of Western Europe and Japan, only 8 percent of American manufacturing was exposed to foreign competition in the early 1960s. But, as Joseph S. Nye (1983) argues, growth of European and Japanese industry relative to the United States was inevitable, because these countries started from a base of virtually zero. Thus, U.S. industrial predominance could only be a temporary phenomenon, as the rest of the developed world gradually recovered.

Table I-1 shows that both exports and imports have played an increasing role during the postwar period. As a percentage of GNP, exports (including goods and services) rose from 6 percent in 1948 to more than 10 percent by 1986. Similarly, the import share rose from slightly over 4 percent in 1948 to around 14 percent in 1986. In this sense, Nye's prediction is apparently coming true: the United States, with the passage of time, is more closely resembling the countries of Western Europe and Japan in being both vulnerable to imports and export dependent. Table I-1 also indicates why international competitiveness has become such an important issue in the United States in the late 1980s. After peaking at slightly over 12 percent in 1980, the export share has subsequently continued to decline, while imports, as a percentage of GNP, have continued to grow at a rapid rate, resulting in unprecedented trade deficits.

While U.S. foreign direct investment has been a noteworthy postwar phenomenon, the presence of foreign assets in the United States has emerged in the 1980s as one of the most controversial political issues. U.S. assets held abroad, as a percentage of GNP, have remained relatively constant since 1981, but the ratio of foreign assets in the United States to GNP has increased substantially during recent years. As a result of the relatively high value of the Japanese yen, and in anticipation of a U.S. wave of protectionism, a number of Japanese companies purchased American firms at the end of 1987 and in early 1988. For example, in March 1988, the Bridgestone Corporation purchased Firestone for $2.6 billion, Sony bought CBS Records for $2 billion, and Aoki Corporation purchased Westin Hotels for $1.5 billion.[2]

The United States has responded in part to exposure of its markets to foreign competition with increased protectionist activity. The Senate and House of Representatives established a precedent by enshrining the notion of "fair" trade rather than free trade as the overriding goal of government policy in the trade legislation passed in April 1988. It is now easier for domestic industries to apply for and receive trade protection. For example, the President would be virtually bound to adhere to the determination and recommendation of the U.S. International Trade Commission, which serves as a government adjudicator in hearing complaints from industries allegedly injured by foreign competition.

2. "Japanese Shop for U.S. Companies," *International Herald Tribune*, April 29, 1988, p. 11.

Considering the performance of firms in international trade as responding to the nature of competition represents a marked contrast to the more traditional explanation of trade flows posited by the Heckscher-Ohlin model. The Heckscher-Ohlin theory suggests that international trade is determined by the relative abundance and scarcity of factor endowments. According to the theory, the proportion of productive factors determines the trade structure. A country having an abundance of physical capital relative to labor will tend toward export of capital-intensive goods; labor abundance relative to physical capital leads to the export of labor-intensive goods. While the focus of the model was originally on capital and labor inputs (Deardorff 1984), it was later expanded to include human capital, skilled labor (Keesing 1966; Lowinger 1971), and technology (Gruber, Mehta, and Vernon 1967; Vernon 1966) as decisive factors. Virtually all of the empirical research has been limited to testing the static predictions of the Heckscher-Ohlin model (Baldwin 1971 and 1979; Stern 1976). Not only have most of the empirical studies involved only one point in time, but they have generally not incorporated the nature of competition into the analysis.

The studies testing the Heckscher-Ohlin theory implicitly assume that either perfect competition prevails in every market or that the degree of competition is not relevant in determining trade flows. Responding to this questionable assumption, several empirical studies have been attempted to identify the determinants of imports or import share through including elements of market structure, most notably market concentration, into a more traditional factor endowment model (Hufbauer 1970; Baumann 1976; Pugel 1978; White 1974; Caves et al. 1980).

The development of the international oligopoly models, which consider the market shares of domestic and foreign firms in the world market as a Cournot-equilibrium outcome of an international oligopoly game, has led to an emphasis on the market structure and organization of industry as decisive determinants of trade (Brander 1981; Lyons 1981; Brander and Krugman 1983; Helpman and Krugman 1985, chap. 5). Research by Krugman (1979), Helpman (1981), Lancaster (1980), and Ethier (1982) has shown that the presence of scale economies, imperfect competition, and product differentiation in countries with identical endowments of capital and labor is actually conducive to intra-industry trade. Even with the development of these international oligopoly models, the few empirical analyses have been limited to static cross-section models that examine competition as an equilibrium outcome (Yamawaki

Table I-1. U.S. Export Share, Import Share, and International Investment, 1948-1986
(In Percentages)

	Exports/ GNP	Imports/ GNP	U.S. Assets Abroad/GNP	Foreign Assets in U.S./GNP
1948	6.0	4.3	-	-
1955	5.1	5.1	-	-
1960	5.9	6.1	-	-
1965	6.3	6.5	-	-
1970	7.4	8.6	-	-
1975	9.6	8.9	-	-
1980	12.2	10.4	0.16	0.18
1981	12.1	10.6	0.24	0.19
1982	11.4	10.6	0.26	0.22
1983	10.6	11.2	0.26	0.23
1984	10.6	13.0	0.24	0.24
1985	10.1	13.1	0.23	0.27
1986	10.1	14.2	-	-

a. Both the export and import shares are in real terms, while the U.S. Assets Abroad/GNP and Foreign Assets in U.S./GNP are based on nominal measures in the numerator and denominator. The export and import figures include both goods and services.

Source: U.S. Department of Commerce, Bureau of Economic Analysis.

and Audretsch 1988; Audretsch and Yamawaki 1988). In reviewing the international oligopoly literature, Markusen (1986) argues that factor endowments are most decisive in determining what he terms "North-South" trade flows and least important in influencing "East-West" trade.

The internationalization of U.S. markets is examined in the papers that follow. The first section of the book offers alternatives to the Heckscher-Ohlin theory. In particular, Stephen P. Magee proposes a novel theory describing international trade in manufactured goods. His proposed model, the competence theory of comparative advantage, suggests that competent labor produces exports and less competent labor produces import-competing products. L. Fernando Ruiz-Mier and Albert N. Link provide a model of strategic trade in imperfectly competitive markets and find that cooperative R&D agreements could, under certain conditions, improve the strategic position of domestic firms relative to their foreign counterparts. Harry P. Bowen and Leo Sveikauskas provide a detailed study of inter-industry trade for thirty-five countries, and find that the model correctly reveals factor abundance in about three-quarters of the cases.

An empirical analysis of trade flows and trade policy, with special emphasis on bilateral trade relationships, is provided in the second section of the book. While Keith E. Maskus, Deborah Battles, and Michael H. Moffett focus on bilateral trade between the United States and Japan, the United States and Korea, and Korea and Japan, and emphasize the role that different types of labor categories play, David B. Audretsch and Hideki Yamawaki examine the significance of R&D rivalry in determining U.S.-Japanese bilateral trade patterns. Alan V. Deardorff and Robert M. Stern use the Michigan Model of World Production and Trade to consider alternative scenarios for trade liberalization, especially those that are likely to emerge in the eighth GATT (Uruguay) round of multilateral trade negotiations.

The final section of this volume examines foreign direct investment in the United States. While a voluminous literature exists for U.S. foreign direct investment overseas, the opposite case is a much more recent phenomenon, and therefore researchers are only just beginning to study it with scientific scrutiny. Richard E. Caves examines the short-run sensitivity of U.S. foreign investment to exchange-rate fluctuations and finds that U.S. foreign investment increasingly consists of buying up established businesses and responded to opportunities to arbitrage between the markets for such assets abroad and in the U.S. Rachel McCulloch analyzes Japanese investment in the U.S. and finds little support for the alarmist view that Japan is "buying up" America. Not only does she find that U.S. foreign investment does not typically consist of a direct investment, she writes that Japan ranks third in foreign investment in the United States, behind the United Kingdom and the Netherlands.

While each of the ensuing papers offers a unique perspective on the internationalization of U.S. markets, an important conclusion emerges from the studies considered together. The relationship between the U.S. and its trading partners has clearly evolved from the model of American dominance in the 1950s and 1960s to one more closely resembling parity among the developed nations. Thus, more than ever, firm strategies and government policies play an important role in determining international competitiveness.

David B. Audretsch and Michael P. Claudon

REFERENCES

Audretsch, David B., and Hideki Yamawaki. 1988. "R&D, Industrial Policy, and U.S.-Japanese Trade." *Review of Economics and Statistics* 70 (August): 438-47.

Baldwin, Robert E. 1971. "The Determinants of the Commodity Structure of U.S. Trade." *American Economic Review* 61 (March): 126-46.

——. 1979. "Determinants of Trade and Foreign Investment: Further Evidence." *Review of Economics and Statistics* 61 (February): 40-8.

Baumann, Harry G. 1976. "Structural Characteristics of Canada's Pattern of Trade." *Canadian Journal of Economics* 9 (August): 498-524.

Brander, James A., and Paul R. Krugman. 1983. "A 'Reciprocal Dumping' Model of International Trade." *Journal of International Economics* 15 (November): 313-21.

Caves, Richard E., Michael E. Porter, and A. Michael Spence, with John T. Scott. 1980. *Competition in the Open Economy.* Cambridge: Harvard University Press.

Deardorff, Alan V. 1984. "Testing Trade Theories and Predicting Trade Flows." 1984. *Handbook of International Economics,* vol. 1. Ed. Ronald Jones and Peter B. Kenen. Amsterdam: North-Holland.

Ethier, Wilfred. 1982. "National and International Returns to Scale in the Modern Theory of International Trade." *American Economic Review* 72 (June): 389-405.

Gruber, W. H., D. Mehta, and Raymond Vernon. 1967. "The R&D Factor in International Trade and International Investment of the United States." *Journal of Political Economy* 75 (February): 20-37.

Helpman, Elhanan. 1981. "International Trade in the Presence of Product Differentiation, Economies of Scale, and Monopolistic Competition." *Journal of International Economics* 11 (August): 305-40.

Helpman, Elhanan, and Paul R. Krugman. 1985. *Market Structure and Foreign Trade: Increasing Returns, Imperfect Competition, and the International Economy.* Cambridge: MIT Press.

Hufbauer, Gary C. 1970. "The Impact of National Characteristics and Technology on the Commodity Composition of Trade in Manufactured Goods." *The Technology Factor in International Trade.* Ed. Raymond Vernon. Universities National Bureau Conference Series, No. 22. New York: Columbia University Press.

Keesing, Donald B. 1966. "Labor Skills and Comparative Advantage." *American Economic Review* 56 (May): 249-58.

Krugman, Paul R. 1979. "Increasing Returns, Monopolistic Competition, and International Trade." *Journal of International Economics* 9 (November): 469-79.

Lancaster, Kelvin. 1980. "Intra-Industry Trade Under Perfect Monopolistic Competition." *Journal of International Economics* 9 (May): 151-75.

Lowinger, T. C. 1971. "The Neo-Factor Proportions Theory of International Trade: An Empirical Investigation." *American Economic Review* 61 (September): 675-81.

Lyons, Bruce. 1981. "Industrial Behavior, the Technology of Demand, and the Pattern of International Trade Between Identical Countries." *Recherches Economique de Louvain* 47 (September): 243-58.

Markusen, James R. 1986. "Explaining the Volume of Trade: An Eclectic Approach." *American Economic Review* 76 (December): 1002-11.

Nye, Joseph S. 1983. "The Multinational Corporation in the 1980s." *The Multinational Corporation in the 1980s.* Ed. Charles P. Kindleberger and David B. Audretsch. Cambridge: MIT Press.

Pugel, Thomas. 1978. *International Market Linkages and U.S. Manufacturing: Prices, Profits, and Patterns.* Cambridge, MA: Ballinger.

Stern, Robert M. 1976. "Testing Trade Theories." *International Trade and Finance: Frontiers of Research.* Ed. Peter B. Kenen. New York: Cambridge University Press, 3-50.

Thurow, Lester C. 1985. "Healing with a Thousand Bandages." *Challenge* 28 (November/December): 22-31.

Vernon, Raymond. 1966. "International Investment and International Trade in the Product Life Cycle." *Quarterly Journal of Economics* 80 (May): 190-207.

White, Larry. 1974. "Industrial Organization and International Trade: Some Theoretical Considerations." *American Economic Review* 64: 1013-20.

Yamawaki, Hideki, and David B. Audretsch. 1988. "Import Share Under International Oligopoly with Differentiated Products: Japanese Imports in U.S. Manufacturing." *Review of Economics and Statistics* 70 (November): 569-79.

I ALTERNATIVES TO THE HECKSCHER-OHLIN THEORY

The Heckscher-Ohlin model is one of the most powerful theories in economics. It has been, and remains, the foundation for understanding international trade flows. The importance of the theory of comparative advantage has been matched by serious criticisms, beginning with the Leontief Paradox, which pointed out that, in fact, the actual patterns of U.S. trade did not correspond to the predictions of the theory. The papers in this section continue in this tradition of challenging the contemporary interpretation of the laws of comparative advantage.

In the first paper, Stephen P. Magee argues that the traditional theory of comparative advantage inappropriately treats all factors of production equally. Instead, he introduces the competence theory, which ignores all input factors except for human capital. Thus, he emphasizes the competence of individuals rather than production competence. While the Heckscher-Ohlin model predicts that a nation will export goods containing its abundant factor, Magee's theory of competence states that a nation will produce import-competing goods containing less-skilled labor and export products containing skilled labor.

L. Fernando Ruiz-Mier and Albert N. Link suggest that strategic trade policy can improve national welfare, at least under certain conditions. In particular, they examine whether the relaxation of government antitrust intervention can promote the strategic position of domestic firms. This is an especially relevant question, because there was substantially less enforcement of the antitrust laws under the Reagan administration. Among other things, cooperative research joint ventures were legalized by the National Cooperative Research Act of 1984 during President Reagan's tenure. Based on a game-theoretic model, Ruiz-Mier and Link conclude that, under certain conditions, joint R&D agreements can promote the international competitiveness of domestic firms. Similarly, government subsidies of R&D can improve the strategic position of domestic firms vis-à-vis foreign competitors. Thus, while Magee emphasizes the role of skilled labor in international competition, Ruiz-Mier and Link focus on R&D policies, both by firms and government.

In the last paper in this section, Harry P. Bowen and Leo Sveikauskas examine the empirical methods that have traditionally been used to test the theory of comparative advantage. By comparing the patterns of factor abundance inferred from a cross-section repression model at the disaggregated industry level with the factor abundance as suggested by net trade in factor services, Bowen and Sveikauskas conclude that both approaches generally reveal similar results. However, the consistency in results tends to be stronger for certain input factors, such as capital and land, than for other factors, such as measures of the component of skilled labor. Since Magee argues that skilled labor is in fact the only decisive factor determining international competitiveness, Bowen and Sveikauskas' results may shed some doubt on many of the accepted inferences about factor abundance.

1 THE COMPETENCE THEORY OF COMPARATIVE ADVANTAGE

Stephen P. Magee

The theory of comparative advantage is one of the oldest propositions in economics. It states that countries export what they do best and import what they do worst. Recently, Bowen, Leamer, and Sveikauskas (1988) have shown that the Leontief Paradox appears to hold across a wide range of countries and factors. That is, the Heckscher-Ohlin-Samuelson theory of comparative advantage is not a good predictor of trade patterns. An alternative theory describing international trade in manufactured goods is proposed here. The competence theory of comparative advantage in this paper suggests that competent labor produces exports and less competent labor produces import-competing products. More precisely, countries export manufactured goods produced by skilled labor and produce import-competing manufactured goods produced by unskilled labor. Countries export their high-wage labor and protect their low-wage labor from imports. Empirical evidence for the theory is provided.

Results from endogenous tariff theory reported in Magee, Brock, and Young (1989) indicate the relationship between country factor endowments and national tariff rates. Since tariffs protect the import-competing factor, I develop here the principle of "revealed comparative advantage" to infer the competence theory of comparative advantage from statistical relationships between national tariff rates and country factor endowments.

The theory is simple: it ignores all factors of production except varying skills of labor. Richer models are possible incorporating multiple factors. For a discussion of these extended Heckscher-Ohlin models, see Jones and Neary (1984).

The competence theory is based on four assumptions:

1. Most theories of comparative advantage focus on production competence or country factor endowment competence rather than the competence of individuals. For example, the Ricardian theory is based on production competence: if output per man of autos is higher in Japan than in the United States (other output ratios being identical), then Japan will export automobiles. The Heckscher-Ohlin-Samuelson theory is based on country competence: the greater the capital endowment of Japan, the more likely it will export capital-intensive goods such as automobiles. The competence theory is based more on the skills of individuals than on country characteristics.
2. This paper is about manufactured goods only and draws on the insights for trade patterns from Vernon's product cycle (1966, 1979).
3. Skills are relative while competence is absolute. Relative skills determine comparative advantage while absolute competence determines wages. Skilled labor in high-income countries is more competent than skilled labor in lower-income countries because of the positive externalities of education and culture. But, as in the original theory of comparative advantage, workers will specialize in exportables or import-competing production based on their relative advantage. In the long run, wages will be determined on world markets by absolute competence.
4. We generally think of imports and domestic production of import-competing goods as if they were the same. Import-competing production facing competition from higher-income countries requires highly skilled domestic workers; exports require skilled labor; and import-competing production facing goods from lower-income countries requires unskilled workers. Thus, import-competing production requires both more skill and less skill than exports. However, sophisticated imported manufactured goods have fewer domestically produced counterparts than older manufactured imports because of rapid turnover in new and sophisticated products and slow changes in older products. Thus, countries typically export goods that are more skilled-labor intensive than import-competing production.

The competence theory emphasizes asymmetries and hierarchical relationships. Every country exports goods that are more skilled-labor intensive than import-competing production; advanced countries export goods to lower-income countries that the latter are incapable of producing; skilled labor in the United States earns more in long-run equilibrium than skilled labor in lower-income countries; advanced countries have permanently higher income than developing countries; wages in import-competing production will be permanently lower than in export production; and all these results occur despite factor-price equalization holding within competence categories. In addition, skilled labor adapts more rapidly than unskilled labor.

THE HIERARCHY OF LABOR, PRODUCTION, AND COUNTRIES

The theory assumes a hierarchy of three labor skills in every country: (1) highly skilled (HS), (2) skilled (SK), and (3) unskilled (US). Each category is more skilled than lower categories and earns more than lower categories. In equilibrium, no class of labor will migrate to a higher skill category because the costs of acquiring the higher skill will exceed the perceived benefits.

To simplify, assume that each type of labor specializes in the production of the following goods and services:

Highly Skilled	Redistributive Activity and New Importables	(R)
Skilled	Exportables	(X)
Unskilled	Older Import-Competing Goods	(M)

The most competent and the least competent in each country are engaged in services, while labor in the middle engages in international trade. Redistributive activity includes politics, legal activity, tax evasion, and other white-collar activities aimed at transferring wealth. It also includes industries that have high returns because of past political activity—for example, artificial scarcity, such as doctors in the United States. New importables include new products, typically from higher-income countries. Exportables include all managerial labor and engineers, among other groups, and foreign direct investment activities. There is a fourth (lower) category (not shown) of simple services, which includes manual labor and menial jobs in the nontraded goods sector.

The products exported by each country are endogenous. Skilled labor in each country decides what it can make, what it can sell, and where it can sell it (this aspect follows the work of Helpman and Krugman [1985] on the imperfect competition theory of international trade). In effect, trade is simply a veil through which labor competes across countries. There are three types of countries, arranged by levels of development: developed countries (DCs), newly industrializing countries (NICs), and less-developed countries (LDCs).

Jones and Neary (1984) argue that modern trade theory rests on four "core" propositions: Heckscher-Ohlin-Samuelson; factor-price equalization; Stolper-Samuelson; and Rybczynski. We now consider each of these and derive the parallels for the competence theory.

THE COMPETENCE THEORY OF TRADE

The Heckscher-Ohlin-Samuelson theory states that countries export products containing the country's abundant factor. *The competence theory states that countries export goods containing skilled labor and produce import-competing goods typically containing less-skilled labor.* Because of the hierarchical nature of the theory, there is the following asymmetry: because skilled labor can change its products rapidly while unskilled labor cannot, import-competing production is typically in older products; hence, import-competing production usually competes with goods from lower-income countries, while exports are sent both to higher- and lower-income countries.

Starting from autarky, the exports of a country compete less directly with production in lower-income countries (because export labor is more "competent" in higher-income countries) than with production in higher-income countries (because the latter is higher priced). As a pedagogical device, think of exportables as younger products and import-competing products as older ones. Thus, exports penetrate lower-income countries because of their superior quality (they are unique) and higher-income countries because of their lower price. In short, *the export strategy is to compete down based on quality and up based on price.*

Trade and its relation to labor can be divided into three groups: (1) imports from higher-income countries are the most highly skilled and are not produced locally, (2) exports utilize the next most skilled labor, and (3) import-competing production faces imports from lower-income countries and uses even less skilled labor.

Following Vernon (1966, 1979), there is a continuing evolution of a country's imports from higher-income countries into more sophisticated products. As a given imported product ages, it is replaced with domestic production in the form of direct foreign investment, still controlled by foreigners. This may utilize highly skilled labor. However, once imports of the good cease, the good is nontraded and is no longer counted as import-competing. Older industries that compete with imports from lower-income countries live longer, pay lower wages, and have more permanent representation in import-competing statistics. For closure of the model, obviously the theory could not apply to the very lowest-income countries. For them, import-competing production is more skilled-labor intensive than exportables.

The gains from trade for skilled labor are: (1) skilled labor can create new products that unskilled labor cannot, and (2) skilled labor looks at the returns it could earn from competing locally with less-skilled labor and then looks at the much larger pool of less-skilled labor it can prey upon on world markets. The gains to skilled labor are: (1) higher returns from producing goods not made in lower-income countries, and (2) in underpricing goods made in higher-income countries.

FACTOR-PRICE EQUALIZATION

The competence theory suggests that labor competes with higher-status labor in lower-income countries and lower-status labor in higher-income countries. *International competition will bring about equalization of wages for equal levels of competence.* Countries with greater talent will have higher average wages than those with less talent.

Competence definitions of skills are all relative to talent within a country. But skilled labor in a DC is more talented than skilled labor in an NIC. Thus, all labor on any row of Table 1-1 is assumed to be of equal "competence." For row 3, skilled labor (SK) in an NIC has the same talent as highly skilled labor (HS) in an LDC or unskilled labor (US) in a DC. In autarky, wages on any row in the table are highest in the most developed countries (DCs) and lowest in the least (LDCs). In the long run, and in the absence of new product development by skilled workers, unskilled workers in the DCs will earn the same as skilled workers in the NICs, and both will earn the same as highly skilled workers in the LDCs.

One might understand why US wages in the DCs for US would be driven to equality with SK wages in the NICs because of international trade. I argue that these two groups ultimately earn the same wages as skilled labor (politicians) in the LDCs, which also equals skilled labor competing with high-tech LDC importables. Regarding equality of LDC politicians' wages with those of high-tech LDC engineers, the argument is that the biggest barrier to skilled labor's penetration of lesser-developed country markets is the political system. The definition of a political equilibrium is that the marginal value of forces for and against change is balanced. Thus, in equilibrium, the value of the marginal-skilled worker hired in an NIC to penetrate an LDC market will just equal the value of the marginal-skilled politician. There is anecdotal support for this, because foreign direct investment by multinationals generally occurs at wages above those of skilled workers in local export industries. Also, local politicians become either direct or indirect employees of foreign multinationals as part of the entry process, which contributes to the arbitrage process.

THE STOLPER-SAMUELSON THEOREM

The Stolper-Samuelson theorem—revealed comparative advantage using country factor endowment ratios—states that trade restrictions make the scarce factor better off and the abundant factor worse off. Consider the standard neoclassical model in which there were two factors of production: skilled labor and unskilled labor. According to Stolper-Samuelson, unskilled labor is the scarce factor in the advanced countries and would favor trade restrictions there, while skilled labor is the scarce factor in developing countries and would favor trade restrictions there.

I propose here to infer patterns of comparative advantage from patterns of protection. Caves (1976) and Baldwin (1976) showed the empirical origins, while Brock and Magee (1978) provided the first theoretical model of endogenous tariffs. Special-interest politics was incorporated into a full general equilibrium model of endogenous tariffs by Young and Magee (1986). The method of revealed comparative advantage employed here comes from the endowment theory of tariffs developed by Magee, Brock, and Young (1989).

The Stolper-Samuelson theorem in general economic-political equilibrium asserts that we should observe the inverted U-shaped relationship between tariff rates and country unskilled/skilled

Table 1-1. Stylized Trade and Wage Patterns Across Countries:
Relative Skills[a] Within Countries and Five Absolute Competence Levels

Absolute Competence Level[b]	Countries: Developed (DCs)			Newly Industrializing (NICs)			Less-Developed (LDCs)	
1	**HS**	politics						
2	**SK**	exports —>		**HS**	politics & import-competing			
3	**US**	import-competing	<— exports	**SK**	exports —>		**HS**	politics & import-comp
4				**US**	import-competing	<— exports	**SK**	exports
5							**US**	nontraded

a. Relative skill levels within countries: highly skilled (**HS**), skilled (**SK**), unskilled (**US**).

b. International factor-price equalization occurs within each of the five absolute competence levels.

labor endowment ratios shown in Figure 1-1 (Magee, Brock, and Young 1989, chap. 16). The Magee, Brock, and Young inverted-U theorem is the following: Low-income countries export unskilled-labor goods and import skilled-labor goods; the greater the endowment ratio of skilled labor, the more powerful the political pressures for import protection and the higher the country average tariff rates. For the high-income countries, the reverse is true: they export skilled-labor goods, and the higher the country's skilled-labor ratio, the greater the clout of skilled labor for export promotion and the weaker the power of low-wage labor for protection.

The competence theory, in contrast, suggests a declining monotonic relationship for tariff rates against skilled-labor ratios across all countries. The reason is that import competition falls most heavily on unskilled labor. Since developed countries have the lowest relative endowment of unskilled labor, they should have the least political clout of unskilled labor for protection and the greatest political clout for export promotion.

The relationship between country factor endowment ratios and tariffs can reveal whether Heckscher-Ohlin or the competence theory better reveals underlying comparative advantage in a cross-country sample. Consider Figure 1-2. Following Leamer (1985), I use country illiteracy rates in deriving skilled/total labor endowment ratios. Notice the negative and relatively monotonic relationship between tariff rates and skilled-labor endowment ratios. Figure 1-2 suggests that protection helps unskilled labor in all countries, not just the advanced ones. This provides "revealed comparative advantage" evidence for the competence theory, that is, that import-competing production is less skilled-labor intensive than exports for almost all countries.

Reasonable scholars would object that the monotonic relationship in Figure 1-2 proves nothing because other variables are not held constant. To account for this, Magee, Brock, and Young (1988) estimated a cross-section tariff equation for the fifty-eight countries in Figure 1-2. The skilled-labor coefficient was positive for both advanced and developing countries (although it was not quite significant for the developing countries), taking into consideration the following variables: (1) the share of government revenue coming from import duties, (2) the country's capital/labor ratio, and (3) the ratio of imports to GNP.

Figure 1-1. Relationship Between Tariff Rates and Country Unskilled/Skilled Labor Endowment Ratios

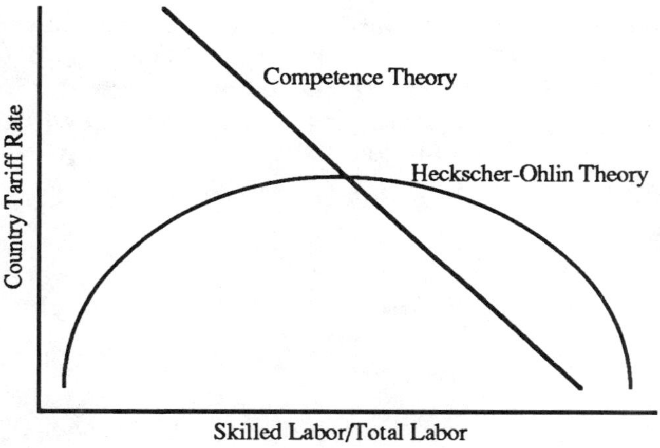

Thus, even after accounting for these development-dependent indicators, the theory appears to have support. The results in Figure 1-2 are not attributable to the level of development effects. *The Stolper-Samuelson theorem in the competence theory states that tariffs protect unskilled labor in almost all countries.*

THE RYBCZYNSKI THEOREM

The Rybczynski theorem states that an increase in a country's endowment of a factor will lead to increased production of the good that uses that factor intensively and a decrease in output of the good that uses that factor less intensively. *Our modified Rybczynski theorem states that an increase in one of the labor types will lead to increased output of that industry's product.* Several insights follow from this work, two of which are considered here. First, Mancur Olson (1982) argues that older, advanced societies experience increases in redistributive activity. Brock and Magee (1984) formalize Olson's work, showing that increases in redistributive activity can paradoxically increase GNP in the short run. Notice in Table 1-1 that an increase in labor devoted to redistributive activity in the DCs will pull skilled labor out of exports and into the highly skilled category. Such advanced countries should display secular declines in the trade balance in partial equilibrium. For NICs, increased skilled labor devoted to redistributive activity will reduce labor available to compete with high-tech imports. This will increase imports and (to the extent that skilled labor is also pulled up and into redistributive activity) cause exports to decline. Again, the trade balance will deteriorate. Second, while I do not explore the question here, the economic development literature has long considered whether export promotion or import substitution is the superior strategy.

Figure 1-2. Tariffs vs. Country Skilled-Labor Ratios

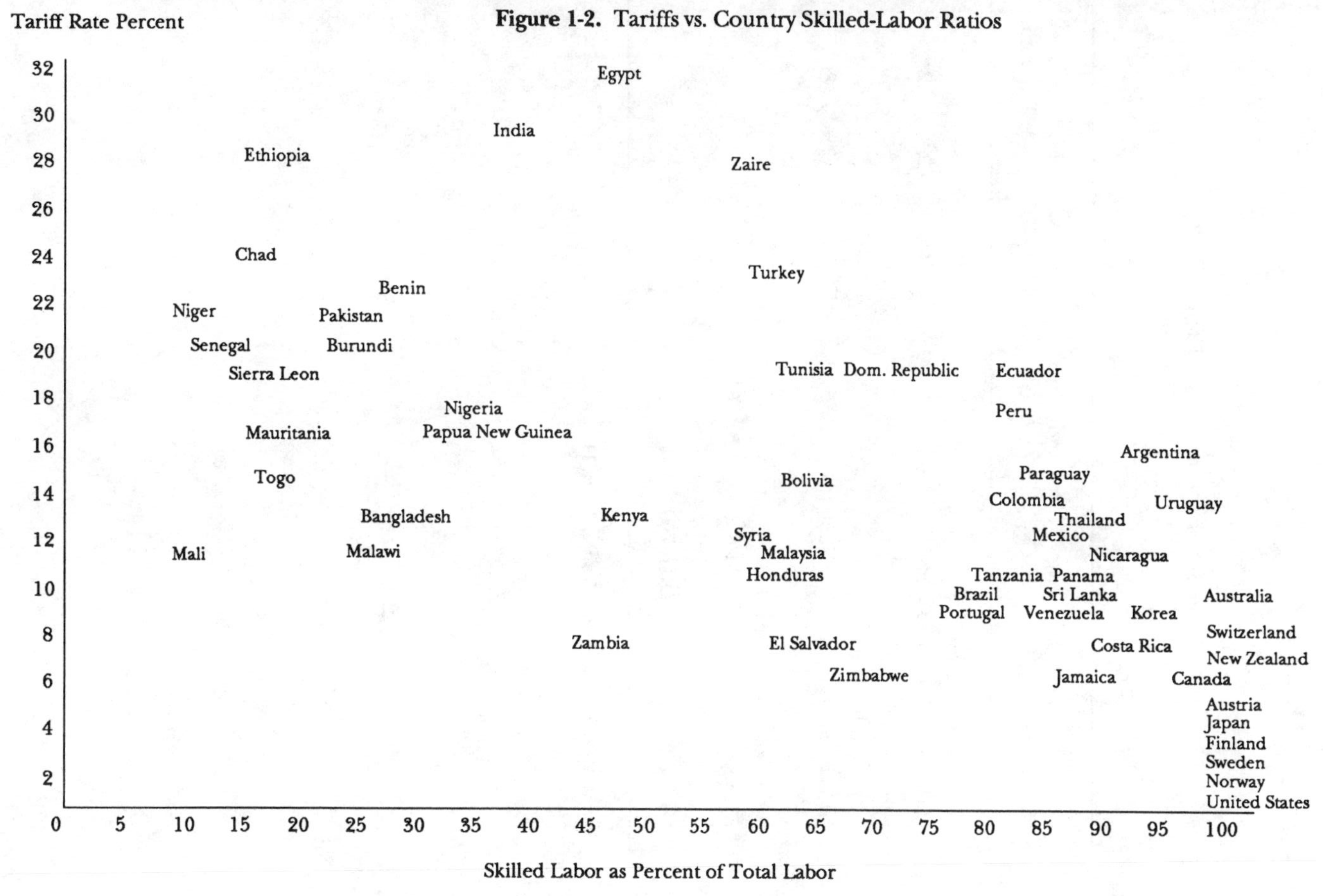

APPENDIX

Table 1-A. Patterns of World Trade, 1985

Country Groupings	Avg. GDP Per Capita	Industry as % of GDP	Services as % of GDP	Mfd. Exp. as % of Tot. Exp.
Low & Mid-Income (Ethiopia - Lebanon)	$510	25	46	22
Upper Middle Income (Brazil - Singapore)	$1,850	35	54	48
Ind. Mkt. Economies (Spain - U.S.)	$11,800	36	61	77
(U.S.)	$16,700	(31)	(67)	(75)

Source: World Bank (1988), Tables 3 and 11.

REFERENCES

Baldwin, Robert E. 1985. *The Political Economy of U.S. Import Policy.* Cambridge: MIT Press.

Bowen, Harry P., Edward E. Leamer, and Leo Sveikauskas. 1988. "Multicountry, Multifactor Tests of the Factor Abundance Theory." *American Economic Review* 78 (December): 791-809.

Brock, William A., and Stephen P. Magee. 1978. "The Economics of Special-Interest Politics: The Case of the Tariff." *American Economic Review* 68 (May): 246-50.

——. 1984. "The Invisible Foot and the Waste of Nations." *Neoclassical Political Economy.* Ed. David C. Colander. Cambridge, MA: Ballinger Publishing, 177-85.

Caves, Richard E. 1976. "Economic Models of Political Choice: Canada's Tariff Structure." *Canadian Journal of Economics* 9 (May): 278-300.

Helpman, Elhanan, and Paul R. Krugman. 1985. *Market Structure and Foreign Trade: Increasing Returns, Imperfect Competition, and the International Economy.* Cambridge: MIT Press.

Jones, Ronald, and Peter Neary. 1984. "The Positive Theory of International Trade." *Handbook of International Economics,* vol. 1. Ed. Ronald Jones and Peter B. Kenen. Amsterdam: North Holland.

Krugman, Paul R., and Maurice Obstfeld. 1988. *International Economics: Theory and Policy.* New York: Scott, Foresman.

Magee, Stephen P., William A. Brock, and Leslie Young. 1989. *Black Hole Tariffs and Endogenous Policy Theory.* Cambridge: Cambridge University Press.

Magee, Stephen P., and Leslie Young. 1983. "Multinationals, Tariffs and Capital Flows with Endogenous Politicians." *The Multinational Corporation in the 1980s.* Ed. Charles P. Kindleberger and David B. Audretsch. Cambridge: MIT Press, 21-37.

Olson, Mancur. 1982. *The Rise and Decline of Nations.* New Haven: Yale University Press.

Vernon, Raymond. 1966. "International Investment and International Trade in the Product Cycle." *Quarterly Journal of Economics* 80 (May): 190-207.

——. 1979. "The Product Cycle Hypothesis in a New International Environment." *Oxford Bulletin of Economics and Statistics* 41 (November): 255-67.

World Bank. 1988. *World Development Report, 1987.* London: Oxford University Press.

Young, Leslie, and Stephen P. Magee. 1986. "Endogenous Protection, Factor Returns and Resource Allocation." *Review of Economic Studies* 53: 407-19.

2 R&D POLICY AND TRADE ADVANTAGE

L. Fernando Ruiz-Mier and Albert N. Link

The international economic environment has experienced considerable change in recent years. The growth of the rest of the world relative to the United States has altered the U.S. trade position. The United States has become more trade dependent while the rest of the world's trade dependence on the United States has declined. This reversal in the U.S. trade position together with the increased internationalization of the world economy has altered the view of U.S. trade policy. One of the reasons the new position of the United States in the world economy calls for a reconsideration of policies is the recognition that certain policy areas previously considered domestic in nature (such as antitrust laws and other types of regulation) are now realized to affect the trade position of the United States.

Recognizing that domestic policies also have an impact on trade and incorporating these effects in the formulation of policies constitutes an internationalization of domestic policies. The internationalization of domestic policies is a natural consequence of the increased internationalization of markets for goods and services. For example, strong antitrust laws geared to promote competition in domestic markets may no longer be effective as markets become internationalized and domestic firms begin to compete with foreign firms.[1] Some of the issues associated with the internationalization of policies are linked to the strategic trade literature. The general idea is that in certain markets domestic firms are players in an "international market game," and that domestic policies, by altering the environment in which domestic firms operate, can confer upon firms a comparative advantage (or disadvantage). Under certain conditions, it may be in a country's interest to tailor policies or adopt "industrial policies" so as to place its firms in a favorable position.

This paper is generally concerned with the internationalization of domestic policy. We focus on the specific case of policies related to research and development (R&D). Industries in which R&D plays a significant strategic role are, more often than not, imperfectly competitive. In an international setting in which the number of firms is small, the strategic interaction between firms will result in domestic policies affecting the outcome in international markets. This confers a strategic role to governments, which can, by adopting different policies, alter the strategic environment in which domestic firms make decisions. Once this is recognized, the question is one of determining which policy, if any, should be adopted.

The recent trade literature provides a rationale for activist trade and industrial policies.[2] It is suggested that strategic trade policy can, under certain conditions, improve a country's welfare (relative to free trade). One way in which policies can improve a country's position is by enhancing the ability of domestic firms to secure a larger share of world markets in which rents are present. Rents would presumably be possible if the market in question is imperfectly competitive. Various writers have illustrated the possibility that subsidies or other policies can increase a country's rent share, thereby increasing its welfare at the expense of other countries. In markets where rents exist, a trade subsidy provides firms with a credible strategy that allows them to expand output. Rival firms respond by contracting their output, thereby increasing the price and hence the profits that the expanding firm can obtain. This adjustment has been referred to as the "strategic" effect by Brander (1986).

1. Dixit (1984) discusses the relationship between trade and antitrust policies in imperfectly competitive markets. He finds that under certain conditions the merger of two domestic firms in an oligopolistic market may lead to a welfare gain.

2. Grossman and Richardson (1985) provide an excellent survey and discussion of the strategic trade literature.

Spencer and Brander (1983) consider the case of R&D subsidies in an environment such as the one described above. They show that an R&D subsidy will, by increasing the level of R&D chosen by domestic firms, lead to domestic firms capturing a larger share of the international market. The increased profits associated with a larger market share imply that subsidies are welfare improving. The optimal subsidy is the one that maximizes domestic rents earned from exports. The model presented by Spencer and Brander is an illustration of how a subsidy, which can normally be regarded as a domestic policy, becomes a trade policy.

The theoretical possibility that, in the presence of market imperfections, strategic trade policies could improve a country's welfare is now generally accepted. However, because of the difficulties associated with implementing a theory, the step between the recognition of this theoretical possibility and the recommendation of an activist trade policy is not trivial. If an activist trade policy is to be successful, policymakers must have sufficient information to allow them to accurately pick the industries that should be targeted.

Given that the major criticism of a subsidy rests with the fact that relevant information may not be available and/or reliable, it is tempting to ask whether there is an alternative way in which the government can alter the strategic environment, thereby conferring domestic firms an advantage. Ideally, this alternative approach would require less information and less government intervention. This paper examines whether the relaxation of antitrust legislation, in particular allowing firms in the domestic industry to form a cooperative research joint venture (RJV), is one effective way to improve the strategic position of domestic firms.[3]

The case of industrial policies aimed at R&D is particularly interesting because it is believed that R&D policy is central to any discussion of the international trade position of the United States in high-technology industries.[4] Furthermore, as discussed by Audretsch and Yamawaki in Chapter 4 of this volume, there is some support for the view that R&D has been successfully employed by firms as a strategic instrument to enhance market share.

To study the effects of allowing domestic firms to engage in joint research ventures, we employ a simple yet illustrative structure. In particular, we consider the case of two domestic firms competing against one foreign firm. The three firms produce the same

3. For a detailed discussion of cooperative research activity among U.S. manufacturing firms, see Link and Bauer (1988).

4. See, for example, Branson and Klevorick (1986).

product for the same foreign market.[5] Our model can be viewed as a three-stage game. In the first stage, domestic firms choose whether to participate in the cooperative research agreement. The second stage consists of firms choosing the optimal levels of R&D to maximize profits. The final stage consists of each firm choosing the profit-maximizing level of output, given the production costs associated with the R&D performed in the previous stage. Our analysis closely follows that of Spencer and Brander (1983), as well as drawing on the work of Katz (1986) on cooperative research.

THE NATURE OF R&D

To describe the problem and introduce some notation, let us consider a single firm's choice of R&D level. Let r^i denote the ith firm's expenditure on R&D. The effective level of R&D available to firm i, denoted $t^i(\cdot)$, is given by

$$(1) \qquad t^i(r^1,\ldots,r^n) = r^i + \phi \sum r^j \qquad i, j=1,\ldots,n \quad i\neq j \qquad 0 \leq \phi \leq 1.$$

Equation (1) illustrates the fact that a firm could capture, in part, knowledge resulting from other firms' R&D activities. The degree to which the output of other firms' R&D activities spill over to firm i is quantified by the parameter ϕ. We assume, for simplicity, that there are no spillovers unless an RJV is established.[6] In such a case, ϕ captures the extent to which one member benefits from R&D undertaken by other member firms, and n is the number of firms that have joined the RJV.

The result of both direct and indirect R&D efforts is that of lowering production costs (R&D is process improving). Abstracting from risk considerations, the relationship between R&D and costs is presumed to be deterministic and given by

$$(2) \qquad c^i = c(t^i).$$

5. Although the number of firms is different, these assumptions are the same as those in Brander and Spencer (1984). The assumption that the industry's output is sold outside the domestic market allows for a simple measure of the industry's contribution to domestic welfare, namely industry profits.

6. The absence of an RJV, the case of $\phi > 0$, could capture the public-good nature of technical knowledge that sometimes results in firms choosing a level of R&D lower than the socially optimal. When this is the case, n refers to the number of firms in the industry.

We assume that $c_t < 0$, $c_{tt} > 0$, $c_t(t) \rightarrow -\infty$ as $t \rightarrow 0$ and $c_t(t) \rightarrow 0$ as $t \rightarrow \infty$, where subscript t denotes the derivative with respect to t. Furthermore, we assume that unit production costs are independent of output levels.

EQUILIBRIUM IN THE ABSENCE OF AN RJV

Consider first industry equilibrium in the absence of cooperative agreements. This case can be represented by a simple two-stage oligopoly model similar to that in Brander and Spencer (1984). It is assumed that firms make Cournot-Nash conjectures in each of the two stages. In the first stage, firms independently choose their levels of R&D, which leads to cost reductions. In the second stage, each firm chooses its output level given its R&D level and the output levels of its competitors.

The Output Stage

We start with the analysis of the output stage in which R&D levels are treated as exogenous. Letting x^i denote the ith firm's output level and $x=(x^1, x^2, x^3)$ the vector of outputs, the profit (flow) of firm i can be expressed as

$$(3) \qquad \Pi^i (x; t^i (r^i)) = R^i (x^1, x^2, x^3) - c^i (t^i)x^i - r^i$$

with $R^i_j < 0$ and $R^i_{ij} < 0$ $(i \neq j)$.

Equilibrium in the output market is the result of each firm maximizing its profits with respect to output, given the output of its rivals. Such equilibrium is characterized by the following first-order conditions

$$(4) \qquad \Pi^i_i = R^i_i - c^i = 0 \qquad\qquad i = 1, 2, 3.$$

Let D_1 denote the matrix of second-order terms associated with the system[7]

7. To simplify notation we have dropped the superscripts. Note that the superscript would be the same as the first subscript in all cases.

$$D_1 = \begin{pmatrix} \Pi_{11} & \Pi_{12} & \Pi_{13} \\ \Pi_{21} & \Pi_{22} & \Pi_{23} \\ \Pi_{31} & \Pi_{32} & \Pi_{33} \end{pmatrix} .$$

It is assumed that D_1 is negative definite. That is, the principal minors of D_1 of order k have sign $(-1)^k$, for all k=1, 2, 3. Among other things, this requires that $\Pi_{ii} < 0$ and that own marginal effects on profits exceed cross effects ($\Pi_{ii} < \Pi_{ij} < 0$ for i, j=1, 2, 3).[8]

Since the solutions to x^1, x^2 and x^3 are functions of r^1, r^2 and r^3, we can write

$$(5) \quad x^1 = q^1(r^1, r^2, r^3), \qquad x^2 = q^2(r^1, r^2, r^3), \qquad x^3 = q^3(r^1, r^2, r^3).$$

Substituting (5) into (4) and totally differentiating, we obtain an expression for the effect of changes in one firm's R&D on its own and on the other firms' output levels

$$q_i^i = \frac{dq^i}{dr^i} = \frac{c_t^i\{\Pi_{hh}\Pi_{jj} - \Pi_{hj}\Pi_{jh}\}}{|D_1|} > 0 \quad h, i, j = 1, 2, 3 \quad h \neq i \neq j$$

(6)

$$q_j^i = \frac{dq^j}{dr^i} = \frac{c_t^i\{\Pi_{ji}\Pi_{hh} - \Pi_{hi}\Pi_{jh}\}}{|D_1|} < 0 \quad h, i, j = 1, 2, 3 \quad h \neq i \neq j.$$

Our discussion thus far has shown that output, and hence market share, depends on marginal costs. Marginal costs, in turn, depend on r, the level of R&D expenditures independently undertaken by the firm. More specifically, equation (6) shows that an increase in a firm's own R&D level will result in an increase in the firm's output and a decrease in the output of its competitors. Thus, a firm's market share is directly related to its R&D level and inversely related to the R&D level of its competitors.

8. $\Pi_{ii} < 0$ and $\Pi_{ii} < \Pi_{ij} < 0$ are the assumptions adopted by Spencer and Brander to guarantee equilibrium in the two-firm case. As discussed by Spencer and Brander, equilibrium will be unique if such conditions hold globally. Our assumption concerning D_1 is the equivalent assumption for the case of three firms.

The R&D Stage

Consider now the stage in which firms choose R&D levels. Firms recognize the effect that R&D levels have on output levels and take this information into account when choosing R&D levels. Incorporating this information, the profit function of firm i can be expressed as

$$(7) \qquad V^i = \Pi^i \{q^1(r), q^2(r), q^3(r); t^i(r^i)\}$$

where $r=(r^1, r^2, r^3)$.

At this stage, firms choose R&D levels so as to maximize profits given the R&D levels of rival firms. The first-order conditions of a Nash equilibrium in R&D levels are

$$V^i_i = R^i_1 q^1_i + R^i_2 q^2_i + R^i_3 q^3_i - c^i q^i_i - c^i_t q^i - 1 = 0 \qquad i=1, 2, 3.$$

Given that $R^i_1 - c^i = \Pi^i_i = 0$ and that $\Pi^i_j = R^i_j$, the previous conditions can be expressed as

$$(8) \qquad V^i_i = \Pi^i_j q^j_i + \Pi^i_h q^h_i - c^i_t q^i - 1 = 0 \qquad i, j, h = 1, 2, 3 \quad i \neq j \neq h.$$

The second-order conditions are $V^i_{ii} < 0$ where

$$(9) \qquad V^i_{ii} = R^i_j q^j_{ii} + R^i_h q^h_{ii} + q^j_i \left(\frac{dR^i_j}{dr^i}\right) + q^h_i \left(\frac{dR^i_h}{dr^i}\right) - c^i_t q^i_i - c^i_{tt} q^i$$

and

$$(10) \qquad \frac{dR^i_j}{dr^i} = R^i_{ji} q^i_i + R^i_{jj} q^j_i + R^i_{jh} q^h_i \qquad i, j, h = 1, 2, 3 \quad i \neq j \neq h.$$

Letting D_2 denote the matrix of second-order terms associated with the R&D stage, we have

$$D_2 = \begin{pmatrix} V_{11} & V_{12} & V_{13} \\ V_{21} & V_{22} & V_{23} \\ V_{31} & V_{32} & V_{33} \end{pmatrix}.$$

We assume that D_2 has the same properties as D_1, thus guaranteeing that the second-order conditions hold. This assumption also implies that own effects of R&D on marginal profit dominate cross effects. The two assumptions concerning the properties of D_1 and D_2 ensure stability of equilibrium of the output and R&D stages, respectively. These assumptions are the three-firm analog to the assumptions adopted by Spencer and Brander.

The resolution of the R&D stage determines the optimal levels of R&D for each of the three firms. In the symmetric case, the three firms will choose the same level of R&D expenditures. Denoting this cost by r^o

$$r^o = r^1 = r^2 = r^3$$

which implies that the level of effective R&D is also identical across firms

$$t^o = t^1 = t^2 = t^3.$$

The equality of R&D levels across firms will, in turn, lead to equal market shares. It should be noted that, given the nature of the Nash equilibrium, firms have no incentives to depart from their choices of R&D levels.

Spencer and Brander have shown that an R&D subsidy will lead a firm to choose a higher level of R&D, thereby enabling it to capture a larger share of the market. This is because a government can alter the strategic environment in which firms are making choices. In the case of a subsidy, the government provides a "credible threat," which affects rival firms' behavior in a way that a "self-subsidy" on the part of the firm cannot.

The theoretical possibility that, in the presence of market imperfections, strategic trade policies could improve a country's welfare is now generally accepted. There is, however, some disagreement among trade theorists about the desirability of an activist trade policy.[9] The reservations and criticisms are for the

9. See, for example, Grossman (1986) and Krugman (1987).

most part associated with the difficulties that would arise in applying the theories in practice. If an activist trade policy is to be successful, policymakers need to be provided with information of sufficient detail and quality so as to allow them to pick the industries that should be targeted. The difficulties involved in gathering the necessary information, together with the incentives to manipulate information in an attempt to seek rents on the part of special interest groups, suggests that a lot of caution has to be exercised when considering industries as potential candidates for targeting.

In the case of the particular example with which we are dealing, Spencer and Brander established that R&D subsidies can be welfare improving. This result is obtained under the assumption that the opportunity cost of government revenue is unity.[10] The gains associated with a subsidy will be smaller as the opportunity cost of government revenues increases.

We mentioned earlier that when introducing a subsidy the government alters the strategic environment in which firms are operating. Given that the major criticism of a subsidy is that the relevant information may not be available and/or reliable, it is desirable to determine whether there is an alternative way in which the government can alter the strategic environment, thereby conferring domestic firms an advantage. Ideally, such an alternative would require less information and a lesser degree of active government intervention.

RESEARCH AGREEMENTS

In this section, we specify the nature of cooperative research agreements and consider the case of the two domestic firms establishing such an agreement. A research agreement has to specify rules for sharing both the costs and results of R&D, as well as the particular way in which R&D will be performed. In general, these sharing rules, which characterize a research joint venture, will be chosen optimally by member firms. For the purpose of simplicity, we shall not model the choice of rules. Thus, when evaluating the RJV option, firms consider only one type of agreement.[11]

10. Spencer and Brander (1983) discuss this assumption in their conclusion and are careful to point out that it weakens the case for recommending an active policy.

11. Restrictions on the particular types of agreements that firms may adopt could reflect government regulations.

Our description of cooperative research is a modified version of that of Katz (1986). Each of the firms engaged in cooperative research has an R&D department. Firms share the cost of R&D and the result of R&D efforts according to the following rules.

Cost Sharing

Any RJV will be characterized by linear cost-sharing rules. Total expenditures on R&D for the ith firm engaged in an RJV is given by

$$\lambda r^i + \frac{(1-\lambda)}{(n-1)} \Sigma\, r^j \qquad 0 \leq \lambda \leq 1$$

where n is the number of firms that are members of the agreement, λ is the share of the costs of its own R&D that a firm must bear, and $(1-\lambda)/(n-1)$ is the share of another member's R&D costs that each firm must bear. For the two-firm case, we shall consider the above expression reduces to

$$(11) \quad \lambda r^i + (1-\lambda) r^j \qquad i, j=1, 2 \quad i \neq j.$$

When firms do not enter into RJV agreements, they must bear the full cost of their R&D activities.

R&D Sharing

When an RJV is formed, member firms share the results of each other's R&D activities. A firm's effective level of R&D is thus a function of its own R&D efforts as well as those of other member firms. The specific form in which R&D results are shared is captured by

$$t^i (r^1,\ldots, r^n) = r^i + \phi\, \Sigma\, r^j \qquad i, j=1,\ldots,n \quad i \neq j \qquad 0 \leq \phi \leq 1.$$

When the RJV consists of only two firms, we have

$$(12) \quad t^i (r^1, r^2) = r^i + \phi\, r^j \qquad i, j=1, 2 \quad i \neq j \qquad 0 \leq \phi \leq 1.$$

As noted above, the parameter ϕ captures the extent to which the results of one firm's R&D can be passed on to another member firm. Based on the two rules discussed above, a cooperative research joint venture can be characterized by (λ, ϕ).

EQUILIBRIUM IN THE PRESENCE OF AN RJV

Our consideration of equilibrium in the presence of a cooperative research agreement is limited to the case of a symmetric outcome. In such a case, both member firms will have identical levels of effective R&D. Letting 1 and 2 denote the two domestic firms and 3 denote the foreign firm, the profit functions can be written as

$$(13) \quad \Pi^i(x; t^i(r^1, r^2)) = R^i(x^1, x^2, x^3) - c^i(t^i)x^i - \lambda r^i - (1-\lambda)r^j \qquad i, j=1, 2 \quad i \neq j$$

for the domestic firms, and

$$(14) \quad \Pi^3(x; t^3(r^3)) = R^3(x^1, x^2, x^3) - c^3(t^3)x^3 - r^3$$

for the foreign firm.

In the output stage, firms will choose their profit-maximizing levels of output taking R&D levels as given. The optimal output levels will depend on the effective R&D levels and can be written as

$$(15) \quad x^i = q^i(t^1(r^1, r^2),\ t^2(r^1, r^2),\ t^3(r^3)) \qquad i=1, 2, 3.$$

The effects of changes in R&D levels of domestic firms on output are given by

$$q_i^i = \frac{\{c_t^i\{\Pi_{jj}\Pi_{33} - \Pi_{3j}\Pi_{j3}\} - c_t^j\,\phi\{\Pi_{ij}\Pi_{33} - \Pi_{3j}\Pi_{i3}\}\}}{|D_1|} > 0$$

$$(16) \quad q_i^j = -\frac{\{c_t^i\{\Pi_{ji}\Pi_{33} - \Pi_{3i}\Pi_{j3}\} - c_t^j\,\phi\{\Pi_{ii}\Pi_{33} - \Pi_{3i}\Pi_{i3}\}\}}{|D_1|} \gtrless 0$$

$$q_i^3 = \frac{\{c_t^i\{\Pi_{ji}\Pi_{3j} - \Pi_{3i}\Pi_{jj}\} - c_t^j\,\phi\{\Pi_{ii}\Pi_{3j} - \Pi_{3i}\Pi_{ij}\}\}}{|D_1|} < 0.$$

To interpret the above expressions, let i=1 and j=2. A comparison of the expression for q_i^1 to the corresponding expression for the case of no RJV shows that the increase in a firm's output due to a higher level of R&D is smaller when the firm participates in an RJV. The reason for this is that an increase in firm 1's level of R&D benefits firm 2 by increasing its effective R&D.

Note also that the cross-effect between member firms is ambiguous. The sign of q_i^j is given by the sign of the numerator in the right-hand side. The sign of this term is, in turn, linked to ϕ. In particular, a sufficiently large ϕ will lead to an increase in firm 2's output as a response to a higher R&D level chosen by firm 1. Unless otherwise stated, we shall assume that ϕ is sufficiently small so that $q_i^j < 0$.

Finally, the expression for q_i^3 reveals, as expected, that the reduction of firm 3's output due to an increase in the R&D level of a competing firm will be greater when the competing firm is a member of an RJV.

The effects of changes in the level of R&D of the foreign firm on its own and its rivals' output levels are given by

$$(17) \qquad q_3^3 = \frac{c_t^3 \{\Pi_{11}\Pi_{22} - \Pi_{12}\Pi_{21}\}}{|D_1|} > 0$$

and

$$(18) \qquad q_3^i = \frac{c_t^3 \{\Pi_{ij}\Pi_{j3} - \Pi_{jj}\Pi_{i3}\}}{|D_1|} < 0 \qquad i, j=1, 2 \quad i\neq j.$$

Thus, the foreign firm's choice of output is directly related to its level of R&D, whereas the choice of output of its rivals is inversely related to its R&D levels.

In the presence of a cooperative research agreement, the R&D stage consists of firms choosing their optimal R&D levels given the established R&D sharing rules and taking the R&D levels of other firms as given. The profit function for an RJV member firm is given by

$$(19) \qquad V^i = \Pi^i(q; t^i(r^1, r^2)) = R^i(q^1, q^2, q^3) - c^i(t^i)q^i - \lambda r^i - (1-\lambda)r^j \qquad i, j=1, 2 \quad i\neq j$$

with first-order conditions

$$\text{(20)} \quad V_i^i = R_j^i q_i^j + R_3^i q_i^3 - c_t^i q^i - \lambda = 0 \qquad i, j=1, 2, \quad i \neq j$$

and

$$\text{(21)} \quad V_3^3 = R_1^3 q_3^1 + R_2^3 q_3^2 - c_t^3 q^3 - 1 = 0.$$

Substituting equation (16) into (20), and comparing the resulting expression with the corresponding one for the case of no RJV (both evaluated at t^o), yields

$$\text{(22)} \quad (c^{j\prime}\phi/|D_1|)\ \{R_j^i \Psi_{jj} + R_3^i \Psi_{j3}\} + (1-\lambda)$$

where $\Psi_{jj} = \{\Pi_{ii}\Pi_{33} - \Pi_{3i}\Pi_{i3}\}$ and $\Psi_{j3} = \{\Pi_{3i}\Pi_{ij} - \Pi_{ii}\Pi_{3j}\}$. Expression (22) reveals the additional feedbacks that, in the presence of an RJV, affect the optimal choice of r.

Assume, again, for the sake of exposition, that i=1 and j=2. When firm 1 partially shares the results of R&D with firm 2, the reduction in the second firm's output level is smaller than what it would have been if no sharing had taken place. This negative effect on the revenues of the firm undertaking R&D is given by $(c^{j\prime}\phi/|D_1|)R_j^i\Psi_{jj}$. At the same time, the adjustment of output of firm 2, by leading to a lower output level on the part of firm 3, has a positive effect on firm 1's revenues as indicated by $(c^{j\prime}\phi/|D_1|)R_3^i\Psi_{j3}$. Thus, the term $(c^{j\prime}\phi/|D_1|)\{R_j^i\Psi_{jj} + R_3^i\Psi_{j3}\}$, which can be shown to be negative, captures the additional indirect effect that a change in a firm's R&D expenditures has on its own profits when a firm shares the results of R&D.

The sign of expression (22) depends on the magnitude of the effect discussed above relative to the share of R&D not paid by the firm. In particular, this expression will be positive when the negative impact of a firm's R&D activity on its revenues brought about by the sharing of its R&D results with the other member firm is smaller than the share of the cost of R&D paid by the other firm. We refer to this case as $T > 0$, where $T=(c^{j\prime}\phi/|D_1|)\{R_j^i\Psi_{jj} + R_3^i\Psi_{j3}\} + (1-\lambda)$.

The effect that a cooperative research agreement has on R&D levels depends on the sign of T as well as on the properties of the demand faced by firms. Let t^d and t^f represent the optimal levels of R&D of domestic and foreign firms when domestic firms form an RJV and, as before, t^o denote the equilibrium level of R&D in the absence of an RJV. It can be shown that if $\{R_j^i\Psi_{jj} + R_3^i\Psi_{j3}\}/|D_1|$ and

$\{R_j^i\Psi_{ij} + R_3^i\Psi_{i3}\}/|D_1|$ are not greatly affected by changes in t^d, the assumptions about $c(\cdot)$ imply that equilibrium will be characterized by $t^d > t^o > t^f$ if $T > 0$.[12] If, on the other hand, $T < 0$, the equilibrium will be characterized by $t^d < t^o < t^f$ (see Appendix A).

The above result implies that allowing domestic firms to engage in cooperative research will result in domestic firms capturing a larger share of the market, and consequently rents, when the negative impact of a firm's R&D activity on its revenues brought about by the sharing of the results of its R&D with the other member firm is smaller than the share of the cost of R&D paid by the other firm.

How would the establishment of an RJV affect the industry and domestic firms when T=0? Note that allowing firms to engage in cooperative research affects firms in two ways in our model. First, the effective level of R&D available to each firm is likely to be different from that which firms would choose in the case of no RJV. Second, allowing firms to share the results of R&D leads to a reduction of duplicative efforts. When T=0, the effective level of R&D available to domestic firms is t^o. Thus, an RJV will not affect marginal costs. Firms, however, will face lower per-unit costs because expenditures on R&D are lower. This results in profits increasing even though the share of the market captured by domestic firms has not changed.

Should the government allow RJVs? Our analysis suggests that it is to a country's advantage to allow for cooperative research when $T \geq 0$. Determining whether this condition is satisfied, however, is not a trivial matter. Nonetheless, the focus on the expression for T allows us to ask a further question. When is the condition $T \geq 0$ more likely to be satisfied? Inspection of T reveals that whether this condition is met depends, in part, on the values of the parameters ϕ and λ. T is more likely to be greater than zero the smaller both ϕ and λ are. Note that if $\phi=0$, each firm will be "subsidized" by the other firm with no R&D being shared. In this case, domestic firms could increase their market share and profits at the expense of the foreign firm. The outcome in this case would be similar to that presented by Spencer and Brander, with the difference that here firms subsidize each other as opposed to the

12. Changes in t^d will lead to changes in the output of both domestic and foreign firms. How $\{R_j^i\Psi_{jj} + R_3^i\Psi_{j3}\}/|D_1|$ and $\{R_j^i\Psi_{ij} + R_3^i\Psi_{i3}\}/|D_1|$ are affected by these changes depends on demand. If, for example, market demand is given by $P(X) = \alpha + \beta X$, where $X = x^1 + x^2 + x^3$, equation (20) reduces to $V_i^i = (\beta x^i/|D_1|)\{(\Psi_{ij}+\Psi_{i3}) + \{\Psi_{jj} + \Psi_{j3}\} - c^{i\prime}q^i - s$ with β, $|D_1|$ and Ψ's constant. We assume that the effect of changes in t^d on x^i are sufficiently small relative to the effect on $c^{i\prime}$.

government providing the subsidies. We would expect this case not to be likely since it is the sharing of R&D results that presents the incentive for firms to enter RJVs and share the costs of R&D. In fact, firms are likely to optimally choose both ϕ and λ.

Assuming that both ϕ and λ are jointly chosen by firms participating in a research joint venture, a second question of interest is whether firms would voluntarily enter an RJV if $T < 0$. As we mentioned earlier, this case is characterized by the level of effective R&D available to each domestic firm being smaller than that of the foreign firm. As a result, domestic firms will have higher marginal costs and will capture a smaller share of the market. Whether profits of domestic firms increase under these circumstances will depend on the magnitude of the reduction of the firms' R&D (fixed) costs due to both R&D sharing and lower R&D levels relative to the increase in (marginal) costs due to a lower level of R&D, and the decreased revenues due to a smaller market share. Because the establishment of an RJV is voluntary, we would expect no RJV to be formed in the event that an RJV results in domestic firms realizing smaller profits than those they would obtain in the absence of an RJV.

R&D SUBSIDIES

We have shown thus far that the effects of an RJV will depend on the particular form of the R&D agreement (λ, ϕ) as well as demand conditions. In particular, we have seen that when $T > 0$ an RJV will result in an increase in the effective R&D levels of domestic firms. This result occurs because when choosing its level of R&D each firm considers only its own share of its R&D costs. Thus, the two firms are, in effect, subsidizing each other. In this section, we study how the industry equilibrium under an RJV compares to that under government subsidies.

Let s be the fraction of R&D costs paid by the government. Thus, the government's total subsidy is given by sr. In the presence of subsidies, a domestic firm's profit functions can be written as

$$(23) \quad V^i(r^1, r^2, r^3, s) = R^i(q^1, q^2, q^3) - c^i(r^i)q^i - (1-s)r^i \qquad i, j=1, 2$$

with first-order conditions

$$(24) \quad V^i_i = R^i_j q^j_i + R^i_3 q^3_i - c^i_t q^i - (1-s) = 0 \qquad i, j=1, 2, \quad i \neq j.$$

The effect of subsidies on domestic and foreign R&D levels can be shown to be given by (see Appendix B)

$$\frac{dr^1}{ds} = \frac{V_{33}(V_{12}-V_{22})}{|D_2|} > 0$$

$$(25) \quad \frac{dr^2}{ds} = \frac{V_{33}(V_{21}-V_{11})}{|D_2|} > 0$$

$$\frac{dr^3}{ds} = \frac{V_{31}(V_{22}-V_{12}) + V_{32}(V_{11}-V_{21})}{|D_2|} \gtrless 0$$

when $V_{3i} \gtrless 0$ $\qquad$ i=1, 2.

Thus, a domestic R&D subsidy will lead to an increase in the R&D levels of domestic firms and decrease (increase) foreign R&D provided $V_{3i} < 0$ ($V_{3i} > 0$).

The Optimal Domestic R&D Subsidy

Let B denote net domestic benefit. Then we can write

$$(26) \quad B(s) = V^1(r^1, r^2, r^3, s) + V^2(r^1, r^2, r^3, s) + s(r^1, r^2).$$

That is, in the presence of a subsidy, the net domestic benefit is the profits of the domestic firms less the subsidy.

Differentiating equation (26) with respect to s, and solving for s, the optimal R&D subsidy can be shown to be given by (see Appendix C)

$$(27) \quad s = \frac{(V_3^1 + V_3^2)\dfrac{dr^3}{ds} + V_2^1\dfrac{dr^2}{ds} + V_1^2\dfrac{dr^1}{ds}}{\dfrac{dr^1}{ds} + \dfrac{dr^2}{ds}}.$$

The above equation shows that for the optimal subsidy to be positive, domestic R&D subsidies must lead to lower foreign R&D. The optimal subsidy is equal to the increase in the profits of domestic firms resulting from the reduction of the foreign firm's R&D (brought about by the subsidy-induced increase in domestic R&D)

minus the decrease in profits of domestic firms brought about by the negative impact of one firm's increased R&D on the other firm's profits.

We should note that when there is only one domestic firm equation (27) reduces to

$$(28) \qquad s = V_f^h \frac{\frac{dr^f}{ds}}{\frac{dr^h}{ds}}$$

where h and f denote the domestic and foreign firms respectively (expression [28] is equivalent to that derived by Spencer and Brander).

A comparison of equations (27) and (28) reveals that, because of the negative effect that subsidizing one domestic firm has on the profits of the other domestic firm, the optimal subsidy will be smaller when the domestic industry consists of two firms instead of one.

The Optimal-Subsidy-Equivalent Cost-Sharing Rule

One of the parameters characterizing an RJV is λ, the share of own R&D costs paid by a member firm. The effect that changes in λ (given constant ϕ) has on the R&D levels of the foreign and the domestic firms is given by

$$\frac{dr^1}{d\lambda} = \frac{V_{33}(V_{22}-V_{12})}{|D_2|} < 0$$

$$(29) \qquad \frac{dr^2}{d\lambda} = \frac{V_{33}(V_{11}-V_{21})}{|D_2|} < 0$$

$$\frac{dr^3}{d\lambda} = \frac{V_{31}(V_{12}-V_{22}) + V_{32}(V_{21}-V_{11})}{|D_2|} \gtrless 0$$

when $V_{3i} \gtrless 0 \qquad i=1, 2.$

Comparison of (25) and (29) shows that when firms do not share R&D results

$$(\phi=0), \frac{dr^i}{d\lambda} = -\frac{dr^i}{ds} .$$

Let s* denote the optimal government R&D subsidy. Comparison of the first-order conditions given by equations (20) and (24) reveals that, for the case $\phi=0$, there exists a cost-sharing rule λ^*, given by $\lambda^*=(1-s^*)$, that replicates the industry equilibrium obtained under an optimal subsidy. In fact, it can be shown that, when f=0 and firms choose λ optimally so as to maximize joint profits, the cost-sharing rule equivalent to the optimal subsidy exists (see Appendix D).

FURTHER EXTENSIONS: ALTERNATIVE COOPERATIVE RESEARCH AGREEMENTS

An interesting question is whether there is more than one R&D agreement that leads to the same level of effective R&D, and hence market share. In particular, it would be interesting to determine the research agreements that lead to the same level of effective R&D obtained with an optimal subsidy. Although the outcome in the equilibrium market would be the same, if such agreements exist, the profits of the domestic industry would be different. Achieving the same level of effective R&D in the presence of R&D sharing would involve a lower R&D cost, and consequently would be associated with higher industry profits. Presumably, the profit-maximizing agreement would include an R&D sharing rule that sets $\lambda=1$, thereby minimizing the cost of achieving a given level of effective R&D. Ideally, the choice of an R&D agreement should be modeled as part of the decision process of the domestic firms.

CONCLUSION

Following the strategic trade literature, we have focused on an international market in which, because of the imperfectly competitive nature of the market, firms enjoy rents in the form of profits. This paper addresses the question of whether permitting cooperative research agreements in high-technology industries would, by altering the strategic environment in which domestic firms operate, enable them to capture a larger share of international markets. We have shown that, under certain conditions, cooperative research agreements could improve the strategic position of domestic firms vis-à-vis foreign competitors. We have referred to this as an example of the internationalization of domestic policies.

Allowing for an RJV to be formed could lead to an outcome similar to that obtained under government subsidies of R&D. Thus, RJVs could provide an alternative to government subsidies as a means of strengthening the competitive position of domestic firms. The attractiveness of RJVs lies in that government plays a passive role. The decision concerning the desirability and the level of "subsidies" is left to the participating firms, which presumably have better information available than do policymakers. Furthermore, in the presence of RJVs, because of the sharing of R&D, the cost of obtaining a given level of effective R&D will be smaller. To the extent that the lower cost is associated with increased profits, cooperative research ventures can provide an additional source of domestic welfare gains.

APPENDIX A: THE EFFECT OF AN RJV ON EFFECTIVE R&D LEVELS

The following is an outline of a proof of the result for the case of $T > 0$. The case $T < 0$ proceeds in a similar way.

Equilibrium in the R&D stage obtains when t^d and t^f are such that (20) and (21) are satisfied. Define $H(t^d, t^f)$ and $F(t^d, t^f)$ as

$$H(t^d, t^f) = R^i_j q^j_i + R^i_3 q^3_i - c^i_t q^i - \lambda \;\; ; \;\; F(t^d, t^f) = R^3_1 q^1_3 + R^3_2 q^2_3 - c^3_t q^3 - 1$$

Evaluating the above two expressions at $t^d_o = t^o = t^f_o$ yields $F(t^d_o, t^f_o) = 0$, but, since $T > 0$, it must be that $H(t^d_o, t^f_o) > 0$. Given the properties of $c(\cdot)$ and our assumptions that $\{R^i_j \Psi_{jj} + R^i_3 \Psi_{j3}\}/|D_1|$ and $\{R^i_j \Psi_{ij} + R^i_3 \Psi_{i3}\}/|D_1|$ are not greatly affected by changes in t^d, there exists a t^d, say t^d_1, such that $t^d_1 > t^o$ and $H(t^d_1, t^f_o) = 0$. This will result in $F(t^d_1, t^f_o) < 0$. There is, however, a t^f, say t^f_1, such that $t^f_1 < t^o$ and that $F(t^d_1, t^f_1) = 0$. The above procedure generates sequences $\{t^d\}$ and $\{t^f\}$ that converge and have limit points that satisfy the first-order conditions.

APPENDIX B. THE EFFECT OF SUBSIDIES ON R&D LEVELS (NO RJV)

The profit functions of domestic firms are now given by

$$V^i(r^1, r^2, r^3, s) = R^i(q^1, q^2, q^3) - c^i(r^i)q^i - (1\text{-}s)r^i \quad i, j=1, 2.$$

The three-equation system of first-order conditions is

$$V^1_1 = R^1_2\, q^2_1 + R^1_3\, q^3_1 - c^1_t\, q^1 - (1\text{-}s) = 0$$

$$V^2_2 = R^2_1\, q^1_2 + R^2_3\, q^3_2 - c^2_t q^2 - (1\text{-}s) = 0$$

$$V^3_3 = R^3_1\, q^1_3 + R^3_2\, q^2_3 - c^3_t q^3 - 1 = 0.$$

Differentiation of the above system with respect to r^1, r^2, r^3 and s yields

$$\begin{pmatrix} V_{11} & V_{12} & V_{13} \\ V_{21} & V_{22} & V_{23} \\ V_{31} & V_{32} & V_{33} \end{pmatrix} \begin{pmatrix} dr^1/ds \\ dr^2/ds \\ dr^3/ds \end{pmatrix} = \begin{pmatrix} -1 \\ -1 \\ 0 \end{pmatrix}.$$

Application of Cramer's rule yields

$$\frac{dr^1}{ds} = \frac{V_{33}(V_{12}-V_{22}) + V_{32}(V_{23}-V_{13})}{|D_2|} > 0$$

$$\frac{dr^2}{ds} = \frac{V_{33}(V_{21}-V_{11}) + V_{31}(V_{13}-V_{23})}{|D_2|} > 0$$

$$\frac{dr^3}{ds} = \frac{V_{31}(V_{22}-V_{12}) + V_{32}(V_{11}-V_{21})}{|D_2|} \gtrless 0 \text{ when } V_{3i} \gtrless 0 \quad i=1, 2.$$

It should be noted that in the symmetric case $(V_{23}-V_{13})=0$. The effect of changes in λ on r^1, r^2 and r^3 can be found in a similar way.

APPENDIX C. THE OPTIMAL SUBSIDY

Net domestic benefit is given by

$$B(s) = V^1(r^1, r^2, r^3, s) + V^2(r^1, r^2, r^3, s) + s(r^1, r^2).$$

Differentiating the above expression with respect to s and equating to zero to find the optimal subsidy yields

$$\frac{dB}{ds} = (V_3^1 + V_3^2)\frac{dr^3}{ds} + (V_2^1 - s)\frac{dr^2}{ds} + (V_1^2 - s)\frac{dr^1}{ds} = 0$$

which can be rearranged to show the optimal subsidy

$$s = \frac{(V_3^1 + V_3^2)\frac{dr^3}{ds} + V_2^1\frac{dr^2}{ds} + V_1^2\frac{dr^1}{ds}}{\frac{dr^1}{ds} + \frac{dr^2}{ds}}.$$

APPENDIX D. THE CHOICE OF COST-SHARING RULE THAT MAXIMIZES JOINT PROFITS

Joint profits are given by

$$\mathbf{V}^* = \mathbf{V}^1(r^1, r^2, r^3, \lambda) + \mathbf{V}^2(r^1, r^2, r^3, \lambda)$$

where boldface is used to distinguish this case from the case of a subsidy. Differentiating the above expression with respect to λ yields

$$\frac{d\mathbf{V}^*}{ds} = (\mathbf{V}^1_3 + \mathbf{V}^2_3)\frac{dr^3}{ds} + (\mathbf{V}^1_2 - s)\frac{dr^2}{ds} + (\mathbf{V}^2_1 - s)\frac{dr^1}{ds} = 0.$$

Making use of the fact that $\mathbf{V}^1_2 = V^1_2 - (1-\lambda)$, $\mathbf{V}^2_1 = V^2_1 - (1-\lambda)$, $\mathbf{V}^1_3 = V^1_3$ and $\mathbf{V}^2_3 = V^2_3$, where V^i_j represents the corresponding term in the case of a subsidy, the above expression can be written as

$$\frac{d\mathbf{V}^*}{ds} = (V^1_3 + V^2_3)\frac{dr^3}{ds} + (V^1_2 - (1-\lambda))\frac{dr^2}{ds} + (V^2_1 - (1-\lambda))\frac{dr^1}{ds} = 0.$$

Solving for $(1-\lambda)$ yields

$$(1-\lambda) = \frac{(V^1_3 + V^2_3)\dfrac{dr^3}{ds} + V^1_2\dfrac{dr^2}{ds} + V^2_1\dfrac{dr^1}{ds}}{\dfrac{dr^1}{ds} + \dfrac{dr^2}{ds}} = s^*.$$

REFERENCES

Brander, James A., and Barbara J. Spencer. 1984. "Export Subsidies and International Market Share Rivalry." *Journal of International Economics* 18, no. 1/2: 83-100.

Brander, James A. 1986. "Rationales for Strategic Trade and Industrial Policy." *Strategic Trade Policy and the New International Economics.* Ed. Paul R. Krugman. Cambridge: MIT Press.

Branson, William H., and Alvin K. Klevorick. 1986. "Strategic Behavior and Trade Policy." *Strategic Trade Policy and the New International Economics.* Ed. Paul R. Krugman. Cambridge: MIT Press.

Dixit, Avinash K. 1984. "International Trade Policy for Oligopolistic Industries." *Economic Journal* 94 (supplement).

Grossman, Gene M. 1986. "Strategic Export Promotion: A Critique." *Strategic Trade Policy and the New International Economics.* Ed. Paul R. Krugman. Cambridge: MIT Press.

Grossman, Gene M., and J. David Richardson. 1985. "Strategic Trade Policy: A Survey of Issues and Early Analysis." Princeton *Special Papers in International Economics,* no. 15 (April).

Katz, Michael L. 1986. "An Analysis of Cooperative Research and Development." *Rand Journal of Economics* 17, no. 4: 527-43.

Krugman, Paul R. 1987. "Targeted Industrial Policies: Theory and Evidence." *The New Protectionist Threat to World Welfare.* Ed. D. Salvatore. Amsterdam: North-Holland.

Link, Albert N., and Laura L. Bauer. 1988. *Cooperative Research in U.S. Manufacturing: An Assessment of Policy Initiatives and Corporate Strategies.* Lexington, MA: Lexington Books.

Spencer, Barbara J., and James A. Brander. 1983. "International R&D Rivalry and Industrial Strategy." *Review of Economic Studies* 50: 707-22.

3 INTER-INDUSTRY REGRESSION ESTIMATES OF FACTOR ABUNDANCE

Harry P. Bowen and Leo Sveikauskas

I. INTRODUCTION

Many studies have attempted to test the Heckscher-Ohlin theory or, more generally, to infer a country's abundant resources, by regressing industry trade balances on factor input requirements in a single year. Inferences about a country's abundance in a factor are then based on the sign of its estimated coefficient. However, Leamer and Bowen (1981) and Aw (1983) recently demonstrated that unless each factor is specific to each industry, such inferences are inappropriate in a model with more than two factors. Since industries do in fact use several inputs, whether the sign of an estimated coefficient reveals a country's true factor abundance will depend on the extent to which industries' use of several inputs confounds the relationship between a coefficient's sign and the country's true supply of that factor.

Despite this caution, many economists have continued to use the inter-industry regression methodology in recent years. Balassa (1979, 1986) has studied the relationship between factor intensity and trade in a large number of countries, often with quite strong

The authors would like to thank K. C. Fung, Tom Pugel, and participants at the Tenth Annual Middlebury Conference on Economic Issues for their comments. The views expressed here do not necessarily reflect those of the U.S. Department of Labor.

results. Baldwin and Hilton (1984) have reinterpreted the standard methodology to provide evidence on factor price differences among particular countries. Finally, Harkness (1978, 1983) has continued to argue that inter-industry regressions provide information on factor abundance.

Balassa's work in particular suggests that the regression methodology provides useful information on factor abundance. In contrast, work using net trade in factor services (Bowen, Leamer, and Sveikauskas 1987) suggests factor abundance contributes little to an understanding of trade patterns. The contrast between these conclusions means that it is important to examine these two approaches in some detail to determine the conditions under which the regression approach is useful, when it is not useful and, more generally, what the regression approach really means and contributes.

This paper presents some initial results that are part of a broader ongoing study examining the relationship between factor abundance as suggested by a regression approach and factor abundance as suggested by the trade in factor services. This broader analysis examines the importance of different levels of input aggregation, among other items. The present paper also reports results for input requirements defined at the 80-order level of the U.S. input-output table and for four alternative models reflecting alternative aggregation of factor inputs. Our results provide some initial empirical evidence on the likelihood that a regression of industry trade balances on factor inputs requirements reveals the abundance of a factor as measured by the net trade in factor services.

Section II reviews the theory behind our empirical work. Section III presents the results of estimating an inter-industry regression for each country, while Section IV examines the extent to which the coefficient signs predict factor abundance. We examine reasons why the signs of the coefficients may fail to predict factor abundance in Section V and offer remarks in Section VI.

II. THEORY

In general, country i's net trade in factor services can be written:

$$(1) \qquad A_i'T_i = A'_iQ_i - A'_iC_i$$

where

T_i = Nx1 vector of net trades
A_i = NxK matrix of factor input requirements
Q_i = Nx1 vector of final outputs
C_i = Nx1 vector of final demands.

Following Leamer and Bowen (1981), if it is assumed that the matrix A is identical across countries[1] and that countries have identical homothetic tastes, then (1) can be written

(2) $A'T_i = (E_i - \alpha_i E_w)$

where

E_i = Kx1 vector of factor supplies in country i
$E_w = \Sigma_i E_i$, a Kx1 vector of world factor supplies
α_i = country i's share of world expenditure.

Defining a country to be abundant in factor k if its share of the world amount of factor k exceeds its consumption share α_i, (2) implies the well-known Heckscher-Ohlin-Vanek (H-O-V) theory: a country will be a net exporter of the services of its abundant factors and a net importer of the services of its scarce factors. Therefore, if (2) is assumed to hold, a country's true factor abundance can be determined by examining the signs of either the factor content vector $A'T_i$ or the excess factor supply vector $(E_i - \alpha_i E_w)$.

As Leamer and Bowen (1981) note, many researchers wishing to infer a country's true factor abundance observe T_i and A but do not compute $A'T_i$. Instead, they regress the trade vector on the input requirements:

(3) $T_i = A\beta + \varepsilon$

where β is the Kx1 vector of regression coefficients (excluding a constant term) and ε is the Nx1 vector of errors. The vector of estimated coefficients β^* are then assumed to have the same sign as the corresponding elements of the factor content vector $A'T_i$, or since (2) is assumed to hold, the same sign as the elements of the excess factor supply vector $(E_i - \alpha_i E_w)$. However, this assumed equality

1. This assumes either factor-price equalization or that input requirements are technologically fixed and internationally identical.

of signs between the vector of coefficients and either the vector of factor contents or the vector of excess factor supplies is not an implication of the H-O-V theory since β^* is

$$(4) \qquad \beta^* = (A'A)^{-1}A'T_i$$

which by equation (2) is

$$(4) \qquad \beta^* = (A'A)^{-1}(E_i - \alpha_i E_w).$$

Whether the elements of the estimated coefficient vector have the same sign as the corresponding elements of the factor content vector or the vector of excess factor supplies depends on the matrix $(A'A)^{-1}$. As suggested by Leamer and Bowen and proved rigorously by Aw (1983), a necessary and sufficient condition for the vector β^* to have the same sign as the vector of factor contents is that $(A'A)^{-1}$ be a diagonal matrix with strictly positive elements.

Since the actual input requirements matrix A used in such regression studies is never diagonal, at issue is the extent to which the presence of the off-diagonal elements of $(A'A)^{-1}$ cause the sign of each element of β^* to differ from the sign of the corresponding elements of the factor content vector or the excess factor supply vector.

We explore in this paper the extent of conformity between the sign of regression coefficients and the sign of factor contents by first estimating equation (3) for each of thirty-five countries, using as data the 1967 net trade in sixty-four industries in agriculture, mining, and manufacturing, and the 1967 matrix of total (direct plus indirect) factor input requirements for the United States. We then compute the factor content vector for each country and compare the sign of each element of this vector to the sign of the corresponding regression coefficient. Our measure of conformity between the signs of the elements of these two vectors is then the proportion of correct sign matches.

We consider four alternative models defined according to the level of aggregation of the factor input data. Our most general model (Model 1) uses data on the total requirements of thirteen factor inputs: capital, nine categories of labor (professional/ technical, managers, sales, clerical, craftsmen, operatives, laborers, services, and farmers), and three categories of land (arable, pasture, and forest). Model 2 collapses the three land categories into one variable, LAND. Model 3 further collapses the labor categories into two variables, WHITE (professional/technical, managers, sales, and clerical) and BLUE (craftsmen, operatives, laborers, services, and farmers). Finally, Model 4 aggregates all the labor inputs into one variable, LABOR.[2]

The main line of recent theoretical trade literature (see, for example, Leamer 1987) has emphasized a three-input model: capital, labor, and land, which in our analysis corresponds to Model 4. In contrast, much of the empirical trade literature has tended to favor a three-factor model: capital, human capital, and raw labor. Our four-factor model, Model 3, is closest to this three-factor model and differs only by the inclusion of the aggregate land variable.

The equations we estimate include a constant term, whereas the factor content vector $A'T_i$ for each country i is computed using only the matrix of factor input requirements. Below we will indicate some sensitivity analysis of this difference for our results, but at this stage we are unwilling to impose the constraint of no intercept.

III. INTER-INDUSTRY REGRESSIONS

We are primarily interested at present in the following question: How does aggregation of the factor input data affect the explanatory power of the equations? Not all of the regression tables are included here due to space constraints, but the major results and conclusions will be reported.[3]

For Model 1, the equation (3) estimates for six countries (Belgium-Luxembourg, Canada, Finland, Norway, Sweden, and Yugoslavia) are not significant at the 10 percent level, and of these, Finland and Canada have negative R-bar squares. Five countries have an R-bar square in excess of .90 (Argentina, New Zealand, Iceland, Nigeria, and Brazil) and seventeen countries have an R-bar square in excess of .50. The fact that the R-bar square is only .523 for the United States is somewhat surprising given that the factor input data relate to the United States.

When the three land variables are aggregated into one variable, LAND (Model 2), the regressions for Austria, Egypt, Korea, and the United States become insignificant. In addition, the R-bar square

2. The data used here are essentially those used in Bowen, Leamer, and Sveikauskas (1987), which are discussed in detail in the Data Appendix to that paper. The only differences in the present data are that we use the 80-order input-output table for the United States in 1967, and we use use data on thirty-five countries instead of twenty-seven as in the preceding study.

3. Detailed results for the interindustry regressions estimating equation (3) for Models 1-4 are available from the editors upon request.

declines by more than .10 in sixteen countries. Such results suggest it is important to keep the land variables separate.

When the labor data are aggregated into WHITE and BLUE (Model 3), the equations for Austria and Korea become significant again (at the 90 percent confidence), but the equation for Greece becomes insignificant. The equation for the United States remains statistically insignificant.

Finally, consideration of the three-input model, CAPITAL, LABOR, and LAND, which aggregates WHITE and BLUE, results in only a slightly further reduction of R-bar square. In particular, most countries have a reduction of less than .02, the only exception being Switzerland, which has a reduction of .05.

Going from Model 1 to the the four-input model (Model 3) produces a major reduction in explanatory power of more than .10 (including those that are no longer significant) for fourteen of the thirty-five countries. The suggested conclusion is thus that aggregation of the input data does result in an important loss of explanatory power. Much of the reduction is due to aggregation of the land variables.[4]

It is also of interest to examine the signs of the coefficients estimated for each model. For Model 1, each of the twenty-five countries with a significant capital coefficient has a negative sign. Similarly, all significant coefficients for PROFTECH, MANAGERS, SALES, CLERICAL, and CRAFTSMEN have the same sign. However, for the remaining labor categories and for the land variables, the coefficient signs vary across countries.

This same pattern of signs recurs for CAPITAL and the labor categories in Model 2. For Model 3, the sign of CAPITAL is again consistently negative when significant. Aggregation of the labor variables leads to few changes in the sign of LAND's coefficient. Where significant, the sign of WHITE is negative and the sign of BLUE varies across the sample. Finally, further aggregation of the labor data into a single variable, total labor, tends to leave the sign of coefficients for CAPITAL and LAND undisturbed.

Aggregation of the labor and land categories generally appears to leave the sign for capital essentially undisturbed and does not lead to an appreciable change in the number of significant coefficients.

4. In the future we may scale the trade data to reflect the importance of various commodities in world trade. This correction may alter some of the initial empirical results presented here.

IV. PREDICTING FACTOR ABUNDANCE

We now proceed to the the basic empirical results of this paper. Tables 3-1 and 3-2 report the frequency of correct sign matches between the sign of the factor content vector and the sign of the corresponding vector of estimated regression coefficients. Table 3-1 reports the proportion of successes when the elements of these two vectors are compared for each factor, while Table 3-2 reports proportions when the elements are compared for each country. The first four columns of each table show the proportion of sign matches when all signs are considered, that is, without regard to the level of significance. The last four columns of each table show proportions only for the coefficients whose sign is significant at the 10 percent level (one-tail).

For example, the first column of Table 3-1 indicates that for capital the proportion of correct sign matches between the sign of capital's coefficient and the net trade in capital services across the thirty-five countries is 80 percent for Model 1 and 74 percent for Model 4. However, when we consider only those cases in which the sign of capital's coefficient is significant at the 10 percent level, the proportion of sign matches is 88 percent for Model 1 and 86 percent for Model 4.

Table 3-1 indicates that across models the signs for capital and the aggregate land variable frequently match the sign of the net export of their services. The likelihood of a correct sign match typically increases if only significant signs are considered. Among the disaggregated land variables, the sign for arable land frequently predicts the sign of the net trade in arable land, but for pasture land and forest land the frequency of a sign match is considerably less.

Generally, the coefficient signs of the disaggregated labor variables infrequently match the sign of the net trade in their services, though the likelihood of a sign match increases if only significant signs are considered. The results for WHITE, BLUE, and LABOR suggest that these difficulties occur for labor in general and do not essentially reflect difficulties in measuring one or another of the broad occupational groups accurately.

Finally, the bottom row of Table 3-1 shows that for the total overall sample the likelihood that a coefficient's sign will correctly match the sign of the factor content is higher in the more aggregate models, and that this probability increases if only significant signs are considered.[5]

When signs are compared within each country (Table 3-2), the proportion of correct matches for Model 1 exceeds .75 for three countries (Belgium-Luxembourg, Japan, and Greece) and is below .5 for six countries (Argentina, Australia, Austria, Denmark, Egypt, and Ireland). When only significant signs are considered for this model, the proportions increase marginally for most countries. Part of the increase occurs because the more aggregated models give less weight to the labor variables that predict factor abundance less frequently.

To summarize the importance of considering only significant signs, Tables 3-3 and 3-4 show the difference between the proportion of correct sign matches when all signs are considered and when only significant signs are considered for each model. For example, considering only the significant signs for capital in Table 3-3 raises the proportion of successes by .08 for Model 1 and by .12 for Models 2 and 3. There does not appear to be any consistent pattern of increase or decrease in Table 3-3. It all depends on the factor under consideration.

When the differences in proportions are considered for each country (Table 3-4), there also does not appear to be a consistent pattern of increases when only significant signs are considered. The proportion of correct inferences actually falls for many countries.

The proportion of correct sign matches generally appears sensitive to the number of regressors and choice of factor or country. The more aggregated the model, the higher the likelihood of a correct inference. This conclusion is sensitive to the smaller sample size of the more aggregated models. However, even when the overall proportion of sign matches is considered, there does not appear to be an appreciable increase in the proportion of successes either when all signs or only those signs that are significant are considered.

V. SOURCES OF INCORRECT PREDICTIONS OF FACTOR ABUNDANCE

Because the extent to which the sign of a factor's regression coefficient fails to match the sign of the net trade in its services is

5. This occurs in part because the more aggregated models contain fewer labor inputs and therefore give less weight to those inputs where sign matches are the weakest.

Table 3-1. Proportion of Sign Matches Factor by Factor

	All Signs				Significant Signs[a]			
Factor / Model	1	2	3	4	1	2	3	4
CAPITAL	0.80	0.77	0.77	0.74	0.88 (24)[b]	0.89 (18)	0.89 (19)	0.86 (21)
LABOR				0.54				0.50 (10)
WHITE			0.74				0.86 (7)	
BLUE			0.51				0.50 (12)	
PROFTECH	0.40	0.40			1.00 (6)	1.00 (4)		
MANAGERS	0.63	0.54			1.00 (2)	1.00 (1)		
SALES	0.37	0.37			0.63 (8)	1.00 (5)		
CLERICAL	0.66	0.71			1.00 (2)	1.00 (2)		
CRAFTS	0.49	0.49			0.75 (4)	0.67 (3)		
OPERATIVE	0.29	0.29			0.25 (8)	0.25 (4)		
LABORERS	0.49	0.34			0.43 (14)	0.67 (9)		
SERVICE	0.60	0.63			0.57 (14)	0.64 (11)		
FARMERS	0.43	0.37			0.30 (23)	0.39 (18)		
LAND		0.89	0.97	0.97		0.96 (28)	1.00 (28)	0.97 (30)
ARABLE	0.91				0.97 (31)			
PASTURE	0.74				0.74 (27)			
FOREST	0.69				0.63 (16)			
TOTAL	0.58	0.53	0.75	0.75	0.68 (179)	0.76 (103)	0.86 (66)	0.85 (61)

a. Significant at 10 percent level.
b. Numbers in parentheses are sample sizes for listed proportions.

Table 3-2. Proportion of Correct Sign Matches Country by Country

Country	All Signs				Significant Signs			
Model	1	2	3	4	1	2	3	4
ARG	0.46	0.36	0.50	0.33	0.40 (10)[a]	0.50 (2)	0.50 (2)	0.50 (2)
AUSL	0.46	0.45	1.00	1.00	0.46 (13)	0.57 (7)	1.00 (3)	1.00 (2)
AUST	0.46	0.27	0.25	0.33	0.67 (3)	0.50 (2)	0.50 (2)	0.50 (2)
BLUX	0.85	0.91	1.00	1.00	0.75 (4)	1.00 (2)	1.00 (1)	1.00 (1)
BRAZ	0.54	0.64	1.00	1.00	0.80 (5)	0.75 (4)	1.00 (2)	1.00 (2)
BRMA	0.62	0.55	1.00	1.00	0.86 (7)	0.57 (7)	1.00 (2)	1.00 (2)
CAN	0.62	0.45	0.75	0.67	0.00 (0)	0.00 (0)	1.00 (2)	0.00 (1)
DEN	0.46	0.36	0.75	0.67	0.44 (9)	0.50 (2)	1.00 (2)	1.00 (2)
EGPT	0.46	0.55	0.50	0.33	0.80 (5)	0.50 (2)	0.00 (0)	0.00 (0)
FIN	0.62	0.73	1.00	0.67	1.00 (2)	0.00 (0)	0.00 (0)	0.00 (0)
FRA	0.54	0.55	0.75	0.67	0.50 (4)	0.50 (4)	1.00 (1)	1.00 (1)
GER	0.69	0.64	0.50	0.67	0.33 (3)	0.50 (2)	0.50 (2)	0.50 (2)
GRCE	0.77	0.64	1.00	1.00	1.00 (4)	1.00 (2)	1.00 (3)	1.00 (2)
HOKO	0.62	0.55	0.50	0.33	0.80 (5)	0.60 (5)	0.50 (2)	0.50 (2)
ICE	0.54	0.45	0.75	1.00	0.44 (9)	0.50 (2)	0.00 (1)	1.00 (2)
IRE	0.38	0.27	0.50	0.67	0.50 (6)	0.00 (1)	0.00 (1)	0.00 (1)
ITLY	0.54	0.45	0.75	1.00	0.75 (4)	0.67 (3)	1.00 (3)	1.00 (3)
JAP	0.77	0.64	1.00	1.00	0.75 (4)	1.00 (3)	1.00 (3)	1.00 (3)
KORA	0.62	0.55	0.75	0.67	1.00 (2)	0.50 (2)	0.67 (3)	0.67 (3)
MEX	0.54	0.64	0.75	0.67	0.50 (2)	0.00 (1)	1.00 (2)	0.00 (1)

Table 3-2. *Continued*

Country		All Signs				Significant Signs			
	Model 1	2	3	4	1	2	3	4
NETH	0.54	0.55	0.75	1.00	0.60 (5)	0.67 (3)	1.00 (3)	1.00 (2)
NUZE	0.54	0.27	0.75	1.00	0.44 (9)	0.33 (3)	0.00 (1)	1.00 (2)
NIGR	0.54	0.55	0.50	0.67	0.60 (10)	0.67 (3)	0.00 (1)	0.00 (1)
NOR	0.62	0.64	1.00	1.00	1.00 (4)	1.00 (3)	1.00 (3)	1.00 (3)
PLIP	0.62	0.55	0.75	0.67	0.67 (3)	0.50 (4)	1.00 (2)	1.00 (2)
PORT	0.62	0.45	0.75	0.67	0.60 (5)	0.33 (3)	1.00 (1)	1.00 (1)
SING	0.62	0.45	1.00	1.00	0.71 (7)	0.57 (7)	1.00 (4)	1.00 (3)
SPAN	0.54	0.36	0.50	0.33	0.67 (3)	1.00 (1)	0.50 (2)	0.50 (2)
SWE	0.62	0.73	0.75	1.00	0.75 (4)	0.50 (2)	1.00 (1)	1.00 (1)
SWIT	0.54	0.55	0.75	0.67	1.00 (1)	1.00 (1)	0.50 (2)	1.00 (1)
THAI	0.54	0.45	1.00	1.00	0.63 (8)	0.50 (8)	1.00 (3)	1.00 (3)
TURK	0.62	0.73	1.00	1.00	0.75 (4)	1.00 (3)	1.00 (3)	0.00 (1)
UK	0.54	0.45	0.50	0.67	0.83 (6)	1.00 (2)	1.00 (2)	1.00 (2)
US	0.62	0.55	0.50	0.33	0.60 (5)	0.67 (3)	0.00 (0)	0.00 (1)
YUG	0.54	0.55	0.75	0.67	1.00 (1)	1.00 (1)	1.00 (1)	0.50 (2)
TOTAL	0.58	0.53	0.75	0.75	0.64	0.62	0.83	0.79
	(455)	(385)	(140)	(105)	(176)	(100)	(66)	(61)

a. Numbers in parentheses are sample sizes used to compute proportions.

Table 3-3. Difference in Proportions of Correct Sign Matches
(All Signs Versus Significant Signs Factor by Factor)[a]

	Model			
Factor	1	2	3	4
CAPITAL	0.08	0.12	0.12	0.11
LABOR				-0.04
WHITE			0.11	
BLUE			-0.01	
PROFTECH	0.60	0.60		
MANAGERS	0.37	0.46		
SALES	0.25	0.63		
CLERICAL	0.34	0.29		
CRAFTS	0.26	0.18		
OPERATIVE	-0.04	-0.04		
LABORERS	-0.06	0.32		
SERVICE	-0.03	0.01		
FARMERS	-0.12	0.02		
LAND		0.08	0.03	-0.00
ARABLE	0.05			
PASTURE	-0.00			
FOREST	-0.06			
TOTAL	0.11	0.23	0.11	0.10

a. Numbers are the difference between the proportion of correct sign matches when all signs are considered and when only significant signs are considered.

determined by the elements of $(A'A)^{-1}$, we present here an initial analysis to see if one or more of the elements of this matrix play a special role in the nonconformity of signs. For simplicity, our analysis focuses on the four-input model (Model 3).

Table 3-5 shows the computed factor contents $A'T_i$ and the estimated sign of each coefficient for each country and factor. From Table 3-5, one can determine where the sign of a particular regression coefficient is opposite that of the associated factor content. For example, Argentina's trade reveals it to be a net exporter of the services of all four factors, yet the estimated coefficients for CAPITAL and BLUE imply that these factors are instead imported.

Premultiplying a row of $(A'A)^{-1}$ times $A'T_i$ generates a vector, the sum of which yields the value of a factor's regression coefficient. For example, column 1 of the table for CAPITAL (Table 3-6), shows a "pseudo" estimate of CAPITAL's coefficient formed by adding only

Table 3-4. Difference in Proportions of Correct Sign Matches
(All Signs Versus Significant Signs Country by Country)[a]

	Model			
Country	1	2	3	4
ARG	-0.06	0.14	0.00	0.17
AUSL	0.00	0.12	0.00	0.00
AUST	0.21	0.23	0.25	0.17
BLUX	-0.10	0.09	0.00	0.00
BRAZ	0.26	0.11	0.00	0.00
BRMA	0.24	0.03	0.00	0.00
CAN	0.00	0.00	0.25	-0.67
DEN	-0.02	0.14	0.25	0.33
EGPT	0.34	-0.05	0.00	0.00
FIN	0.38	0.00	0.00	0.00
FRA	-0.04	-0.05	0.25	0.33
GER	-0.36	-0.14	0.00	-0.17
GRCE	0.23	0.36	0.00	0.00
HOKO	0.18	0.05	0.00	0.17
ICE	-0.09	0.05	-0.75	0.00
IRE	0.12	-0.27	-0.50	-0.67
ITLY	0.21	0.21	0.25	0.00
JAP	-0.02	0.36	0.00	0.00
KORA	0.38	-0.05	-0.08	0.00
MEX	-0.04	-0.64	0.25	-0.67
NETH	0.06	0.12	0.25	0.00
NUZE	-0.09	0.06	-0.75	0.00
NIGR	0.06	0.12	-0.50	-0.67
NOR	0.38	0.36	0.00	0.00
PLIP	0.05	-0.05	0.25	0.33
PORT	-0.02	-0.12	0.25	0.33
SING	0.10	0.12	0.00	0.00
SPAN	0.13	0.64	0.00	0.17
SWE	0.13	-0.23	0.25	0.00
SWIT	0.46	0.45	-0.25	0.33
THAI	0.09	0.05	0.00	0.00
TURK	0.13	0.27	0.00	-1.00
UK	0.29	0.55	0.50	0.33
US	-0.02	0.12	0.00	-0.33
YUG	0.46	0.45	0.25	-0.17

a. Numbers are the difference between the proportion of correct sign matches when all signs are considered and when only significant signs are considered.

Table 3-5. Factor Contents and Coefficient Signs for Model 3

Country	Net Trade In Factor				Coefficient Sign			
	CAPITAL	WHITE	BLUE	LAND	CAPITAL	WHITE	BLUE	LAND
ARG	782427	4191	21363	12223652345	-	+	-	+
AUSL	-1809995	-34935	-52087	12894256558	-	-	-	+
AUST	-1368152	-12460	-20498	-2217972321	+	+	+	-
BLUX	-1564428	-1701	15153	-4998913504	-	-	+	-
BRAZ	-680131	-2704	11294	11900663931	-	-	+	+
BRMA	-64357	-904	-1679	773268280	-	-	-	+
CAN	-29705	-56605	-101676	6080605094	+	-	-	+
DEN	-1868349	-12056	-26243	9836887655	-	+	-	+
EGPT	-421495	-5851	-7218	121031591	+	-	+	+
FIN	-545217	-4791	3879	-1065252025	-	-	+	-
FRA	-7908344	-10329	-9123	-5719983430	-	-	+	-
GER	92747	165554	279141	-37158025936	-	+	-	-
GRCE	-1458067	-17879	-36806	385844920	-	-	-	+
HOKO	-1639242	-10140	-2097	-5189094261	+	-	+	-
ICE	-118810	-1724	-3765	978487957	-	+	-	+
IRE	-720788	-7800	-14173	2376210571	-	+	+	+
ITLY	-7001410	15381	65318	-14951959173	-	-	+	-
JAP	-9897816	52980	130423	-22030542755	-	+	+	-
KORA	-1560582	-14690	-28244	-1040302878	-	-	+	-
MEX	-763341	-21806	-33986	4781879027	-	-	+	+

Table 3-5. *Continued*

	Net Trade In Factor				Coefficient Sign			
	CAPITAL	WHITE	BLUE	LAND	CAPITAL	WHITE	BLUE	LAND
NETH	-3177739	-19855	-66137	7162358554	-	+	-	+
NUZE	-258561	-4303	-6075	8040838403	-	+	-	+
NIGR	315912	-1204	627	2559901832	-	-	-	+
NOR	-2251766	-25639	-63484	1191668003	-	-	-	+
PLIP	-1010823	-11592	-18995	2009541281	-	-	+	+
PORT	-941518	-8077	-8205	-389704765	-	-	+	-
SING	-842586	-8714	-22757	-1009483203	-	-	-	-
SPAN	-5175127	-44653	-85676	-582606880	-	-	+	+
SWE	-1641759	-6392	-3354	-4828779665	-	-	+	-
SWIT	-2177239	-443	-35492	-5777909333	-	+	-	-
THAI	-615265	-10080	-20704	3690380831	-	-	-	+
TURK	-286414	-6805	-6763	3332417320	-	-	-	+
UK	-17269226	-48687	-168732	-51868065162	-	+	+	-
US	6057256	196847	276194	-3474332415	-	+	-	-
YUG	-1018495	-10597	-12894	279654701	-	-	+	+

the components for CAPITAL, WHITE, BLUE, and LAND. We choose to compute this "pseudo" estimate of a factor's regression coefficient because the intercept component is directly related to a country's trade imbalance. Specifically, since our regressions include a constant term, the first element of the matrix product $A'T_i$ is a country's trade balance. The second column in Table 3-6 shows the computed net trade in capital for each country, while the last column shows the actual regression coefficient for capital (the sum of the five vector elements).

It is seen from Table 3-7 that the sign of capital for Argentina is negative, and the sign of its net trade in capital services is positive. The intercept component and the land component of the coefficient for Argentina are negative in row 1 of Table 3-6. One interpretation of this is thus that there is a "factor complementarity" between capital and land that causes the sign of estimated capital coefficient for Argentina to differ from the sign of its net trade in capital services.[6] This same pattern appears for Germany and the United States.

While the reader is encouraged to examine these tables, we note the following curiosity: in Table 3-6, the sign of the "pseudo" regression coefficient (column 1) for a factor matches the sign of the net trade in that factor for each country in every case but one (LAND for the United States). The exact reason for this is currently a mystery to us. However, since the intercept component is directly related to any imbalance in a country's trade, this raises the question of how one should account for trade imbalances when running these cross-section regressions.

In this context, two questions come to mind. First, should one estimate the regressions excluding the constant term? Second, since the intercept term component of $(A'A)^{-1}$ always multiplies the trade imbalance element of the vector A'T, would normalization of the net trade data so that the computed trade balance is zero yield the "correct" coefficient estimate for each factor?

6. In subsequent work, we intend to use a somewhat different method to examine for factor complementarities. Specifically, factor complementarity can be defined in terms of the elements of the matrix A'A, and we propose to test for complementarity as follows: set the elements a_{ji} and a_{ij} to zero for a pair of factors i and j. Then, if this altered version of the matrix A'A, once inverted and premultiplied by the vector $A'T_i$, is sufficient to reverse the sign of the regression coefficient for factor i, we shall conclude that this sign reversal is specifically due to a complementarity between factor i and factor j. To conclude that any specific result is due solely to a complementarity with factor j, we shall also require that the sign of a regression coefficient is not altered if A'A is redefined to set a_{ji} and a_{ij} to zero for any other combination of factors i and j.

Table 3-6. Components of Coefficient Estimate *(In Thousands)*

Country	CAPITAL (1)[a]	CAPITAL (2)[b]	CAPITAL (3)[c]	WHITE (1)	WHITE (2)	WHITE (3)	BLUE (1)	BLUE (2)	BLUE (3)	LAND (1)	LAND (2)	LAND (3)
ARG	45	782.4	-12.7	5984	4.19	546.8	1689	21.4	-2718	51	12223652	50
AUST	-98.5	-1368	63.3	-9289	-12.5	5956	-2284	-20.5	2527	-10	-2217972	-6
CAN	-188	-29.7	5.27	-26789	-56.6	-8512	-7239	-102	-1471	17	6080605	22
DEN	-137	-1868	-30.8	-8011	-12.1	1973	-3202	-26.2	-50.87	42	9836888	44
EGPT	-35.8	-421.5	.326	-3679	-5.85	-269.2	-797.1	-7.22	279.0	0	121032	1
FRA	-380	-7908	-166	-22112	-10.3	-1909	-5688	-9.12	687.6	-17	-5719983	-13
GER	561	92.7	-203	74707	166	2711	20372	279	-2347	-132	-3.7158E+10	-149
HOKO	-91	-1639	1.46	-9091	-10.1	-373.6	-1196	-2.10	1555	-22	-5189094	-20
ICE	-12.4	-118.8	-1.69	-920.4	-1.72	85.70	-354.7	-3.77	-371.8	4	978488	4
IRE	-60.3	-720.8	-4.72	-4877	-7.80	360.4	-1500	-14.2	152.6	10	2376210	11
ITLY	-229	-7001	-137	-9003	15.4	-374.1	117.3	65.3	2840	-54	-1.4952E+10	-52
KORA	-118	-1561	-7.32	-10603	-14.7	-174.1	-2951	-28.2	339.8	-5	-1040303	-2
MEX	-106	-763.3	-1.34	-11362	-21.8	-1491	-2987	-34.0	127.5	18	4781879	20
NETH	-235	-3178	-47.2	-15249	-19.9	2462	-6640	-66.1	-1051	31	7162359	35
NUZE	-32.9	-258.6	-11.7	-1183	-4.30	812.0	-753.5	-6.08	-124.1	33	8040838	34
NIGR	9.6	315.9	-1.65	538.6	-1.20	-523.3	183.6	.627	-151.5	10	2559902	10
PLIP	-83.9	-1011	-11.7	-7377	-11.6	-571.0	-2028	-19.0	119.4	8	2009541	9
PORT	-64.1	-941.5	-2.59	-5894	-8.08	-94.36	-1209	-8.21	621.1	-2	-389705	-1
SPAN	-381	-5175	-47.7	-32643	-44.7	-1243	-9287	-85.7	622.2	-3	-582607	4
SWE	-84.7	-1642	-35.8	-7270	-6.39	-2661	-1248	-3.35	206.4	-20	-4828780	-19
SWIT	-117	-2177	-9.74	-6035	-.443	4045	-3583	-35.5	-402.2	-21	-5777909	-19
THAI	-65.7	-615.3	-11.3	-5571	-10.1	-441.4	-1900	-20.7	-280.9	15	3690381	16
UK	-938	-17269	-199	-69210	-48.7	508.0	-21503	-169	498.0	-206	-5.1868E+10	-190
US	858	6057	-134	107682	197	141378	23706	276	-5813	9	-3474332	-12
YUG	-76.5	-1018	-3.71	-717.1	-106	-312.0	-1598	-12.9	566.2	1	279655	2

a. (1) = Sum Excluding Intercept b. (2) = Factor Content c. (3) = Coefficient

As a partial check of the constant term issue, Model 3 was re-estimated without a constant term. Table 3-8 shows that when all coefficient signs are considered, the proportion of correct sign matches remains the same for twenty-two of the thirty-five countries, and that for the remaining thirteen countries, the proportion of correct sign matches is reduced. This relative insensitivity of the proportion of correct sign matches also appeared when only significant signs where considered.

As for the second issue, one possible correction for the trade imbalance would be to subtract from each element of a country's trade vector the amount (1/N)*B, where N is the number of observations (industries), and B is the country's trade balance. While this would set to zero the first element of the vector A'T (the trade balance component), it is well known that such a correction only affects the estimate of the intercept and leaves unaffected the coefficient estimates for each of the factor inputs. Of course, other normalizations are possible. For example, Baldwin (1971) computed the net trade in each industry as the difference between the export share and the import share. Whether this is an appropriate correction remains to be explored.

An alternative method for adjustment for trade imbalances may be to correct the computed factor contents A'T rather than the trade vector T. As shown in Bowen, Leamer, and Sveikauskas (1987), if one assumes that preferences are homothetic and internationally identical, then the trade balance correction implied by the H-O-V model is:

(5) $A'T_i - \lambda_i E_w$

where λ_i is the ratio of country i's trade balance to world expenditure (GNP). In addition to imposing the assumption of identical tastes, an unsatisfying feature of this adjustment is that errors in measuring world endowments or world GNP may lead one to incorrectly infer a country's true adjusted factor content vector. Nonetheless, as an initial check of this adjustment, we used the Bowen, Leamer, and Sveikauskas (1987) data on the capital supplies and GNP of twenty-seven countries to compute "world" capital and "world" GNP. We then adjusted the factor content data with respect to capital according to (5) for each of the countries listed in Table 3-7.

For three of the twenty-five countries listed in Table 3-7, the adjustment for the trade imbalance reversed the sign of their net exports of capital services. In particular, the sign of the net exports

Table 3-7. Factor Contents and Coefficient Signs for Model 3

	Net Trade In Factor				Coefficient Sign			
Country	CAPITAL	WHITE	BLUE	LAND	CAPITAL	WHITE	BLUE	LAND
ARG	782427	4191	21363	12223652345	-		-	
AUST	-1368152	-12460	-20498	-2217972321	+	+	+	
CAN	-29705	-56605	-101676	6080605094	+			
DEN	-1868349	-12056	-26243	9836887655		+		
EGPT	-421495	-5851	-7218	121031591	+		+	
FRA	-7908344	-10329	-9123	-5719983430			+	
GER	92747	165554	279141	-37158025936	-		-	
HOKO	-1639242	-10140	-2097	-5189094261	+		+	
ICE	-118810	-1724	-3765	978487957		+	+	+
IRE	-720788	-7800	-14173	2376210571		+	+	
ITLY	-7001410	15381	65318	-14951959173		-		
KORA	-1560582	-14690	-28244	-1040302878			+	
MEX	-763341	-21806	-33986	4781879027			+	
NETH	-3177739	-19855	-66137	7162358554		+		
NUZE	-258561	-4303	-6075	8040838403		+		
NIGR	315912	-1204	627	2559901832	-		-	
PLIP	-1010823	-11592	-18995	2009541281			+	
PORT	-941518	-8077	-8205	-389704765			+	
SPAN	-5175127	-44653	-85676	-582606880			+	+
SWE	-1641759	-6392	-3354	-4828779665			+	
SWIT	-2177239	-443	-35492	-5777909333		+		
THAI	-615265	-10080	-20704	3690380831				+
UK	-17269226	-48687	-168732	-51868065162		+	+	
US	6057256	196847	276194	-3474332415	-		-	
YUG	-1018495	-10597	-12894	279654701			+	

of capital services switched from positive to negative for Germany and the United States, and from negative to positive for Canada. Thus, for these countries, the trade balance adjustment leads to conformity between the sign of these countries' capital coefficient and the sign of their net exports of capital services. However, even after adjustment, the sign of the capital coefficient for Argentina, Austria, Egypt, Hong Kong, and the Philippines remained opposite that of their net trade in capital services. These results suggest that while some form of trade balance correction is needed, the precise form is a matter for further study.

VI. CONCLUSION

Detailed study of inter-industry regressions for thirty-five countries indicates that, overall, the sign of regression coefficients provides a fairly adequate measure of factor abundance as revealed by countries' net trade in factor services. In particular, coefficients whose sign is significant (at a not unreasonable level of significance) correctly reveal factor abundance 65 to 85 percent of the time, depending on the model considered.

However, these overall patterns in turn reflect a diversity of results. Regression coefficients for capital and land generally predict factor abundance quite well. On the other hand, regression coefficients for occupational groups, or their aggregates, such as white-collar workers, blue-collar workers, or labor in general, do not predict factor abundance satisfactorily.

The weakness of the disaggregated labor measures of factor inputs in predicting factor abundance contrasts with the results obtained by Balassa based upon a capitalized wage measure of human capital. It is possible that occupational-based measures of labor quality, despite their broad use in much of the empirical trade literature, do not provide a sufficiently reliable measure of the subtle use of labor quality in production. Conversely, one could also question whether the capitalized wage measure provides a reliable and consistent measure of labor quality.[7] In any event, the role of labor quality in trade clearly requires much further work.

More generally, the evidence that regression coefficients often provide useful information suggests that the factor complementarities emphasized by Leamer and Bowen and by Aw are typically not too severe. It remains to be seen how close these

7. In their study of U.S. trade patterns, Branson and Monoyios (1977) conclude that either measure appears to provide the same explanatory power.

Table 3-8. Proportion of Correct Sign Matches Country by Country for Model 3

Country	Constant Included	Constant Excluded
ARG	0.50	0.50
AUSL	1.00	0.75
AUST	0.25	0.75
BLUX	1.00	1.00
BRAZ	1.00	0.75
BRMA	1.00	0.75
CAN	0.75	0.75
DEN	0.75	0.75
EGPT	0.50	0.75
FIN	1.00	1.00
FRA	0.75	0.50
GER	0.50	0.75
GRCE	1.00	0.75
HOKO	0.50	0.75
ICE	0.75	0.75
IRE	0.50	0.50
ITLY	0.75	0.75
JAP	1.00	1.00
KORA	0.75	0.75
MEX	0.75	0.50
NETH	0.75	0.75
NUZE	0.75	0.75
NIGR	0.50	0.75
NOR	1.00	0.75
PLIP	0.75	0.75
PORT	0.75	0.75
SING	1.00	1.00
SPAN	0.50	0.50
SWE	0.75	0.75
SWIT	0.75	0.75
THAI	1.00	1.00
TURK	1.00	1.00
UK	0.50	0.50
US	0.50	0.50
YUG	0.75	0.75
TOTAL	0.53	0.74

complementarities are to being "severe," what complementarities are most relevant, and how these interactions may vary with the level of development. In addition, our work suggests that a country's trade imbalance may play an important role in determining the sign of a coefficient and thus raises the issue of how one should correct the data for such imbalances. Our continuing work will address these issues.

REFERENCES

Aw, Bee-Yan. 1983. "The Interpretation of Cross-Section Regression Tests of the Heckscher-Ohlin Theory with Many Goods and Factors." *Journal of International Economics* (February): 163-7.

Balassa, Bela. 1979. "The Changing Pattern of Comparative Advantage in Manufactured Goods." *Review of Economics and Statistics* (May): 159-66.

——. 1986. "Comparative Advantage in Manufactured Goods: A Reappraisal." *Review of Economics and Statistics* (May): 315-19.

Baldwin, Robert E. 1971. "Determinants of the Commodity Structure of U.S. Trade." *American Economic Review* (March): 126-46.

Baldwin, Robert E., and R. Spence Hilton. 1984. "A Technique for Indicating Comparative Costs and Predicting Changes in Trade Ratios." *Review of Economics and Statistics* (February): 105-10.

Bowen, Harry P., Edward E. Leamer, and Leo Sveikauskas. 1987. "Multicountry, Multifactor Tests of the Factor Abundance Theory." *American Economic Review* 78 (December): 791-809.

Branson, William H., and Nicholas Monoyios. 1977. "Factor Inputs in U.S. Trade." *Journal of International Economics* (May): 111-31.

Harkness, Jon. 1978. "Factor Abundance and Comparative Advantage." *American Economic Review* (December): 784-800.

——. 1983. "The Factor-Proportions Model with Many Nations, Goods and Factors: Theory and Evidence." *Review of Economics and Statistics* (May): 298-305.

Leamer, Edward E. 1984. *Sources of International Comparative Advantage: Theory and Evidence.* Cambridge: MIT Press.

——. 1987. "Paths of Development in the Three-Factor, n Good General Equilibrium Model." *Journal of Political Economy* (October): 961-99.

Leamer, Edward E., and Harry P. Bowen. 1981. "Cross-Section Tests of the Heckscher-Ohlin Theorem: Comment." *American Economic Review* (December): 1040-3.

Stern, Robert M., and Keith E. Maskus. 1981. "Determinants of U.S. Foreign Trade, 1958-76." *Journal of International Economics* (May): 207-24.

Vanek, Jaroslav. 1968. "The Factor Proportions Theory: The N-Factor Case." *Kyklos* (October): 749-55.

II EMPIRICAL ANALYSIS OF TRADE FLOWS AND POLICY

While there has been a plethora of contributions to the theory of international trade, as reflected in the previous section, empirical analyses have remained relatively scarce. This does not suggest that empirical analysis is unimportant, but rather implies that it is difficult to assemble large data bases of high quality and apply them to test the predictions of the theoretical models. In this section, empirical analyses of both trade patterns and policies are provided. In particular, all four papers focus on bilateral trade and trade policies between the United States and Japan. This group of papers is important not only because it focuses on bilateral trade, but because it provides much more detailed analyses and richer data sets than have been previously undertaken.

David B. Audretsch and Hideki Yamawaki consider how the strategic aspect of Japanese and U.S. R&D expenditures affected U.S.-Japanese bilateral trade during the late 1970s. They examine how the allocation of R&D expenditures in each country has contributed to promoting its own trade advantage. Not only do they find that industrial policy in Japan served to improve its trade advantage, but also that the contribution of R&D toward increasing international competitiveness for each country depends on how it is allocated.

Keith E. Maskus, Deborah Battles, and Michael Moffett focus on the U.S.-Korea bilateral trade relationship and the U.S.-Japanese bilateral trade pattern. They estimate models of the direct factor-intensity characteristics of trade and the sources of intra-industry trade. One of their important findings is that the level of labor skills plays an important role in determining intra-industry trade within these bilateral contexts.

Alan V. Deardorff and Robert M. Stern use the Michigan Model of World Production and Trade to examine various scenarios for the multilateral removal of tariffs and nontariff barriers by the major industrialized and developing countries. Because it represents one of the few studies attempting to quantify the impact of trade liberalization, their paper has obvious policy implications. With the impending completion of an integrated European market in 1992 and the accompanying fears in the United States and Japan that their once reliable trading partners will be replaced by "Fortress Europe," Deardorff and Stern's paper is particularly timely.

4 THE ALLOCATION OF R&D EXPENDITURES AND U.S.-JAPANESE TRADE

David B. Audretsch and Hideki Yamawaki

I. INTRODUCTION

While expenditures on research and development (R&D) have been considered to be an important determinant of trade flows for at least two decades (Gruber, Mehta, and Vernon 1967; Hufbauer 1970), very recent literature (Teece 1987; Griliches 1986) suggests that innovation and R&D may be perhaps the most decisive determinants of trade between advanced developed countries such as Japan and the United States. For example, Spencer and Brander (1983), and Audretsch and Yamawaki (1988) argue that R&D expenditures, both in the United States as well as those undertaken by its trading partners, may influence trade flows. The purpose of this paper is to examine how the strategic aspect of Japanese and U.S. R&D expenditures affected U.S.-Japanese bilateral trade during the late 1970s. In particular, we investigate which component of Japanese R&D—expenditures on process innovation, product quality improvements, new products or new technology, and technology

We are grateful to Richard Caves, Thomas Pugel, and J. David Richardson, as well as the rest of the participants at the Tenth Annual Middlebury Conference on Economic Issues, April 7-9, 1988, for their helpful comments. We thank Michael Karge and Jianping Yang for their research and computational assistance. We are also grateful to Edward J. Ray for making some of the data available to us.

transfer—proved to be most effective. We are then able to compare these results with the effectiveness of similar U.S. expenditures on basic R&D, applied R&D, private R&D, and government R&D. Unfortunately, the lack of comparable data excludes the possibility of comparing exactly the same components of R&D in Japan and the United States.

We examine in Section II the structure of U.S.-Japanese bilateral trade for 1977, along with the historical trend in R&D for both countries. In Section III, we combine standard international trade models with industrial organization measures to derive a cross-section regression model estimating U.S.-Japanese bilateral trade. Using 213 four-digit standard industrial classification (SIC) industries, the model is estimated in Section IV. We find that the allocation of R&D resources in both countries influences trade. R&D expenditures in Japan are found to be more effective in promoting the trade position when they are allocated toward process innovation and improving the quality of existing products than toward developing new products and technology. Similarly, expenditures on basic R&D in the United States are found to have promoted the U.S. trade advantage more than have expenditures on applied R&D. In addition, government expenditures on R&D are found to be less effective than private expenditures. This provides some evidence supporting Griliches (1986), who found that private R&D and basic R&D contributed more to U.S. productivity increases than did government R&D and applied R&D.

Finally, two results suggest that U.S.-Japanese trade is structurally very different from trade between the United States and other countries. Contrary to the consistent empirical result that U.S. industries utilizing high-skill intensive labor tend to be net exporters, we find that the U.S.-Japanese bilateral trade balance is negatively related to the skill level of the U.S. labor force. Similarly, U.S. net export industries have consistently been identified as relatively labor-intensive, while we find that capital-intensity is positively related to the trade balance in the case of U.S.-Japanese trade.

II. U.S.-JAPANESE TRADE

Neither U.S. imports from nor U.S. exports to Japan are evenly distributed across manufacturing industries. In the first column of Table 4-1, the thirty-five largest four-digit SIC industries importing manufactured products from Japan in 1977 are ranked in

Table 4-1. U.S. Industries with the Largest Value of Japanese Imports, 1977

Industry	U.S. Imports from Japan ($100,000)	Penetration in U.S. (%)	Rank	Total Import Penetration in U.S. (%)
Motor vehicles	46,031.25	5.48	(19)	15.70
Steel mills	21,659.47	4.70	(27)	11.36
Radio & TV sets	20,926.13	23.93	(4)	39.80
Radio & TV comm. equip.	7,875.33	5.30	(21)	10.20
Motorcycles & bicycles	6,868.50	37.01	(2)	47.82
Photographic equipment	5,859.96	6.18	(13)	10.18
Bolts, nuts, rivets & washers	2,527.75	7.09	(11)	11.69
Motor vehicle parts	2,090.54	0.62	(148)	8.37
Optical instruments	2,055.67	14.06	(8)	20.11
Electronic computing equip.	2.046.47	1.97	(63)	6.89
Construction machinery	1,778.73	1.86	(64)	7.41
Calculating machines	1,739.76	18.79	(6)	31.09
Tires and innertubes	1,645.09	1.73	(70)	8.89
Ball and roller bearings	1,518.00	5.72	(17)	11.10
Watches & clocks	1,454.93	6.87	(12)	32.40
Weaving mills	1,316.37	2.09	(60)	4.39
Electronic components	1,241.14	2.40	(54)	6.31
Steel wire	1,220.61	4.83	(23)	12.88
Internal combustion engines	1,097.30	1.47	(80)	12.64
Hand & edge tools	1,049.30	4.72	(26)	10.32
Sporting & athletic goods	1,045.62	3.80	(34)	18.98
Electric housewares & fans	1,012.77	3.92	(32)	8.50
Industrial organic chemicals	996.00	0.44	(185)	2.79
Machine tools (metal cutting)	959.41	3.33	(39)	13.29
Sewing machines	949.97	22.02	(5)	49.84
Fine earthenware food utensils	947.29	44.11	(1)	64.06
Plastics products	920.32	0.39	(193)	2.28
Cyclic crudes	853.25	1.61	(72)	10.29
Medicinals & botanicals	837.78	5.89	(15)	39.13
Semiconductors	815.37	1.58	(76)	25.48
Valves & pipe fittings	723.96	1.33	(86)	5.29
Musical instruments	685.38	7.27	(10)	15.48
Office machines	685.67	2.49	(53)	6.85
Games & toys	680.56	2.29	(55)	13.23
Vitreous china food utensils	675.98	24.96	(3)	38.92

descending order of the absolute level of imports. Thus, the auto industry, with slightly more than $4.6 billion of Japanese imports, was by far the largest importer of Japanese goods. In contrast, the blast furnace and steel mills and the radio and television sets industries had less than half the dollar value of Japanese imports. Each of the next three largest importing industries—radio and television communication equipment, motorcycles and bicycles, and photographic equipment—imported a considerably smaller value of Japanese goods, between $586 million and $788 million. Thus, the size distribution of imports is skewed toward a select group of industries.

The second column in Table 4-1 shows the Japanese import penetration ratio in the United States, defined as U.S. imports from Japan divided by industry value of shipments plus total imports minus total U.S. exports. The ranking of the Japanese import penetration, in descending order, is given in parentheses. For example, although the motor vehicles industry experienced the largest value of imports, measured in absolute dollars, the Japanese import penetration ratio ranked only nineteenth at 5.48 percent. In some industries, such as motor vehicle parts and accessories, industrial organic chemicals, and plastic products, the ranking of the Japanese import penetration ratio is relatively low compared to the absolute dollar value of imports from Japan. In other industries, such as sewing machines, fine earthenware food utensils, and medicinals and botanicals, the ranking of the Japanese import penetration ratio is relatively high compared to the absolute dollar value of imports from Japan. In such industries, the domestic market in the United States is small relative to the value of imports from Japan. Several industries, such as radio and television sets, motorcycles and bicycles, and optical instruments, have both a high absolute dollar value of imports and a high penetration ratio.

The last column in Table 4-1 shows the total import penetration ratio in the U.S., defined as total U.S. imports divided by the industry value-of-shipments plus total imports minus total U.S. exports. In some industries, such as radio and television receiving sets, motorcycles and bicycles, photographic equipment, optical instruments, and vitreous china food utensils, Japanese products comprise the majority of the total import penetration. In other industries, including motor vehicle parts and accessories, tires and innertubes, and internal combustion engines, imports from Japan constitute a relatively small portion of the total import penetration ratio.

Table 4-2 focuses on the pattern of U.S. exports to Japan. In the first column, industries are ranked according to the absolute dollar value of 1977 exports to Japan. Thus, the largest export industry is logging contractors, which shipped over $831 million of products to Japan. The second largest, meatpacking plants, exported only $350 million of goods to Japan. The tenth largest export industry, aircraft, had $119 million of sales to Japan. Like the imports, the size distribution of U.S. exports to Japan is also skewed toward a relatively select group of industries.

The second column in Table 4-2 shows how large the value of U.S. exports to Japan is relative to domestic production—or the Japanese export share. For example, in the logging contractors industry, 13.34 percent of the value of U.S. shipments is sold to Japan. Since the number in parentheses indicates the relative ranking in descending order, the logging contractors industry had the highest export share to Japan. While some industries, such as petroleum refining and motor vehicles, export a relatively large value of goods to Japan, the percentage of total domestic production—0.11 percent and 0.12 percent—is relatively small. In other industries, such as measuring and controlling devices and jewelers' materials, the value of U.S. exports to Japan is relatively large compared to the value of domestic production.

The last column in Table 4-2 shows the ratio of total U.S. exports as a percentage of domestic production—or the total export share. Thus, while logging products ranks highest in terms of exports to Japan both absolutely and as a percentage of domestic production, other industries, such as electronic computing equipment, pulpmills, medicinals and botanicals, specialized industrial machinery, and measuring and controlling devices, have higher total export shares. In only a few industries, such as logging contractors, do sales to Japan constitute the majority of total U.S. exports. More typical is the sawmills industry, where total exports account for 6.63 percent of total domestic production, while exports to Japan account for only 2.53 percent of total domestic production. Thus, although Japanese goods often constitute the majority of U.S. imports, in only a few cases is Japan the destination of the majority of U.S. goods exported.

Several industries appear on both Tables 4-1 and 4-2. Such industries represent the existence of substantial intra-industry trade. For example, while the United States imported $205 million of electronic computing equipment from Japan, it simultaneously exported $279 million in the same industry to Japan. Thus, the Japanese import penetration ratio in the United States was 1.97 percent, while the U.S. exported 2.16 percent of its total domestic production to Japan. Other industries experiencing similar levels of intra-industry trade include photographic equipment, medicinals and botanicals, semiconductors, and cyclic crudes.

As mentioned in Section I, a number of studies have suggested that innovation and R&D expenditures play a crucial role in determining trade flows between developed nations such as the United States and Japan. While this hypothesis is formally tested in Section III, it is clear from Table 4-3 that R&D patterns have evolved differently over the past two decades in the United States and Japan. There are a number of sectors, such as rubber and plastics, nonelectrical machinery, motor vehicles, and instruments, where the ratio of R&D to sales increased considerably for both Japanese and American firms between 1965 and 1982. However, there are also many sectors in which the R&D intensity of Japanese industries—including industrial chemicals, drugs, nonferrous metal, electrical equipment, communications, and transportation equipment other than motor vehicles—rose while that of their American counterparts did not increase over the same period. Similarly, there are also industries, such as those comprising the paper sector, where the R&D intensity increased in American firms but not in their Japanese counterparts. The exact role that the allocation of these expenditures plays in Japan and the United States is examined in the next section.

III. THE MODEL

Although only a few studies have attempted to identify the determinants of bilateral trade between the United States and Japan, a number of studies examining aggregate U.S. trade have generally reached the same conclusion: none of the international trade hypotheses fully explains variations in the trade structure (Baldwin 1971; Stern 1976; Stern and Maskus 1981). Rather, as Baldwin found, ". . . it is necessary to discard the simple single factor trade theories in favor of multifactor trade models" (1971, 143). Hufbauer (1970), Baldwin (1971, 1979), and Stern and Maskus (1981) found that the standard Heckscher-Ohlin theory, human skills hypothesis, and neotechnology theories combine to provide the fullest and most complete explanation of actual trade behavior. According to the Heckscher-Ohlin theory, the endowment of productive factors determines the trade structure. If there exists an abundance of physical capital relative to labor, a country will tend toward export of capital-intensive goods; an abundance of labor relative to physical capital leads to the export of labor-intensive

Table 4-2. U.S. Industries with the Largest Value of Exports to Japan, 1977

Industry	U.S. Exports to Japan ($100,000)	U.S. Exports to Japan as % of Output	Rank	U.S. Total Exports as % of Output
Logging contractors	8,311.87	13.34	(1)	16.34
Meatpacking plants	3,498.68	1.12	(42)	3.90
Electronic computing equip.	2,794.64	2.16	(16)	25.26
Sawmills	2,744.83	2.53	(10)	6.63
Industrial inorganic chemicals	2,274.13	2.62	(8)	13.24
Pulpmills	1,717.83	8.21	(2)	44.25
Photographic equipment	1,461.11	1.47	(28)	14.44
Industrial organic chemicals	1,408.05	0.58	(79)	8.23
Medicinals & botanicals	1,227.34	6.49	(3)	54.22
Aircraft	1,194.68	0.81	(58)	25.98
Aircraft equipment	1,013.23	2.13	(17)	40.76
Petroleum refining	996.72	0.11	(195)	1.14
Motor vehicles	902.56	0.12	(181)	7.41
Special industry machinery	787.94	2.17	(15)	43.26
Canned seafoods	775.57	5.38	(6)	10.53
Semiconductors	751.21	1.41	(32)	27.98
Plastics materials & resins	746.40	0.69	(67)	9.79
Chemical preparations	722.24	1.83	(21)	22.54
Instruments to measure elec.	627.67	2.27	(13)	21.69
Polishes & sanitation goods	615.22	1.95	(19)	8.94
Measuring & controlling devices	607.86	5.44	(5)	66.30
Radio & TV comm. equip.	603.74	0.41	(101)	10.42
Aircraft engines	580.79	0.93	(49)	13.44
Soybean oil mills	560.24	0.74	(61)	17.72
Paperboard mills	525.35	0.74	(62)	9.25
Pharmaceutical preparations	511.89	0.45	(94)	2.79
Plastics products	498.66	0.21	(147)	3.79
Condensed milk	487.12	1.53	(26)	7.04
Cyclic crudes	472.11	0.84	(57)	15.69
Secondary nonferrous metals	439.47	1.24	(34)	7.29
Surgical instruments	416.24	2.27	(14)	21.86
Animal fats & oils	415.44	2.51	(11)	36.06
Sporting goods	407.33	1.68	(25)	8.01
Jewelers' materials	391.22	5.71	(4)	54.04
Construction machinery	384.54	0.30	(121)	29.97

goods (Lowinger 1971). The human skills hypothesis extends the Heckscher-Ohlin theory by including human capital as a third factor. In the presence of a relative abundance of a highly trained labor force and professional personnel, a country is predicted to export skill-intensive goods. Conversely, the abundance of skilled labor tends to promote the importation of skill-intensive goods (Keesing 1966).

The neotechnology theories focus on R&D and the stage of an industry in the product life cycle. Gruber et al. (1967) suggest that R&D expenditures reflect a temporary comparative advantage resulting from products and production techniques that have not yet been adopted by foreign competitors. Thus, industries with a relatively high R&D component are considered to be in the early stages of the product life cycle and are expected to be net exporters (Vernon 1966).

Just as the theory of international trade in the context of monopolistic competition has recently emerged, recent empirical work has sought to incorporate industrial organization concepts in explaining trade behavior. White (1974), Pagoulatos and Sorenson (1976), Pugel (1978), and Caves et al. (1980) show that market structure significantly affects the trade structure, largely through creating barriers to entry.

In trying to identify the effect of Japanese industrial policy and R&D on U.S.-Japanese trade, we have included variables representing each of the major theories and influences discussed above. Specifically, we use:

Dependent Variable

TB: The U.S.-Japanese trade balance, defined as TB=(X-M)/(X+M), where X is U.S. exports to Japan in 1977, and M is U.S. imports from Japan in 1977. Thus, this measure weights net exports, X-M, by the total amount traded between the two countries, X+M. The identical variable was used by Pugel (1978) and Audretsch and Yamawaki (1988). It has the advantage of implicitly controlling for transportability while still indicating the comparative advantage. As Pugel notes, this measure has the disadvantage of perhaps overstating the importance to the low balance of trade of industries in which there is only little international trade.

Table 4-3. R&D-to-Sales (%) in Japan and the U.S., 1965-1982

Industry	1965		1970		1975		1980		1982	
	Japan	U.S.	Japan	U.S.	Japan	U.S.	Japan	U.S.	Japan	U.S.
Food & beverages	0.4	0.4	0.5	0.5	0.5	0.4	0.6	0.4	0.6	0.4
Textiles & apparel	0.7	0.5	0.6	0.5	0.7	0.4	0.8	0.4	1.1	0.4
Paper	0.5	0.8	0.4	0.9	0.5	0.9	0.4	1.0	0.5	1.2
Chemicals	0.2	4.3	0.4	3.8	0.4	3.7	0.3	3.6	0.4	4.3
Industrial	1.5	4.7	1.8	4.0	1.8	3.6	1.9	3.3	2.2	4.0
Drugs	3.0	6.4	3.4	6.7	4.9	6.4	5.5	6.2	5.6	6.2
Petroleum	0.2	0.9	0.3	1.0	0.2	0.7	0.3	0.6	0.2	0.6
Rubbers & plastics	1.0	1.9	1.2	2.3	2.2	2.2	2.1	2.2	2.5	2.2
Stone, clay & glass	0.9	1.6	1.0	1.8	1.3	1.2	1.3	1.4	1.6	1.4
Iron & steel	0.7	0.7	0.6	0.7	1.1	0.6	1.1	0.7	1.5	0.7
Nonferrous metals	1.2	0.9	0.9	1.0	1.0	1.2	1.0	0.7	1.6	0.7
Fabricated metal products	0.8	1.3	0.8	1.2	1.1	1.2	1.2	1.4	1.4	1.3
Nonelectrical machinery	1.0	4.0	1.4	4.0	1.7	4.8	1.9	5.0	2.3	5.5
Electrical equipment	2.3	9.1	3.0	7.3	3.8	6.5	3.7	6.6	4.1	7.7
Communications[a]	2.4	11.4	3.1	8.2	4.2	7.3	3.9	8.7	4.7	9.3
Motor vehicles	1.6	3.1	1.7	3.5	1.8	3.5	2.4	4.9	3.0	4.6
Other transportation equipment	0.7	3.1	1.1	3.5	2.5	1.3	2.2	0.6	1.7	0.6
Instruments	1.6	5.9	2.0	5.7	2.8	5.9	3.0	7.5	4.0	8.9
Other manufacturing	0.6	0.7	0.7	0.8	1.2	0.8	1.2	0.4	1.3	0.4
Manufacturing total	1.1	4.3	1.4	3.7	1.6	3.1	1.7	3.0	2.2	3.8

a. Includes electrical components.

Source: National Science Foundation, *National Patterns of Science and Technology Resources*, various years; and Japan, Bureau of Statistics, Office of the Minister, *Report of the Survey of Research and Development in Japan*, various years.

Independent Variables

K/L: The capital-labor ratio. K/L has been found to be negatively related to U.S. net exports in most empirical studies, giving rise to the famous "Leontief Paradox" (Baldwin 1971; Stern and Maskus 1981). In his study, which excluded trade barriers and industrial policy, Baldwin found a negative but statistically insignificant relationship between K/L and net exports between the United States and Japan.

HUMK: A measure of human capital and skilled labor, defined as the difference between the annual average industry wage per employee and the annual wage for persons with less than eight years of education, capitalized at 10 percent, for 1970. This measure is identical to the one described by Kenen (1970) and used by Baldwin (1971). As Stern reports after surveying the empirical literature, "There seems to be little question now that U.S. exports are relatively more human-capital intensive than imports" (1976, 12). Thus, most studies have found HUMK and other measures of the level of labor skills (see Keesing 1966) to have a positive and significant coefficient.

RD/S: U.S. R&D expenditures divided by sales, 1977. Ray (1981a, 1981b), Baldwin (1971), Gruber et al. (1967), Keesing (1967), and Lowinger (1975) all found a positive relationship between R&D intensity and U.S. exports.

CR4: The four-firm concentration ratio, 1977. White (1974) demonstrated that market concentration is conducive to imports through the incentive of elevated price-cost margins. Accordingly, Koo and Martin (1984) found a negative and statistically significant relationship between CR and net exports.

AD/S: Advertising intensity measured as advertising expenditures divided by 1977 industry value-of-shipments. According to Caves (1974) and Pagoulatos and Sorenson (1976), the mainstream view in industrial organization is that advertising creates an entry barrier and therefore should be negatively related to imports.

NTB: An index of nontariff barriers in the United States divided by an index of nontariff barriers in Japan for 1970. The same variable was also used by Ray (1981a, 1981b), who argues that nontariff barriers should have a larger effect on trade than do tariff barriers. While nontariff barriers may also be endogenous to the contemporary trade structure, as Ray found, the seven-year lag between NTBUS and TB is sufficient to classify NTBUS as a predetermined variable.

BRD: Expenditures on basic R&D in the United States as a percentage of total R&D expenditures (the sum of basic plus applied R&D), 1973. Griliches (1986) found that basic R&D contributes more to U.S. productivity growth than does applied R&D. A positive coefficient of BRD would be consistent with Griliches' finding and would suggest that American industries that allocate a relatively large share of R&D toward basic research tend to have the trade advantage vis-à-vis Japan. Of course, while Griliches (1986) measured the impact of R&D allocation on U.S. productivity growth, we are measuring its influence on U.S. bilateral trade with Japan.

FRD: Federal funds for industrial R&D expenditures, 1973. A negative sign would be consistent with Griliches' (1986) conclusion that government-funded R&D contributes less to American productivity growth than does private R&D.

JIP: A dummy variable taking on a value of one when the industry had been a target for Japanese industrial policy in the form of preferential depreciation allowance status between 1962-1973. Specifically, those industries with 10 percent or more of total depreciation covered by a special depreciation allowance are classified as recipients of preferential status.[1] When an industry was granted such status, it signaled that the MITI considered the industry to be strategic (Ito et al. 1984). According to Ueno, "A subsidy is important in itself, but it is more important as a signal indicating that the industry or the product

1. Specifically, the special depreciation allowance as a percentage of total depreciation between 1962-1973 was 15 percent in shipbuilding, 13 percent in autos, 12 percent in steel, 13 percent in machinery, and 10 percent in textiles. The average in manufacturing industries was 8 percent (Ogura and Yoshino 1984).

receiving the subsidy is publicly recognized as one under government protection" (1980, 388). If Japanese industrial policy has been effective, the regression coefficient is expected to be negative. This variable is further explained in our 1988 paper.

JPRIN: Japanese R&D expenditures on process innovation as a percentage of total R&D expenditures, fiscal 1969.

JQUAL: Japanese R&D expenditures on product quality improvements, as a percentage of total R&D expenditures, fiscal 1969.

JNEW: Japanese R&D expenditures on new products or new technology, as a percentage of total R&D expenditures, fiscal 1969.

JTRAN: Japanese R&D expenditures on technology transfer, as a percentage of total R&D expenditures, fiscal 1969.

The source of each variable and additional explanations are listed in the Appendix.

IV. REGRESSION RESULTS

Using the balance of trade between the United States and Japan (TB) in 1977 as the dependent variable, the cross-section regression results for 213 four-digit SIC manufacturing industries are shown in Table 4-4.[2] Equation 1 includes the standard variables from international trade and industrial organization—K/L, HUMK, RD/S, CR4, and AD/S—as well as the measure of trade resistance, NTB.[3] The positive and statistically significant sign of K/L implies that the United States tends to import goods from Japan in industries that are relatively labor-intensive and export goods to Japan in industries that are relatively capital-intensive. Apparently, the general finding of capital-intensive industries being associated with high levels of U.S. imports—the Leontief Paradox—does not

2. Only 182 industries are used in equations 2, 3, and 5 due to data constraints when using the U.S. R&D allocations.

3. A measure of relative tariff barriers was also included in the regression but proved to be very significant.

Table 4-4. Regressions of the U.S.-Japan Balance of Trade for Components of U.S. and Japanese R&D Expenditures
(Standard Errors Listed in Parentheses)

	REGRESSION				
	OLS			LOGIT	
	1	2	3	4	5
JPRIN	-3.6170	-	-	-19.5340	-
	(1.6295)[b]			(6.9176)[b]	
JQUAL	-3.8892	-	-	-18.9710	-
	(1.9593)[b]			(8.3177)[b]	
JNEW	-2.5811	-	-	-13.3440	-
	(1.8657)			(8.0000)	
JTRAN	-2.9156	-	-	-11.8250	-
	(2.1141)			(8.9747)	
JIP	-0.4436	-0.2125	-0.1481	-1.7811	0.2678
	(0.1462)[b]	(0.1381)	(0.1353)	(0.6206)[b]	(0.0933)[b]
RD/S	-0.0065	0.0585	0.0406	-0.0408	0.2678
	(0.0226)	(0.0213)[b]	(0.0203)[b]	(0.0959)	(0.0933)[b]
AD/S	0.1038	0.1819	0.2872	-0.4567	-0.4592
	(0.3153)	(0.3206)	(0.3249)	(1.3386)	(1.4027)
CR4	-0.0038	-0.0051	-0.0061	-0.0154	-0.0246
	(0.0022)[b]	(0.0023)[b]	(0.0024)[b]	(0.0097)	(0.0105)[b]
K/L	0.6221	0.6442	0.6715	2.5585	2.9620
	(0.2124)[b]	(0.1963)[b]	(0.1988)[b]	(0.9015)[b]	(0.8589)[b]
HUMK	-0.1675	-0.3242	-0.3261	-0.8126	-1.5438
	(0.0774)[b]	(0.0822)[b]	(0.0833)[b]	(0.3287)[b]	(0.3595)[b]
NTB	0.1359	0.0650	0.0649	0.4908	0.2955
	(0.1051)	(0.0241)[b]	(0.0243)[b]	(0.4460)	(0.1055)[b]
BRD	-	0.8188	1.5589	-	-0.4462
		(0.8816)	(1.1241)		(3.8569)
FRD	-	-0.0731	-	-	-0.2264
		(0.0290)[b]			(0.1269)[a]
Intercept	3.4457	0.6972	0.6945	17.6010	3.8332
	(1.6168)[a]	(0.2990)[b]	(0.3033)[b]	(6.8636)[b]	(1.3081)[b]
R^2	0.181	0.239	0.257	0.183	0.217
F	5.269[b]	6.679[b]	6.592[b]	5.311[b]	6.019[b]

a. Statistically significant at the 90 percent level of confidence, two-tailed test.
b. Statistically significant at the 95 percent level of confidence, two-tailed test.

hold in the case of bilateral trade between the United States and Japan.

The negative and statistically significant sign of HUMK implies that U.S. imports from Japan tend to occur in industries requiring a relatively high component of skilled labor, while U.S. exports to Japan tend to occur in industries not utilizing skilled labor. Again, the U.S.-Japanese structure of trade in 1977 is apparently contradictory to the general pattern of U.S. trade, where net export industries have been found to be skilled-labor intensive. The statistically insignificant coefficient of RD/S might suggest that U.S. R&D does not play a significant role in determining U.S.-Japanese bilateral trade, but it should be noted that this variable is highly correlated with several of the Japanese R&D variables included in the model.

The negative and statistically significant coefficient of CR4 supports the findings of Koo and Martin (1984) that, *ceteris paribus,* foreign competitors have a greater incentive to enter concentrated markets. However, the insignificant coefficient of AD/S provides little support for the contention by Caves (1974) that advertising intensity serves as a barrier to foreign entry. The positive, although weak, coefficient of NTB implies that U.S. nontariff barriers are effective at impeding Japanese imports, and Japanese nontariff barriers deter American imports.

As the negative and statistically significant coefficients of JPRIN and JQUAL indicate, an increase in R&D expenditures on either product innovation or product quality improvements, holding the total budget of R&D constant, is associated with an improvement in Japan's bilateral trade position. In contrast, increases in R&D expenditures on developing new products and technology and on technology transfer have no apparent effect on the bilateral trade balance. This supports the thesis of Peck and Tamura (1976) that Japanese R&D expenditures that have been oriented toward improving the quality or reducing the costs of existing products have been more effective than R&D allocated toward developing new products and technology.

One statistical concern with the estimation is that the dependent variable is by definition bounded by one and negative one. Judge et al. (1980) note that under such conditions ordinary least-square estimation could produce inefficient variances of the estimated coefficients and therefore unreliable t-statistics, rendering the necessary hypothesis tests also unreliable. By first transforming the dependent variable to vary between zero and one, where TB*= (TB+1)/2, we then correct for this potential inefficiency by using a logit transformation, where the transformed dependent variable (TB*) is again transformed to ln (TB*/(1-TB*)). As shown in equation 4, the logit transformation has virtually no effect on the results. In terms of coefficient signs and significance, the results yielded in equation 4 are identical to those in equation 1.

Equation 2 addresses the question: Does the allocation of U.S. R&D between basic and applied research, and between federal and private research have any impact on the bilateral trade balance? As the negative and statistically significant coefficient of FRD suggests, private R&D has been more effective in promoting the U.S. trade balance than has federal R&D. It should be noted that the negative coefficient of FRD does not imply that federal R&D expenditures lead to a decrease in the U.S. bilateral trade position. Rather, the results imply that the marginal benefit of an additional dollar of private R&D is greater than that of federal R&D. These results are consistent with the conclusion of Griliches (1986) that private R&D contributed more to U.S. productivity growth than did federal R&D. This result is confirmed even after making the logit transformation in equation 5. The positive but statistically insignificant coefficient of BRD could be attributable to high multicollinearity, since the correlation between FRD and BRD is 0.595. Thus, FRD is omitted from the regression in equation 3, and the coefficient of BRD increases considerably, though it remains insignificant (but significant at the 80 percent level of confidence). This lends some support to the hypothesis that basic R&D has promoted U.S. trade more than has applied R&D. This result is also consistent with Griliches' (1986) findings.

Based on the estimated regressions, two general questions concerning the overall influence of the allocation of R&D budgets in Japan and the United States can be addressed:

1. Was Japan's trade advantage in 1977 promoted by the allocation of R&D among expenditures on process innovation, product quality, new products, and technology transfer?
2. Was America's trade advantage promoted by the allocation of R&D between basic and applied R&D and between federal and private R&D?

Table 4-5 shows the resulting F-statistics from testing each of these hypotheses. The hypothesis that the allocation of Japanese R&D expenditures has no effect on promoting the trade advantage is tested by comparing the explained sum of squares from equation 1 in Table 4-4 with the explained sum of squares when the coefficients of JPRIN, JQUAL, JNEW, and JTRAN are restricted to equal zero. The resulting F-value of 3.490, which is statistically significant at the 95 percent level of confidence, implies that the allocation of expenditures on R&D by Japanese firms influences the trade balance.

By restricting BRD and FRD to equal zero, the resulting F-value of 3.789 implies that the allocation of R&D expenditures between basic and applied R&D and between federal and private funding has an influence on the subsequent U.S. trade performance, at least with respect to bilateral trade with Japan.

V. CONCLUSIONS

Two types of conclusions emerge from this study. The first is that although several patterns regarding the U.S. general trade structure have emerged in the literature, these patterns may not hold in the case of bilateral trade, at least between the United States and Japan. A positive association in the previous literature has consistently been found between the level of skilled-labor content in an industry and U.S. exports. The United States has been considered to hold the comparative advantage in high-skill industries. However, in the case of bilateral trade between the U.S. and Japan, we find the reverse: the U.S. tends to import more from Japan in industries requiring skilled labor.

Similarly, the United States has consistently been found in the previous literature to have a greater value of imports in capital-intensive industries, and a greater value of exports in labor-intensive industries—the Leontief Paradox. Again, this finding is apparently reversed in the case of U.S.-Japanese bilateral trade. The United States tends to export goods in capital-intensive industries to Japan and import goods in labor-intensive industries from Japan.

The second conclusion is that the allocation of the R&D budget among major components apparently affects the trade performance for both Japan and the United States. We find that Japanese R&D expenditures on improving the quality of existing products and on cost-reducing process innovation for existing products were more effective than analogous expenditures on developing new products and technology and on applications from technology transfer. Similarly, just as U.S. R&D expenditures on basic research have proven to be more effective than expenditures on applied research, private R&D has promoted the American trade advantage more than federal R&D.

Table 4-5. Testing for the Overall Significance of the Allocation of Japanese and U.S. R&D

Hypothesis	Restricted Coefficients	Restricted Explained Sum of Squares[a]	Unrestricted Explained Sum of Squares	F
Allocation of Japanese R&D Does Not Promote Trade	$\beta_{JPRIN} = \beta_{JQUAL} = \beta_{JNEW} = \beta_{JTRAN} = 0$	17.741	23.334	3.490[b]
Allocation of U.S. R&D Does Not Promote Trade	$\beta_{BRD} = \beta_{FRD} = 0$	21.801	24.553	3.789[b]

a. Based on regressions not reported.
b. Statistically significant at the 95 percent level of confidence.

Several important qualifications must accompany these conclusions. First, they are valid only in a historical context in that they relate R&D expenditures in the early 1970s to the trade performance of the late 1970s. Second, they refer to the relative success of the allocation of the R&D budget only in terms of U.S.-Japanese bilateral trade. There are surely other important criteria for judging the effectiveness of R&D, including the general trade performance of a country and purely domestic considerations, such as national defense.

Third, the guided missiles and space vehicles industries (all four-digit industries comprising the three-digit SIC sector 376) are not included in our analysis due to lack of data. In fact, federal R&D plays the greatest role in both an absolute and relative sense in these industries. It is quite conceivable that the contribution of federal R&D in these excluded industries is different from that in the industries included in our sample.

Finally, our results do not distinguish between industry characteristics and firm strategies. That is, the relative success of American exports in industries that require a large proportion of basic research does not imply that reallocating the R&D budget from applied to basic research in industries requiring a large proportion of applied research would necessarily improve U.S. trade performance. Further research needs to be undertaken to unravel more clearly the extent to which firms can alter their competitive position by undertaking specific strategies and the extent to which trade is inherently determined by industry characteristics.

APPENDIX: DATA SOURCES AND FURTHER EXPLANATIONS

Data on the values of exports and imports were obtained from Bureau of Census, *U.S. Exports of Domestic Merchandise*, 1977, Report FT610, and *U.S. Imports: Consumption and General SIC-Based Products by World Areas*, 1977, Report FT210.

HUMK and NTBUS were constructed by the U.S. International Trade Commission. The U.S.I.T.C. databank is described by Ray (1981a). HUMK was constructed using total employment data from U.S. Department of Commerce, Bureau of the Census, Annual Survey of Manufactures, 1970, *Industry Profiles*, Washington, D.C., issued 1973. The average annual wage of individuals with less than eight years of education comes from U.S. Department of Commerce, Bureau of the Census, Current Population Reports, *Consumer Income* (Series P-60), Washington, D.C., October 4, 1971. The formula comes from Hufbauer (1970).

NTBUS is an index based on fifteen nontariff barriers, described in U.S. Tariff Commission, *Trade Barriers*, Report to the Committee on Finance of the United States Senate, Part 4, Washington, D.C., April 1974. The quantitative restrictions included and the exact weighting system can also be found in Ray (1981a). TARIF is derived from the tariff schedules listed in GATT, *Tariff Study*, Geneva, 1970.

CR4, AD, and value-of-shipments are all from U.S. Department of Commerce, Bureau of the Census, Annual Survey of Manufactures, *Census of Manufactures*, 1977, Volume 1, Washington, D.C., issued 1982. RD/S is from National Science Foundation, Research and Development in Industry, 1977, Washington, D.C. It is based on two-digit SIC data with values repeated at the four-digit level.

All of the Japanese R&D and technology purchase variables are from Japan, Industrial and Science Agency, *Minkan Kenkyu Kaihatsu jttai chosa hokoku*, 1970. The data are based on a 1970 survey covering 582 large companies with more than Y 500 million of capital. These companies were classified into thirty broadly defined industries, including twenty-seven in manufacturing. This classification system, which lies between the two- and three-digit SIC level, was then made compatible to the four-digit SIC data by repeating the values among the four-digit industries common to each classified Japanese industry.

REFERENCES

Audretsch, David B., and Hideki Yamawaki. 1988. "R&D Rivalry, Industrial Policy and U.S. Japanese Trade." *Review of Economics and Statistics* 70 (August): 438-47.

Baldwin, Robert E. 1971. "The Determinants of the Commodity Structure of U.S. Trade." *American Economic Review* 61 (March): 126-46.

—— 1979. "Determinants of Trade and Foreign Investment: Further Evidence." *Review of Economics and Statistics* (February): 40-8.

Caves, Richard E. 1974. "International Trade, International Investment and Imperfect Markets." *Special Papers in International Economics,* no. 10. Princeton, NJ: Princeton University.

Caves, Richard E., Michael E. Porter, and A. Michael Spence, with John T. Scott. 1980. *Competition in the Open Economy.* Cambridge: Harvard University Press.

Griliches, Zvi. 1986. "Productivity, R&D and Basic Research at the Firm Level in the 1970s." *American Economic Review* 76 (March): 141-54.

Gruber, W. H., D. Mehta, and Raymond Vernon. 1967. "The R&D Factor in International Trade and International Investment of the United States." *Journal of Political Economy* 75 (February): 20-37.

Hufbauer, Gary C. 1970. "The Impact of National Characteristics and Technology on the Commodity Composition of Trade in Manufactured Goods." *The Technology Factor in International Trade.* Ed. Raymond Vernon. New York: Columbia University Press, 145-231.

Imai, Ken'ichi. 1980. "Japan's Industrial Organisation." *Industry and Business in Japan.* Ed. Kazuo Sato. White Plains, NY: M.E. Sharpe, 74-135 and 375-436.

Ito, Motoshige, Masahiro Okuno, Kazuharu Kiyono, and Kotaro Suzumura. 1984. "Sijo no shippai to hoseitekisangyoseisaku" (Market Failure and Industrial Policy).

Keesing, Donald B. 1966. "Labor Skills and Comparative Advantage." *American Economic Review* 56 (May): 249-58.

——. 1967. "The Impact of Research and Development on United States Trade." *Journal of Political Economy* 75 (February): 38-48.

Kenen, Peter B. 1970. "Skills, Human Capital, and Comparative Advantage." *Education, Income, and Human Capital.* Ed. W. L. Hansen. Conference on Research in Income and Welath, Studies in Income and Wealth, vol. 35. New York: Columbia University Press for National Bureau of Economic Research.

Koo, Anthony Y. C., and Stephen Martin. 1984. "Market Structure and U.S. Trade Flows." *International Journal of Industrial Organization* 2 (September): 173-98.

Lowinger, T. C. 1971. "The Neo-Factor Proportions Theory of International Trade: An Empirical Investigation." *American Economic Review* 61 (September): 675-81.

Markusen, James R. 1986. "Explaining the Volume of Trade: An Eclectic Approach." *American Economic Review* 76 (December): 1002-11.

Ogura, Seiritsu, and Naoyuki Yoshino. 1984. "Zeisei to Zaisei toyushi" (The Tax System and Public Finance). *Nihon no sangyo seisaku* (Industrial Policy in Japan). Ed. Ryutaro Komiya, Masahiro Okuno, and Kotaro Suzumura. Tokyo: University of Tokyo Press.

Pagoulatos, E., and R. Sorenson. 1976. "Domestic Market Structure and International Trade: An Empirical Analysis." *Quarterly Review of Economics and Business* 16 (Spring): 45-60.

Peck, Merton J., and Schuji Tamura. 1976. "Technology." *Asia's New Giant.* Ed. Hugh Patrick and Henry Rosovsky, 525-86. Washington, DC: The Brookings Institution.

Porter, Michael E. 1976. *Interbrand Choice, Strategy, and Bilateral Market Power.* Cambridge: Harvard University Press.

Pugel, Thomas A. 1978. *International Market Linkages and U.S. Manufacturing: Prices, Profits, and Patterns.* Cambridge, MA: Ballinger Publishing.

Ray, Edward J. 1981a. "The Determinants of Tariffs and Nontariff Trade Restrictions in the U.S." *Journal of Political Economy* 89 (February): 105-21.

——. 1981b. "Tariff and Nontariff Barriers to Trade in the United States and Abroad." *Review of Economics and Statistics* 63 (May): 161-8.

Stern, Robert M. 1976. "Testing Trade Theories." *International Trade and Finance: Frontiers of Research.* Ed. Peter B. Kenen. New York: Cambridge University Press, 3-50.

Stern, Robert M., and Keith E. Maskus. 1981. "Determinants of the Structure of U.S. Foreign Trade, 1958-76." *Journal of International Economics* 2 (May): 207-24.

Teece, David J., ed. 1987. *The Competititve Challenge: Strategies for Industrial Innovation and Renewal.* Cambridge, MA: Ballinger Publishing.

Vernon, Raymond. 1966. "International Investment and International Trade in the Product Life Cycle." *Quarterly Journal of Economics* 80 (May): 190-207.

White, Larry. 1974. "Industrial Organization and International Trade: Some Theoretical Considerations." *American Economic Review* 64: 1013-20.

Yamawaki, Hideki, and David B. Audretsch. 1988. "Import Share under International Oligopoly with Differentiated Products: Japanese Imports in U.S. Manufacturing." *Review of Economics and Statistics* 70 (November): 569-79.

5 DETERMINANTS OF THE STRUCTURE OF U.S. MANUFACTURING TRADE WITH JAPAN AND KOREA, 1970-1984

Keith E. Maskus, Deborah Battles, and Michael H. Moffett

I. INTRODUCTION

Despite the apparent dramatic changes in the U.S. manufacturing trade structure with Japan and the Asian Newly Industrializing Countries (NICs) that have occurred in recent decades (see, for example, Branson 1987 and Sazanami 1988), there is scant empirical evidence on the underlying industry characteristics associated with these changes. Baldwin (1971) and Hilton (1984) presented results of regression of the U.S.-Japanese trade structure on U.S. industry characteristics for 1962 and 1972, respectively, while Heller (1976) and Urata (1983) related various measures of Japanese trade, disaggregated by country groups, to Japanese factor-use characteristics in the 1960s and 1967 and 1975, respectively.[1] These studies were motivated by the presumption that bilateral trade

We thank Sean Coffey, Rick Herman, and especially Domenic Venturo for assistance in data compilation. We are grateful to Edward Ray, Hideki Yamawaki, and participants at the Tenth Annual Middlebury Conference on Economic Issues.

1. See also Baldwin and Hilton (1984) and Hilton (1984) for attempts to relate bilateral trade patterns to estimated comparative factor-cost differences.

patterns would reflect, in an average sense, the influence of factor intensities as suggested by the Heckscher-Ohlin theory.[2] More recently, papers have appeared on the determinants of U.S. intra-industry trade (IIT) in 1984 with Japan and other areas (Ray 1986) and, interestingly, on the explanation of Japanese import shares in U.S. manufacturing based in oligopolistic behavior (Yamawaki and Audretsch 1988). To our knowledge, there has been no systematic analysis of the industrial characteristics of U.S.-Korean bilateral trade.

This gap in the literature is perhaps best explained by two simple observations. First, because in general no simple and estimatable relationship between factor intensities and the commodity trade pattern can be rigorously derived from the Heckscher-Ohlin model (Aw 1983), either multilaterally or bilaterally, such regressions can only be considered descriptive and subject to the usual questions regarding hypothesis testing. This difficulty would seem also to characterize all of the voluminous empirical literature on IIT, none of which, so far, has derived from a carefully articulated theoretical specification. Second, the practical difficulties of assembling bilateral trade and industrial characteristics on a highly disaggregated and consistent (across countries and across trade and industry data) basis are daunting. Yet such disaggregation and consistency are important if any confidence is to be placed in the correlations discovered in the data.

The purpose of this paper is to perform a data analysis of the relationships between U.S. bilateral trade patterns in manufactures with Japan and Korea in 1970, 1977, and 1984 and industrial characteristics, such as factor shares. For this purpose, we have assembled detailed data on trade and industry variables in all three countries and concorded them to the three-digit U.S. SIC basis. Because the assembly of such a data base was, as suggested, an extremely time-intensive and laborious process, yet necessary for the performance of the analysis, we view that task itself as an initial contribution of the study. The more novel contribution is in allowing a comparison of U.S. versus Japanese or Korean characteristics in explaining bilateral trade rather than

2. Of course, a huge empirical literature has been inspired by variants of the theory, as reviewed by Deardorff (1984). Recent important contributions include Leamer (1984) and Bowen, Leamer, and Sveikauskas (1987) on the cross-country factor content of trade; Noland (1987) on the factor-intensity characteristics of Taiwanese trade; and Saxonhouse (1983), Saxonhouse and Stern (1988), and Staiger, Deardorff, and Stern (1987) on the estimation and effects of Japanese protection. None of this literature is directly concerned with the characteristics of bilateral U.S. trade, however.

considering only the American production structure, as has typically been done.

We adopt two basic modes of analysis. First, we relate bilateral net exports to factor shares as suggested by the factor-proportions model. Despite the theoretical difficulty noted above in interpreting such equations, we might reasonably expect certain differences between Japanese and Korean trade with the United States and in the evolution of that trade. Thus, for example, Korea's emergence as an important industrial competitor, especially in labor-intensive manufactured exports, should be reflected in the labor-intensity of its bilateral trade with the United States. On the other hand, to the extent that the industrial structure of the Japanese economy has come to resemble that of the United States, with competitive strength more closely allied with high-wage, advanced-technology industries, any close links between factor proportions and bilateral net exports should have diminished in favor of greater intra-industry influence on trade.

In that regard, our second task is to examine the characteristics of bilateral intra-industry trade. We relate conventional IIT indices to simple measures of hypothesized influences on such trade. We prefer to operate within the confines of the standard empirical literature on IIT (though we have added human-capital intensity, heretofore ignored as an explanatory variable) to avoid the excessive experimentation that sometimes characterizes that literature. Again, one suggestive hypothesis would be that IIT should constitute a relatively greater, though not necessarily easier to explain econometrically, phenomenon in U.S.-Japanese than U.S.-Korean trade.

We thus have the relatively modest goal of statistically describing the evolution of certain anticipated relationships between bilateral manufacturing trade patterns and industrial characteristics. As will be evident, we have achieved fairly limited success in this effort. Thus, for example, while the factor-proportions regressions perform substantially as expected, we have greater difficulties in identifying some of the determinants of IIT due to the sensitivity of regression coefficients to equation specification.

We discuss aspects of U.S. bilateral trade structure with Korea and Japan in Section II to set the stage for the econometric analysis. The results of the factor-proportions regressions are presented in Section III, while Section IV contains the results of the IIT analysis. Section V consists of closing remarks.

II. TRADE STRUCTURE

Some indication of changes in the U.S. trade pattern by product group is given in Tables 5-1 and 5-2. The data on total and bilateral U.S. nominal trade were assembled, in most cases, from four-digit entries in Schedules A (Imports) and B or E (Exports), which correspond to the Standard International Trade Classification (SITC).[3] These SITC-based trade data were then concorded to the three-digit SIC classification of the United States, from which the classifications in the tables were developed. In particular, consistent with previous work (Stern and Maskus 1981), the manufacturing industries were classified into Ricardo goods (R), Heckscher-Ohlin goods (HO), and Product-Cycle goods (PC). Heckscher-Ohlin goods were further subdivided into labor-intensive and capital-intensive products, based on 1977 nonwage value added per laborer. These classifications were applied to Japanese and Korean industries as well, after they were concorded to the U.S. SIC (see the Appendix for further details).

This rough classification is designed to reflect some broad production characteristics suggested as important by trade theory: a significant natural resource component in Ricardo goods, standardized and internationally common technology in Heckscher-Ohlin goods, and advanced and dynamic technology in Product-Cycle goods. As indicated in Table 5-1, PC goods have increasingly dominated the U.S. export structure, reaching 59 percent of total manufactured exports by value in 1984. Product-Cycle goods have also become more significant in imports, perhaps reflecting growing intra-industry specialization within the group of high-technology products. These gains in the shares of PC goods have been accompanied by a declining relative presence of capital-intensive HO exports and both R and HO imports.

Of more interest here are trends in bilateral trade. Thus, Japan's share in U.S. manufactured imports rose to nearly 22 percent by 1984. Korea's share more than tripled over the same period. Both countries have become relatively more important markets for U.S. exports also, though that expansion has been less rapid. Perspective on the trade patterns by product group may be gained from Table 5-2. As may be expected, Japan and Korea absorbed more than 20 percent of U.S. Ricardo exports by 1984 and were not

3. All value data in this study are expressed in current dollars, a fact that mandates caution in making comparisons across years. Because the econometric analysis is carried out in terms of factor shares or other ratios, we hope this difficulty is largely mitigated. Our inability thus far to assemble data on detailed industrial price deflators accounts for this shortcoming.

Table 5-1. Shares of Nominal Covered U.S. Manufacturing Trade by Product Group and Japan and Korea

Group or Country	Imports 1970	Imports 1977	Imports 1984	Exports 1970	Exports 1977	Exports 1984
Ricardo	27.6	24.4	20.1	15.6	15.2	14.5
HO[a]	53.1	53.4	49.9	30.7	31.9	26.5
(L-INT)	(19.7)	(16.5)	(17.5)	(6.7)	(7.2)	(7.2)
(K-INT)	(33.4)	(36.9)	(32.4)	(24.1)	(24.7)	(19.3)
PC[b]	19.3	22.2	30.0	53.7	52.9	59.0
Total	100.0	100.0	100.0	100.0	100.0	100.0
Japan	18.0	18.2	21.7	7.8	5.9	9.0
Korea	1.1	2.9	3.5	0.9	1.1	2.1

a. HO = Heckscher-Ohlin goods.
b. PC = Product-Cycle goods.

Table 5-2. Japanese and Korean Shares of Nominal Covered U.S. Manufacturing Trade by Product Group

Country	Imports 1970	Imports 1977	Imports 1984	Exports 1970	Exports 1977	Exports 1984
A. Ricardo Goods						
Japan	2.7	1.4	1.8	14.3	14.7	18.1
Korea	0.9	1.2	0.4	1.9	1.3	2.5
B. Heckscher-Ohlin Goods						
Japan	25.8	24.2	26.1	3.8	2.6	4.9
(L-INT)	(9.0)	(4.4)	(3.4)	(1.1)	(1.0)	(2.0)
(K-INT)	(16.8)	(19.8)	(22.7)	(2.7)	(1.6)	(2.9)
Korea	1.6	4.0	5.4	0.6	0.4	1.0
(L-INT)	(1.5)	(3.0)	(3.6)	(0.1)	(0.05)	(0.2)
(K-INT)	(0.1)	(1.0)	(1.8)	(0.5)	(0.35)	(0.8)
C. Product-Cycle Goods						
Japan	18.6	22.2	27.8	8.1	5.4	8.7
Korea	0.4	2.0	2.4	0.8	1.4	2.5

significant suppliers of Ricardo imports. The opposite was true for HO goods; Japan and Korea supplied more than 30 percent of HO imports by 1984, but absorbed only 6 percent of HO exports (though this percentage was higher than previous levels). In Japan's case, however, its one-quarter share of U.S. HO imports had been established by 1970, with little change since then. Within the category of HO imports, Japan's share of labor-intensive goods has fallen, while that of capital-intensive goods (including transport equipment) has expanded. Korea's share of both types of HO imports has grown rapidly. Finally, Japan's share of PC imports rapidly increased, reaching 28 percent by 1984. Korea's presence in PC goods has also expanded markedly, both in U.S. exports and imports.

These changes surely reflect underlying shifts in industrial structure.[4] For example, whereas all three countries experienced increases in the proportions of total manufacturing employment and value added generated by PC goods between 1970 and 1984, these increases were relatively larger in Japan than in the United States and still larger in Korea, according to our data. Korea alone among these three nations has experienced rising employment and value-added shares in HO goods. A detailed consideration of changes in industrial structure is beyond this paper's scope, but several published accounts exist (see, for example, Hong 1987 and Yamazawa 1987). The trade patterns indicated in Tables 5-1 and 5-2 may also be affected by factors we ignore here, most prominently trade barriers.

Within the context of the simple models we consider here, however, some hypotheses are suggested by the trade data. It is apparent that U.S. bilateral trade with Japan and Korea continues to be sharply distinguished across broad commodity groups, with those natural-resource-poor countries importing R goods in exchange for standardized and (increasingly) high-technology goods. Korea's growing specialization in trade with the United States has been greatest in labor-intensive HO goods, while Japan's has been in PC goods. To the extent that this rough product classification captures the factor-proportions basis of bilateral trade, we might expect to observe corresponding changes in the factor-intensity characteristics of net bilateral trade. That possibility is the subject of Section III.

The data in Table 5-2 may also indicate growth in intra-industry specialization and trade. The United States came to export and

4. No particular direction of causation between trade and structure is meant to be implied by this statement.

import more intensively in both HO and PC goods with both countries between 1970 and 1984.

To provide perspective on this last possibility, we assembled data on IIT. Intra-industry trade was measured by the familiar Grubel-Lloyd index across industries, unadjusted for the aggregate trade-balance position:

$$IIT_i = 1 - |X_i - M_i|/(X_i + M_i)$$

where X_i (M_i) indicates exports (imports) in industry i. To achieve a suitably high degree of disaggregation that would substantially overcome trade-overlap problems (Finger and DeRosa 1979), trade data for 1970 and 1977 were assembled from the four-digit SITC classification. Unfortunately, time constraints prevented us from repeating the process for 1984, which data were accumulated from the three-digit SITC categories. As a result, the 1984 indices are likely biased upward and are not directly comparable to the earlier indices.[5] In concording these data to the SIC, care was taken to weight them appropriately to avoid the further positive aggregation bias that results from simply adding trade figures within categories in computing higher-level IIT indices.[6]

Tables 5-3 and 5-4 present basic indicators of the extent and structure of IIT. It appears from Table 5-3 that around one-third of U.S. industries in 1970 could be characterized as "high" IIT sectors, with indices exceeding 50 percent. The number of such sectors has risen over time, though the increase was slight, especially when some account is taken of the aggregation bias in 1984 by counting indices in excess of 60 percent. Bilateral IIT with Japan and Korea has been less pronounced by this measure, again reflecting the sharply defined inter-industry trade patterns noted earlier. Both countries have registered growing numbers of high indices over time, however. The results in Table 5-4 confirm the expectation that IIT characterizes U.S.-Japanese trade more than U.S.-Korean trade. In general, PC goods have been subject to greater IIT than HO goods, and capital-intensive HO goods to greater IIT than their labor-intensive counterparts. This outcome was reversed in the 1984 U.S.-Japanese trade, however, suggesting perhaps the emergence of greater two-way competition in differentiated consumer products.[7]

5. We attempt to control for this problem in the econometric analysis, as discussed later.

6. See the Appendix for further details.

7. The aggregation problem in the 1984 data makes any such interpretations questionable, though presumably the bias should be similar across product groups.

III. FACTOR SHARES IN U.S. BILATERAL TRADE IN MANUFACTURES

We adopt a model in which U.S. net exports by industry are related to factor shares

(1) $$NX_i = b_u UL_i + b_k K_i + b_H H_i + b_m M_i + e_i$$

where NX is a measure of total or bilateral net exports scaled for market size, UL indicates output share paid to unskilled labor, K is the share of physical capital, H indicates the share going to human capital, and M is the share of materials inputs. The net-exports variable was scaled by the sum of U.S. and Japanese shipments in the cases of total U.S. trade and bilateral U.S.-Japanese trade, and by the sum of U.S. and Korean shipments in the case of U.S.-Korean bilateral trade. This procedure more closely approximates the scaling by world market size suggested by Deardorff (1984) than does scaling by national shipments. It amounts to assuming the existence of segmented bilateral markets, which is questionable in many cases. Unfortunately, we were unable to assemble data on production for a broader set of countries. For the purpose of computing unskilled-labor and human-capital shares, data on total compensation and employment were used to compute an average wage in each industry. The minimum average wage across all industries was then taken to reflect the compensation of unskilled laborers. The unskilled-labor share is then this minimum wage times employment as a proportion of industry shipments. The share of human capital is defined as the difference between each industry's wage and the minimum wage, multiplied by employment, divided by the value of shipments[8]

$$H_i = (WAGE_i - MINWAGE)\ L_i/VS_i.$$

Effectively, we assume the absence of human capital in the lowest-wage industry and standardize upon that industry. While more direct measures of payments to unskilled or uneducated labor are commonly used in the literature, it proved difficult to locate such data for Korea and Japan.[9] The physical-capital share was taken to

8. H_i is a flow measure rather than a stock of human capital. Our procedure is equivalent to capitalizing the wage differential at 10 percent and assuming an annual 10 percent return to human capital.

9. The U.S. minimum wages computed here for 1970 and 1977 were virtually identical to their 1970 and 1976 counterparts in Stern and Maskus (1981).

Table 5-3. Number of Three-Digit Industries with Grubel-Lloyd Indices Exceeding 0.5 in the U.S. Total Manufacturing Trade and Bilateral Manufacturing Trade with Japan and Korea

Trade Partner	1970	1977	1984 (>0.6)[a]
Total	43	49	66 (52)
Japan	22	22	35 (30)
Korea	5	12	23 (17)
Total Number of Industries	128	129	115

a. The smaller number of industries in 1984 is due to separate SITC aggregation scheme.

Table 5-4. Average Grubel-Lloyd Indices in U.S. Bilateral Manufacturing Trade by Product Group

Country, Product Group	1970	1977	1984
Japan			
Ricardo	.1499	.1191	.3791
HO	.1855	.2557	.3964
(L-INT)	(.1703)	(.2307)	(.4176)
(K-INT)	(.2112)	(.3099)	(.3617)
PC	.3685	.3382	.3491
Korea			
Ricardo	.0488	.0677	.2771
HO	.1092	.1589	.2485
(L-INT)	(.1109)	(.1065)	(.1479)
(K-INT)	(.1061)	(.1977)	(.4204)
PC	.0839	.2222	.3507

be nonwage value added as a proportion of shipments under the assumption that value added comprises only payments to labor and capital. Balassa (1979) discussed the meaningfulness of this value-added measure and notes that no compelling reasons exist to prefer a measure of capital stock in computing factor intensities or shares.[10] Finally, the materials share is simply cost of materials, as given by value of shipments less value added, as a proportion of shipments.

The focus on factor shares as measures of intensities comes closest to the specification suggested by the factor-proportions theory (Deardorff 1984; Harkness 1978). The measurements of factor shares chosen here fully exhaust output so the constant term is suppressed in equation (1).

One motivation for this study was to investigate whether the use of differing national industrial characteristics improves our understanding of the link between factor intensities and trade performance. It has been common in the literature to use a single country's factor intensities, usually those of the United States, in explaining trade structure across several countries (for example, Baldwin 1979; Balassa 1979, 1986a). In the absence of factor-price equalization or fixed-coefficient production functions, however, such a procedure could seriously misrepresent foreign intensities. This problem necessitates the collection of data on factor shares across countries. We have, therefore, compiled the variables on industry output and factor usage for the United States, Korea, and Japan from national sources (see the Appendix).

Table 5-5 presents simple correlations between U.S. and Japanese and U.S. and Korean factor shares. It is apparent that these shares are strongly correlated, perhaps especially as regards labor and human capital. This finding may be surprising in light of the bonus system in Japan and Korea that has been thought to divorce labor compensation somewhat from employment characteristics (Urata 1983). The positive correlations lend some credence to the practice of using a specific country's intensities in analyzing trade patterns based upon presumed factor-price equalization.[11] There appears to have been an increase in these correlations between the United States and Korea over this period, with no apparent trend in the U.S.-Japanese correlations.

10. We considered also the gross book value of depreciable assets as a stock measure. We estimated our equations using conventional intensity variables, the stocks of physical and human capital per worker, with little change in results.

11. Wages are also highly correlated across industries among these countries, with the correlation becoming much stronger between 1977 and 1984 (rising from 0.34 to 0.73) in the case of the United States and Korea.

Table 5-5. Correlations Between U.S. and Foreign Factor Shares

	U.S.-Japan			U.S.-Korean		
Factor Share	1970	1977	1984	1970	1977	1984
Unskilled labor	0.528[a]	0.501[a]	0.545[a]	0.655[a]	0.624[a]	0.767[a]
Human capital	0.705[a]	0.782[a]	0.718[a]	0.633[a]	0.372[a]	0.616[a]
Physical capital	0.419[a]	0.395[a]	0.387[a]	0.379[a]	0.334[a]	0.593[a]
Materials	0.651[a]	0.752[a]	0.687[a]	0.492[a]	0.393[a]	0.661[a]
Simple average	0.575	0.608	0.584	0.540	0.431	0.659

a. Significantly positive at 1 percent level.

Table 5-6. Regressions of U.S. Scaled Total Net Exports Against U.S. Factor Shares[a]

Year	UL	K	H	M	R^2	F
1970 (n=109)	-0.700[b]	-0.111	0.851[b]	0.012	.35	19.2[b]
	(-6.18)	(-1.52)	(6.02)	(0.38)		
1977 (n=108)	-1.123[b]	-0.027	1.274[b]	-0.025	.24	10.8[b]
	(-4.65)	(-0.14)	(3.59)	(-0.37)		
1984 (n=109)	-1.790[b]	0.020	1.152[b]	-0.064	.36	19.6[b]
	(-7.10)	(0.16)	(4.05)	(-1.29)		

a. Net exports are scaled by the sum of U.S. and Japanese shipments.
b. Significant at 1 percent level.

Of initial interest is the link between factor-intensity characteristics and total U.S. manufacturing trade by sector. Table 5-6 lists the results of such regression in the four-factor model. It is apparent that over this period U.S. trade performance by industry was negatively related to the share of low-wage labor and positively associated with the share of high-wage labor or human capital. The strength of the negative association with unskilled labor grew markedly between 1970 and 1984. The United States may have been a net importer of direct capital services in 1970, but overall trade flows in capital and material were largely balanced. These results substantially confirm and extend the results of the standard three-factor model of intensities and U.S. trade (Stern and Maskus 1981).

We now consider whether U.S. trade with Japan and Korea is consistent with the overall U.S. trade pattern. The results of the bilateral regressions are noted in Table 5-7. Two regressions are reported for each country in each year, corresponding to the use of U.S. factor shares (for example, USUL connotes the unskilled labor share) or foreign (Japanese or Korean) factor shares as independent variables. Two general features of these results are of note. First, consistent with the factor-share correlations noted earlier, the coefficients did not differ greatly when foreign intensities were substituted for U.S. intensities in explaining bilateral net exports. Only five of the twenty-five paired coefficients exhibited opposing signs, and in only one of those cases was either coefficient even marginally significant (materials share in 1970 U.S.-Japanese trade).[12] This finding again supports the practice of using a single country's techniques to explain at least bilateral trade patterns. However, the second feature of note is that the foreign factor shares were jointly capable of explaining considerably less variation in scaled bilateral net exports than were the U.S. shares. Only in the case of 1984 U.S.-Japanese trade, when neither equation performed well, was this result reversed. Although a variety of explanations might be offered for this result, including simply any systematic errors that arise from the fact that the trade data were generated from U.S. sources but the foreign factor share from Japanese and Korean sources, we are unable at this point to resolve it.[13]

12. Although we note coefficients that differ from zero at the 10 percent level, we place somewhat less confidence on the indicated relationships due to the difficulty of interpreting conventional measures of significance in ad hoc regression equations.

13. We also experimented with combined U.S.-Japanese and U.S.-Korean factor shares with unsurprising results: essentially unchanged coefficients with overall equation performance between those of the paired equations.

Table 5-7. Regressions of U.S. Scaled Bilateral Net Exports Against U.S. and Foreign Factor Shares[a]

Country, Equation		USUL	FUL	USK	FK	USH	FH	USM	FM	R^2	F
Japan, 1970 (n=109)	1a.	-0.175[b]	-	-0.029	-	0.145[b]	-	0.014[d]	-	.29	14.2[b]
		(-5.97)		(-1.49)		(3.81)		(1.63)			
	1b.	-	-0.192[b]	-	-0.024	-	0.186[c]	-	-0.005	.08	2.9[c]
			(-2.10)		(-1.00)		(2.55)		(-0.53)		
Korea, 1970 (n=102)	2a.	-0.017[b]	-	0.001	-	0.021[b]	-	0.000	-	.24	10.2[b]
		(-4.96)		(0.41)		(3.52)		(0.09)			
	2b.	-	-0.013[c]	-	-0.003	-	0.017[c]	-	0.000	.07	2.3
			(-1.96)		(-1.00)		(2.10)		(0.22)		
Japan, 1977 (n=108)	3a.	-0.060[c]	-	-0.007	-	-0.049	-	0.016[c]	-	.14	5.5[b]
		(-2.46)		(-0.40)		(-1.38)		(2.29)			
	3b.	-	-0.116[c]	-	-0.011	-	0.013	-	0.004	.05	1.9
			(-1.96)		(-0.73)		(0.25)		(0.67)		
Korea, 1977 (n=108)	4a.	-0.143[b]	-	-0.007	-	0.136[b]	-	0.004	-	.44	27.4[b]
		(-8.25)		(-0.58)		(4.75)		(0.73)			
	4b.	-	-0.130[b]	-	0.017	-	0.075[d]	-	-0.009	.12	4.9[b]
			(-3.39)		(1.24)		(1.84)		(-1.46)		
Japan, 1984 (n=109)	5a.	-0.047	-	0.008	-	-0.113[d]	-	0.006	-	.05	1.8
		(-0.87)		(0.29)		(-1.84)		(0.61)			
	5b.	-	-0.200[c]	-	0.012	-	-0.131	-	0.003	.07	2.5[c]
			(-2.01)		(0.42)		(-1.47)		(0.25)		
Korea, 1984 (n=112)	6a.	-0.288[b]	-	0.002	-	0.264[b]	-	-0.009	-	.31	16.4[b]
		(-6.06)		(0.09)		(3.94)		(-0.81)			
	6b.	-	-0.307[b]	-	0.024	-	0.407[b]	-	-0.023[d]	.20	9.1[b]
			(-4.95)		(0.80)		(2.63)		(-1.81)		

a. Net exports are scaled by the sum of U.S. and either Japanese or Korean shipments, as appropriate.
b. Significant at 1 percent level.
c. Significant at 5 percent level.
d. Significant at 10 percent level.

Turning to the individual coefficients, it is apparent that determinants of the U.S.-Korean trade pattern were similar to those of overall U.S. trade. In particular, U.S. net exports to Korea were negatively related to unskilled-labor intensity and positively related to human-capital intensity. Both of these effects seemed to grow stronger over time, suggesting increasing inter-industry specialization according to labor skills. Again, trade flows in direct capital services and materials were essentially balanced, though U.S. net exports may have become negatively associated with high materials shares by 1984.

A similar pattern emerges with respect to U.S.-Japanese trade, though the relationship between trade and unskilled-labor intensity was not clearly negative in 1984. The one substantial difference between the Japanese and Korean results was that the coefficient on human-capital share had become negative and marginally significant in the former case.[14] Again, no discernible link between physical-capital intensity or the share of materials and bilateral trade could be discovered by the four-input regression model.[15]

No inferences may be drawn from these results about the nature of changes in the underlying causes of bilateral trade, which may include such factors as changes in relative endowments, trade barriers, and technology. We are interested, however, in further investigation of two such possibilities. First, if the regression coefficients reflect bilateral advantages stemming from factor endowments, they should themselves be functions of relative factor supplies, as noted by Balassa (1979, 1986a), in the multilateral trade context. We applied Balassa's one-step technique to the bilateral regression models by stacking the 1977 Japanese and Korean data and interacting the factor shares with measures of relative

14. An apparent difficulty arises in comparing Japanese and Korean results. A substantial portion of Korean exports comes from Japanese-owned affiliates, particularly in the later years. To the extent that specific factors (for example, Japanese management skills) in this offshore production explain rising Korean export sources, the simple direct-factor-intensity model is ill-suited to capture these trends without explicit consideration of investment patterns and Japanese-Korean bilateral trade. This qualification is likely overstated, however, because Japanese direct investment in Korea has been primarily in labor-intensive areas in which Korea has gained comparative advantage anyway. Hence, U.S.-Korean trade flows should largely reflect underlying U.S. and Korean factor intensities as captured by the model.

15. The result on capital intensity accords with Baldwin's (1971) finding, but contrasts with Hilton's (1984) estimation of a positive coefficient, reflecting, by his interpretation, a greater return to capital in Japan than in the United States. One possible source for this discrepancy that bears further investigation is that Hilton employed total factor-intensities while the current paper uses direct factor-intensities.

endowments in 1975 given in Leamer (1984) (see the Appendix for details). The results (not shown) were inconclusive in that, while the coefficients on the endowment variables had the correct signs, none was significant beyond the 15 percent level. We ascribe this result primarily to collinearity; with only two countries there was insufficient variation in the endowments data to estimate sharply any influences of factor supplies on the bilateral coefficients. Thus, whereas some weak evidence exists that factor supplies affect the direct factor-intensity characteristics of U.S. trade with Japan and Korea, resolution of that issue must await further work.

The second possibility is loosely suggested by the inability of the basic regression model to explain U.S.-Japanese trade in 1984. In fact, factor shares appeared to have no clear influence on such trade, either individually or jointly, to the extent that such influences may be captured here. It is conceivable that by 1984 the incentives for inter-industry trade between those countries had been largely supplanted by incentives for intra-industry trade. We turn next to an examination of that issue.

IV. REGRESSION ANALYSIS OF INTRA-INDUSTRY TRADE

In concert with the large number of hypothesized explanations for the existence of IIT and the difficulty of adequately measuring many of them, the literature has advanced an enormous array of empirical determinants of the phenomenon (providing examples are Grubel and Lloyd 1975; Loertscher and Wolter 1980; Balassa 1986b; Marvel and Ray 1987; and the papers in Tharakan 1983). It would be impossible to specify a model incorporating even most of these determinants. Rather, we adopt a standard specification that covers a limited set of potential determinants of IIT that may be of interest in the context of U.S.-Korean and U.S.-Japanese trade.

The first such variable is industry value added per establishment, a proxy for scale economies (Loertscher and Wolter 1980; Tharakan 1983). Most empirical researchers have expected a positive relationship between scale and IIT, but Caves (1981) has argued that large-scale production could readily diminish intra-industry exchange. Marvel and Ray (1987) extended the latter argument and presented econometric evidence of a negative relationship in U.S. trade. They argued that IIT would instead be more characteristic of industries that produce user-specific differentiated goods on a made-to-order basis. It is the selective need for individualized products on the part of commercial customers that allows two-way market penetration. We chose to examine this hypothesis by including the ratio between inventories of work in process plus materials and total inventories. This inventory ratio is taken as a proxy for the made-to-order nature of production by industry.

In the standard conception, IIT is supposed to be positively related to product differentiation in consumer goods. To attempt to capture this phenomenon, we included a dummy variable that classified the three-digit industries into consumer goods, with a value of one, and other goods, with a value of zero.

A fourth variable was a measure of the transportability of industry output, the mile radius within which 80 percent of each U.S. industry's production was sold, as developed by Weiss (1972). The conventional wisdom is that lower transport costs would stimulate greater IIT. As pointed out by Tharakan (1983), however, higher transport costs could stimulate the development of local output varieties in each country, which then later enter two-way trade to satisfy preferences for diversity. Further, higher transport costs may result in greater IIT due to incentives for cross-hauling (Brander and Krugman 1983).

We included as a fifth variable the number of subcategories at the eight-digit level of the SIC, within each three-digit classification, in which the United States registered positive exports in each year studied. The primary purpose of this variable was to control for the aggregation bias inherent in a three-digit categorization of IIT, which, as noted earlier, should be greater in the 1984 data. Similar measures have been used elsewhere as proxies for product differentiation (see, for example, Loertscher and Wolter 1980), but we discount that interpretation.

A final set of variables chosen included the physical-capital-labor ratio, defined as the gross book value of depreciable assets per employee, and the human-capital-labor ratio, defined as the discounted wage differential by industry. Use of the physical-capital-labor ratio has been motivated in several ways in the literature and has been subject to numerous and often confusing interpretations. As it happened, that ratio was inconsequential in our data in explaining U.S. total or bilateral IIT. We thus exclude it from the estimated bilateral equations we report.

To our knowledge, the only previous use of the human-capital-labor ratio is in Toh (1982), who adopted the view that human capital is negatively correlated with the length of production runs (scale economies) and should accordingly be negatively related to IIT. This idea is curious, in that human capital might as easily be positively related to suspected influences on IIT, such as product differentiation through heavy investment in advertising skills. In any event, the appropriate concern should be with human capital as an independent determinant of IIT, and here we take a modified version of the Linder (1961) hypothesis. In particular, we expect human-capital intensity to be a useful proxy for the technological sophistication of a commodity. Human capital then should be positively related to IIT among developed economies and negatively related to IIT between developed and developing economies.[16] We examine this hypothesis in the bilateral trade equations.

The list of independent variables hardly exhausts all suspected determinants of IIT. Perhaps most prominent by its absence is a measure of industry-specific trade barriers, though the direction and causation of a relationship between barriers and IIT are open to question (Caves 1981; Marvel and Ray 1987). Also absent are measures of strategic internationally oligopolistic behavior that might explain market interpenetration and two-way trade (Yamawaki and Audretsch 1988). Unfortunately, time and data constraints prevented the consideration of these variables for this paper.

For purposes of estimation, we used the unadjusted Grubel-Lloyd index as defined above to measure IIT. It is apparent that simple ordinary-least-squares estimation of the IIT equations is inappropriate given the truncated nature of this index. The equations were accordingly estimated with the standard logistic transformation.

We begin in Table 5-8 with equations for total U.S. intra-industry trade as a benchmark for the bilateral regressions. It is evident that scale economies, as measured here (VAPEST) were little related to IIT. Because physical-capital intensity (KL) was strongly correlated with VAPEST, we dropped it from the second equation in each pair. In no case was this procedure sufficient to establish a relation between VAPEST and IIT. But, there was a positive link between the made-to-order nature of manufactured goods (INVRAT) and IIT, results that support the Marvel and Ray (1987) hypothesis.

It is further apparent that U.S. IIT has been positively related to consumer goods, at least until recently, and negatively related to the transportability of products. Categorical aggregation was significant only in 1984, as suspected. Finally, our expectation concerning human capital was borne out: U.S. intra-industry trade tended to be greater in industries with higher human-capital intensity.

16. Thus, while human-capital intensity should be an unambiguously positive determinant of U.S. inter-industry trade (though that interpretation has been clouded in the literature by the correlations between human capital and technological inputs), it should exhibit this bifurcation in explaining IIT.

The bilateral regressions are presented in Tables 5-9 (Japan) and 5-10 (Korea). The first equation in each pair reflects regressions against U.S. product characteristics, and the second equation reflects regressions against Japanese or Korean characteristics. It is interesting that again there is broad consistency between coefficients estimated from U.S. versus Japanese or Korean data. At best, the various hypotheses we have suggested received mixed support. While IIT may have risen over time in both U.S.-Japanese and U.S.-Korean trade, our model could not provide tighter explanations of the phenomenon. Although we had no necessary expectation that U.S.-Japanese IIT would be easier to explain (as opposed to simply higher) than U.S.-Korean IIT, the apparently greater success of the Korean equations came as somewhat of a surprise.[17]

Regarding specific coefficients, it appears that U.S.-Japanese IIT may have had a weak negative relationship with scale economies in 1977. In contrast, U.S.-Korean IIT was positively related to large scale in Korean industry in 1977 and to large scale in U.S. industry in 1984. The bilateral trade patterns were also distinguished by this link to human-capital intensity. The Japanese-U.S. pattern of IIT depended positively on human-capital inputs, whether American or Japanese, before 1984.[18] The Korean relationship was negative in 1970, providing some support for our basic hypothesis, but had become significantly positive by 1984.

Bilateral IIT bore a positive relationship to the inventory ratio for Japan in 1970 and Korea (the U.S. ratio) in 1977, but had become negative for Japan by 1984. Consumer goods were strongly represented in U.S.-Korean IIT in the earlier years, but never in the U.S.-Japanese case. Transportability bore a negative relationship to IIT in both countries, consistent with the overall U.S. trade pattern. Finally, categorical aggregation mattered only in the case of U.S.-Japanese trade, though it had an unexpected negative sign in 1984. It is possible that using U.S. export categories to measure aggregation accounted for this outcome by misrepresenting the actual number of subcategories in U.S.-Japanese exports and imports. It is also conceivable that the variable in fact proxies for product differentiation, and that U.S.-Japanese IIT had become less

17. Obviously, the explanatory powers of the separate equations are not strictly comparable.

18. The general deterioration in 1984 of both the bilateral factor proportions and IIT regressions suggests that our practice of developing trade data from the three-digit SITC rather than the four-digit SITC may have sacrificed considerable variation in the constructed dependent variables.

Table 5-8. Logistic Regressions of U.S. Total IIT Indices Against U.S. Determinants

Year, Equation	C	VAPEST	KL	HL	INVRAT	CONS	TRANS	SUBCAT	R^2	F
1970 (n=132)										
I1a.	0.020	0.018	0.006	0.130[b]	0.152	0.303[b]	-0.055[b]	-0.006	.20	4.5[a]
	(0.12)	(0.57)	(0.093)	(2.01)	(1.22)	(1.93)	(-1.93)	(-0.23)		
I1b.	0.012	0.017	-	0.134[a]	0.152	0.304[b]	-0.058[b]	-	.20	6.3[a]
	(0.08)	(0.62)	-	(3.11)	(1.29)	(2.15)	(-2.24)	-		
1977 (n=129)										
I2a.	-0.374	-0.048	0.019	0.079[a]	0.473[a]	0.372[b]	-0.021	-0.011	.18	3.7[a]
	(-1.62)	(-1.26)	(0.36)	(2.44)	(2.84)	(2.05)	(-0.75)	(-0.33)		
I2b.	-0.357[c]	-0.044	-	0.070[a]	0.503[a]	0.325[b]	-	-	.17	6.3[a]
	(-1.65)	(-1.32)	-	(3.35)	(3.31)	(1.96)	-	-		
1984 (n=131)										
I3a.	-0.496[b]	-0.029	-0.056	0.319[a]	0.208	0.039	-0.226[a]	0.103[a]	.33	8.6[a]
	(-2.11)	(-0.77)	(-0.83)	(4.54)	(1.33)	(0.21)	(-6.42)	(3.24)		
I3b.	-0.540[b]	-0.046	-	0.274[a]	0.240[c]	-	-0.217[a]	0.096[a]	.32	12.0[a]
	(-2.46)	(-1.41)	-	(6.02)	(1.66)	-	(-6.41)	(3.12)		

a. Significant at 1 percent level.
b. Significant at 5 percent level.
c. Significant at 10 percent level.

intensive in highly differentiated goods. At present, however, we consider the result anomalous.

We have achieved only limited success in explaining bilateral intra-industry trade. Although the results were broadly supportive of the hypotheses specified, they were hardly conclusive. Therefore, rather than attempting to depict firmly the underlying determinants of IIT, we note simply that much room remains for refining these estimates.

V. CONCLUSION

Our objective in this paper was to investigate the industrial characteristics of bilateral manufacturing trade with Japan and Korea since 1970. Despite the substantial growth in such trade and the apparent shifts in these trade patterns, relatively few attempts have been made to analyze their underlying determinants. We have attempted this task by estimating simple models of the direct factor-intensity characteristics of trade and of the sources of intra-industry trade. While sharp inferences were difficult to draw in our data set, evidence emerged that bilateral trade has been influenced by differentiated labor skills, with perhaps a diminished influence of relative skills on recent U.S.-Japanese trade. Human capital appears to have contributed to IIT, along with other factors.

As noted earlier, the factor-proportions model allows no unambiguous conclusions about the ultimate sources of changes in trade, such as changing endowments, technology, market structure, or trade barriers, and the complex interactions among them. We have accordingly avoided speculation about these factors. The results presented here, however, should provide a useful context within which to explore further the nature of bilateral trade between the United States and countries of the Asian Pacific region.

Table 5-9. Logistic Regressions of U.S.-Japanese IIT Indices Against U.S. and Japanese Determinants

	1970 (n=108)		1977 (n=106)		1984 (n=108)	
	I4a.	I4b.	I5a.	I5b.	I6a.	I6b.
C	-.102	-.271[c]	-.000	-0.16	.152[a]	.490[a]
VAPEST	-.015	-	-.051[c]	-	-.041	-
VAPESTJ	-	-.070	-	-.046[c]	-	.012
HL	.107[b]	-	.015	-	.020	-
HLJ	-	.196[a]	-	.094[a]	-	.025
INVRAT	.088	-	-	-	-	-
INVRATJ	-	.213[c]	-	-	-	-.266[b]
CONS	-	-	-	-	.063	-
TRANS	-.108[a]	-.100[a]	-.093[a]	-.141[a]	-	-
SUBCAT	-	-	.070[b]	.063[b]	-.058[c]	-.096[a]
R^2	.08	.14	.13	.17	.08	.15
F	2.4[b]	4.2[a]	4.0[a]	5.3[a]	2.3[c]	4.5[a]

a. Significant at 1 percent level.
b. Significant at 5 percent level.
c. Significant at 10 percent level.

Table 5-10. Logistic Regressions of U.S.-Korean IIT Indices Against U.S. and Korean Determinants

	1970 (n=96)		1977 (n=103)		1984 (n=111)	
	I7a.	I7b.	I8a.	I8b.	I9a.	I9b.
C	.019	-.037	-.232[c]	-.118	-.051	-.052
VAPEST	.001	-	-.022	-	.202[a]	-
VAPESTK	-	-.004	-	-.043[b]	-	.029
HL	-.046[c]	-	.013	-	-.013	-
HLK	-	-.061[c]	-	-.023	-	.098[b]
INVRAT	-	-	.225[b]	-	-	-
INVRATK	-	.081	-	.097	-	-
CONS	.303[c]	-	.661[a]	.438[b]	-	-
TRANS	-.068[a]	-.068[a]	-.073[a]	-.084[a]	-.156[a]	-.079[a]
SUBCAT	-	-	-	-	-	-
R^2	.41	.42	.35	.34	.13	.11
F	17.2[a]	16.1[a]	11.1[a]	10.1[a]	5.7[a]	4.3[a]

a. Significant at 1 percent level.
b. Significant at 5 percent level.
c. Significant at 10 percent level.

APPENDIX: DATA SOURCES

Data on U.S. trade in total and with Japan and Korea for 1970 and 1977 were assembled from the four-digit SITC categories listed in U.S. Department of Commerce, Report FT 135, *U.S. General Imports: Schedule A Commodity by Country*; and Report FT 410, *U.S. Exports: Schedule B Commodity by Country*. Trade data for 1984 were taken from Schedule A (imports) and Schedule E (exports) at the three-digit level; these data were provided on computer diskette from the COMPRO system of the U.S. government. The data were concorded to the U.S. three-digit SIC classification by means of concordances developed especially for this purpose, taking into account the 1972 SIC revision. Details are available upon request.

The aggregation of the SITC-based trade data and their concordance to the SIC involved the application of several weights based on commodity trade shares in the various years. In developing IIT indices for the three-digit industries, it was necessary to aggregate across IIT indices for all SITC subcategories, incorporating these weights rather than simply computing aggregate exports and imports for each SIC group and then calculating an IIT index. The latter procedure typically results in dramatically higher aggregate IIT indices than are implicit in the disaggregated trade data.

The classification of industries into Ricardo, Heckscher-Ohlin, and Product-Cycle goods was substantially the same as that used in Stern and Maskus (1981). Heckscher-Ohlin industries were further classified into labor-intensive or capital-intensive sectors based upon their ratios of value added to employment in 1977, as developed from data in Department of Commerce, *Census of Manufacturers*, 1977. The classification of products into consumer goods and nonconsumer goods was based simply on the apparent main uses of industry output.

U.S. data on inventories were taken also from the *Census of Manufacturers* in 1972, 1977, and 1982. Data on employment, payroll, value added, value of shipments, gross book value of depreciable assets, and number of establishments for the United States were taken from various issues of Department of Commerce, *Annual Survey of Manufacturers*. Corresponding data for Japanese industry were taken from MITI, Industrial Statistics Division, "Report by Industries," *Census of Manufacturers* (Kogyo Tokeio Hyo: Sokatsuhen), appropriate years. The 1970 Japanese data on industrial characteristics were for establishments with twenty or more persons engaged; those for 1977 and 1984 were for establishments with thirty or more engaged. Total wages and salaries paid included bonuses and subsidies. Korean industrial characteristics were taken from Economic Planning Board, *Report on Mining and Manufacturing Survey* (Kwanggop t onggye chose pagoso), various years. Wages and salaries included bonuses, allowances, subsidies, and payments in kind. Japanese and Korean value data were converted to millions of dollars by applying end-of-year exchange rates in each year. Concordances were developed for each year between the Japanese SIC and the U.S. SIC and between the Korean SIC and the U.S. SIC. Details are available upon request.

Factor endowments for the Balassa-type one-step regressions were taken from Leamer (1984). Relative endowments were defined as Japanese or Korean per-capita endowments relative to U.S. per-capita endowments. The human-capital endowment was proxied by Leamer's LABOR1 and the unskilled-labor endowment by his LABOR2. Natural-resource endowments were considered separately as the sum of Leamer's land endowments and the sum of minerals outputs. Population statistics were taken from the International Monetary Fund, *International Financial Statistics.* That source also provided exchange-rate data.

The transportability measure was taken from Weiss (1972). The number of finely disaggregated subcategories within each three-digit SIC industry was taken from Department of Commerce, Report FT 610, *U.S. Exports: SIC-Based Products,* various years.

REFERENCES

Aw, Bee-Yan. 1983. "The Interpretation of Cross-Section Regression Tests of the Heckscher-Ohlin Theorem with Many Goods and Factors." *Journal of International Economics* 14: 163-7.

Balassa, Bela. 1979. "The Changing Pattern of Comparative Advantage in Manufactured Goods." *Review of Economics and Statistics* 61: 259-66.

——. 1986a. "Comparative Advantage in Manufactured Goods: A Reappraisal." *Review of Economics and Statistics* 68: 315-19.

——. 1986b. "Intra-Industry Specialization: A Cross-Country Analysis." *European Economic Review* 30: 27-42.

Baldwin, Robert E. 1971. "Determinants of the Commodity Structure of U.S. Trade." *American Economic Review* 61: 126-46.

——. 1979. "Determinants of Trade and Foreign Investment: Further Evidence." *Review of Economics and Statistics* 61: 40-8.

Baldwin, Robert E., and R. Spence Hilton. 1984. "A Technique for Indicating Comparative Costs and Predicting Changes in Trade Ratios." *Review of Economics and Statistics* 66: 105-10.

Bowen, Harry P., Edward E. Leamer, and Leo Sveikauskas. 1987. "Multicountry, Multifactor Tests of the Factor Abundance Theory." *American Economic Review* 77: 791-809.

Brander, James A., and Paul R. Krugman. 1983. "A 'Reciprocal Dumping' Model of International Trade." *Journal of International Economics* 15: 313-21.

Branson, William H. 1987. "Trade and Structural Interdependence Between the United States and the Newly Industrializing Countries." *Trade and Structural Change in Pacific Asia.* Ed. Colin I. Bradford, Jr., and William. H. Branson, 27-60. Chicago: University of Chicago Press.

Caves, Richard E. 1981. "Intra-Industry Trade and Market Structure in the Industrial Countries." *Oxford Economic Papers* 33: 203-23.

Deardorff, Alan V. 1984. "Testing Trade Theories and Predicting Trade Flows." *Handbook of International Economics,* vol. 1. Ed. R. W. Jones and Peter B. Kenen, 467-517. Amsterdam: North-Holland.

Finger, J. Michael, and Dean A. DeRosa. 1979. "Trade Overlap, Comparative Advantage and Protection." *On the Economics of Intra-Industry Trade.* Ed. Herbert Giersch, 213-44. Tubingen: J.C.B. Mohr.

Grubel, Herbert G. and Peter J. Lloyd. 1975. *Intra-Industry Trade: The Theory and Measurement of International Trade in Differentiated Products.* London: MacMillan.

Harkness, Jon. 1978. "Factor Abundance and Comparative Advantage." *American Economic Review* 68: 784-800.

Heller, Peter S. 1976. "Factor Endowment Change and Comparative Advantage: The Case of Japan, 1956-1969." *Review of Economics and Statistics* 58: 283-92.

Hilton, R. Spence. 1984. "Commodity Trade and Relative Returns to Factors of Production." *Journal of International Economics* 16: 259-70.

Hong, Wontack. 1987. "Export-Oriented Growth and Trade Patterns of Korea." *Trade and Structural Change in Pacific Asia.* Ed. Colin I. Bradford, Jr. and William H. Branson, 271-306. Chicago: University of Chicago Press.

Leamer, Edward E. 1984. *Sources of International Comparative Advantage: Theory and Evidence.* Cambridge: MIT Press.

Linder, Staffan B. 1961. *An Essay on Trade and Transformation.* New York: John Wiley and Sons.

Loertscher, Rudolf, and Frank Wolter. 1980. "Determinants of Intra-Industry Trade: Among Countries and Across Industries." *Weltwirtschaftliches Archiv* 116: 280-93.

Marvel, Howard P., and Edward J. Ray. 1987. "Intraindustry Trade: Sources and Effects on Protection." *Journal of Political Economy* 95: 1278-91.

Noland, Marcus. 1987. "Newly Industrializing Countries' Comparative Advantage in Manufactured Goods." *Weltwirtschaftliches Archiv* 123: 679-96.

Ray, Edward J. 1986. "An Empirical Analysis of U.S. Intra-Industry Trade." Manuscript.

Saxonhouse, Gary R. 1983. "The Micro- and Macroeconomics of Foreign Sales to Japan." *Trade Policy in the 1980s.* Ed. William R. Cline, 259-304. Washington, DC: Institute for International Economics.

Saxonhouse, Gary R., and Robert M. Stern. 1988. "An Analytical Survey of Formal and Informal Barriers to International Trade and Investment in the United States, Canada, and Japan." *U.S.-Canadian Trade and Investment Relations with Japan.* Ed. Robert M. Stern. Chicago: University of Chicago Press.

Sazanami, Yoko. 1988. "Trade and Investment Patterns and Barriers in the U.S., Canada, and Japan." *U.S.-Canadian Trade and Investment Relations with Japan.* Ed. Robert M. Stern. Chicago: University of Chicago Press.

Staiger, Robert W., Alan V. Deardorff, and Robert M. Stern. 1987. "An Evaluation of Factor Endowments and Protection as Determinants of Japanese and American Foreign Trade." *Canadian Journal of Economics* 20: 449-63.

Stern, Robert M., and Keith E. Maskus. 1981. Determinants of the Structure of U.S. Foreign Trade, 1958-1976." *Journal of International Economics* 11: 207-24.

Tharakan, P. K. M., ed. 1983. *Intra-Industry Trade: Empirical and Methodological Aspects.* Amsterdam: North-Holland.

——. 1984. "Intra-Industry Trade Between the Industrial Countries and the Developing World." *European Economic Review* 26: 213-27.

Toh, K. 1982. "A Cross-Section Analysis of Intra-Industry Trade in U.S. Manufacturing Industries." *Weltwirtschaftliches Archiv* 118: 281-301.

Urata, Shujiro. 1983. "Factor Inputs and Japanese Manufacturing Trade Structure." *Review of Economics and Statistics* 65: 678-84.

Weiss, Leonard W. 1972. "The Geographic Size of Markets in Manufacturing." *Review of Economics and Statistics* 54: 245-57.

Yamawaki, Hideki, and David B. Audretsch. 1988. "Import Share under International Oligopoly with Differentiated Products: Japanese Imports in U.S. Manufacturing." *Review of Economics and Statistics* 70 (August): 569-79.

Yamazawa, Ippei. 1987. "Japan and Her Asian Neighbors in a Dynamic Perspective." *Trade and Structural Change in Pacific Asia.* Ed. Colin I. Bradford, Jr., and William H. Branson. Chicago: University of Chicago Press.

6 ALTERNATIVE SCENARIOS FOR TRADE LIBERALIZATION

Alan V. Deardorff and Robert M. Stern

I. INTRODUCTION

As the world embarks on the eighth GATT (Uruguay) round of multilateral trade negotiations, it is important to consider the potential economic effects of different negotiating options. In this paper, we report on a series of computational experiments involving alternative liberalization scenarios, using the Michigan Model of World Production and Trade. The Michigan Model is well suited for this kind of analysis because it is a multicountry, multisectoral computational model covering the eighteen major developed and sixteen major developing countries and allowing for a variety of complex general equilibrium interactions, both globally and within individual countries.

An earlier version of this paper was presented to a Workshop on General Equilibrium Trade Modeling held at the University of Western Ontario on March 24, 1988. We would like to thank John Whalley and other participants at the Western Ontario Workshop for their helpful comments. We are grateful also to Bee Aw Roberts and other participants at the Middlebury Conference for their comments. We wish to thank John Alfaro for his computational assistance and Judith Jackson for editorial and typing assistance. Financial assistance was provided in part by a grant from the Ford Foundation to support a program of research on trade policy at the Institute of Public Policy Studies at the University of Michigan.

In the previous GATT rounds, efforts were made to reduce existing nominal tariffs, and, particularly in the Tokyo Round that was concluded in 1979, several agreements (codes) were negotiated involving a variety of nontariff measures. The GATT codes were designed *inter alia* to increase transparency in the use of nontariff measures by the major trading countries, thereby lowering trading costs and improving market access, and to limit the introduction of new barriers. However, little progress was made in reducing or eliminating existing nontariff barriers (NTBs) affecting trade in agricultural or manufactured products. Furthermore, because of the special and differential treatment afforded to developing countries in the GATT, these countries were not obligated to reciprocate the tariff reductions effected by the developed countries. This did not carry over to the GATT codes, however, since participation in the benefits of many of the codes was made conditional on the acceptance of code authority and discipline, which was something that most developing countries were unprepared to accept.

With the negotiations now under way, it is necessary to focus attention on alternative negotiating options. The agenda for the Uruguay Round is rather ambitious. It covers such traditional items as the reduction or elimination of existing tariffs and NTBs on manufactures and agricultural products, and unfinished business from the Tokyo Round, such as the negotiation of a safeguards code. There are also several new agenda items, including rules governing counterfeiting, rights to intellectual property, investment performance requirements, and the liberalization of trade and investment in service industries.

Countries may have different interests with respect to individual agenda items, and it will be necessary for them to weigh the potential benefits and costs of the various options open to them in the negotiations. It may be difficult, however, to assess the options in a precise and comprehensive manner because of the lack of data and the qualitative nature of some of the agenda items at issue. Nonetheless, in view of the importance of merchandise trade in the economies of the major trading countries, it is worthwhile to assess the potential economic effects of alternative liberalization scenarios involving the elimination of existing tariffs and NTBs. At a later point, such quantitative information on trade liberalization may be merged with qualitative judgments on other issues to define what the overall interests of individual nations may be in the Uruguay Round negotiations.[1]

1. The appendix provides a brief description of the Michigan Model and the data on post-Tokyo Round tariffs and NTBs that provide the basis for our policy analysis.

Section II presents the results of various scenarios for the multilateral removal of tariffs and NTBs by the major industrialized and developing countries. Because the results are voluminous, we concentrate our discussion on the effects of the different options on the United States especially, mentioning other nations or regions when appropriate. In Section III, we bring together the various results for the United States and note where the greatest potential benefits might be realized, as well as the problems of adjustment that might be experienced for the different liberalization scenarios. Some suggestions for further research are given in Section IV.

II. COMPUTATIONAL RESULTS OF ALTERNATIVE LIBERALIZATION SCENARIOS

Some Illustrative Features of the Model

To help in interpreting the results for the individual scenarios, it may be useful first to describe how the Model functions when existing tariffs and/or NTBs are removed. Thus, suppose that we consider the complete elimination of post-Tokyo Round tariffs by the major industrialized countries, but assume that existing NTBs in these countries remain in place as do the tariffs in the developing countries. Suppose further that the tariffs are eliminated all at once rather than being phased out over some specified period of time. If we represent NTBs in terms of their tariff equivalents, the analysis of the removal of NTBs would be analogous to the removal of tariffs. The analysis is carried out in terms of comparative statics, and we abstract from the process of adjustment that will occur through time.

With the assumed removal of tariffs, imports will rise as domestic prices are lowered. This will cause increases in world prices, and exports will be stimulated in response. The responses of exports and imports will depend on the sectoral differences in tariffs among the industrialized countries and on elasticities of demand. With NTBs assumed to remain in place, the increase in imports will be moderated depending on the restrictiveness of NTBs as reflected in the NTB coverage indexes that are built into the Model and that serve to limit the responsiveness of imports to tariff removal. While both the prices and quantities of exports and imports will change, we report the changes in the values of exports and imports at constant prices.

When export prices rise relative to the prices of home goods, production for export expands and production of home goods falls. This in turn leads to the expansion of employment in the export sectors and to a decline in employment in the home-good sectors. When the domestic prices of imports fall, there will be a substitution in demand on the part of both households and firms toward imports and away from home goods, depending on the elasticity of substitution.

Thus, broadly speaking, the removal of tariffs results in an increase in the prices of tradeable goods relative to nontradeables and to associated changes in employment. In the Model, we calculate both gross and net changes in employment by sector. The gross change in employment represents the sum of all positive sectoral changes in employment in the economy, and it is intended to serve as an indication of labor-market dislocation and aggregate structural adjustment. It includes those workers who might have to move only between the export and home sectors of their industries. The net change in employment, on the other hand, is the algebraic sum of the expansion and contraction in employment that will occur in home and export sectors of an industry, and it shows which industries on balance will experience an increase or decline in employment as tariffs are removed multilaterally. It should be noted that all of the foregoing changes will reflect both direct as well as indirect effects that operate through the inter-industry (input-output) relations. Also, as noted in the Appendix, because of the way we have endogenized aggregate expenditure, we prevent any change in total employment from occurring.

Although our Model provides information on changes in prices, production, consumption, and trade, it does not readily lend itself conceptually to analysis of changes in economic welfare. The reason is that we permit trade to be unbalanced initially and, when exports and imports respond differentially to exogenous changes in tariffs, the trade balance will change. When exchange rates are flexible in the Model, we allow for adjustment in trade so that the trade balance is restored to its initial position in terms of dollars. When overall prices change, however, there are implied intertemporal changes in the accumulation or decumulation of real assets associated with variations in the real value of the trade balance that are difficult to measure in terms of economic welfare. We have on numerous occasions used an ad hoc procedure for the calculation of welfare based on the static, partial-equilibrium measure commonly used in the literature to calculate changes in consumer and producer surplus. Our experience with this ad hoc measure has been that countries may show an increase or decrease in welfare depending on their trade-balance position because, when tariffs are eliminated, world prices (exclusive of tariffs) tend to rise and consumer prices to fall. To avoid ambiguities in interpreting this ad hoc welfare measure, we have chosen not to use it in the results of our following analysis. Instead, we report the changes in each country's terms of trade for each of the experiments.

As already noted, the elimination of tariffs will tend to increase world prices and cause consumer prices to fall, with corresponding changes in exports and imports. Depending on the change in a country's trade balance, its currency will either depreciate or appreciate to restore the trade balance to its original position. This means that there will be an induced change in a country's exports and imports brought about by the change in the exchange rate that will follow the response of trade to the removal of tariffs. This exchange-rate-induced change in trade can be substantial in some cases, as will be evident in some of our results. As an indication of the changes in exchange rates that may occur for a country in given circumstances, we calculate the weighted percentage change in each country's effective exchange rate, using bilateral exports and imports to weight the changes in bilateral exchange rates that occur.

Since tariff removal will have a significant impact on domestic prices, we calculate an index of the percentage change in import and home prices, using sectoral imports and production as weights to construct the aggregate index. This provides a measure of how each country's price level might be affected by the policy changes being analyzed.

While our analysis of tariff removal concentrates especially on the effects on employment, other factors of production will be affected as well. To provide a more complete indication of the adjustment problems that individual industries may encounter, we also calculate the changes in per-unit value added across sectors. These represent the incentives for factors of production to move among sectors in response to the removal of the entire structure of tariffs. This is familiar from the theory of effective protection, but, rather than just considering the partial equilibrium effects involved, our Model permits us to take into account the many important interactions that occur both within and between countries.

A final point worth noting is that, because our Model does not distinguish imports by country of origin, we cannot examine changes in tariffs or NTBs on a bilateral or preferential basis. Because such NTBs as the Multifibre Arrangement (MFA) and the U.S. Voluntary Export Restraint (VER) on Japanese cars are essentially bilateral in character, we chose to treat them as export taxes from the standpoint of the exporting countries and to analyze their removal accordingly.

Presentation of Computational Results

We explored the economic effects of several different liberalization scenarios in our computations. These scenarios were chosen to illustrate what might be expected to occur if it were possible to eliminate completely existing tariffs and/or NTBs in the world's major trading countries. We realize, of course, that the scenarios selected may not in fact correspond to what is being proposed or may actually be implemented in the Uruguay Round negotiations. Nonetheless, our results may be useful in helping individual nations choose among the available options that may best serve their own interests and in developing a consensus about which options might be mutually beneficial for the various nations participating in the negotiations. The scenarios to be analyzed are:

1. Elimination of all post-Tokyo Round (1987) tariffs in the eighteen major industrialized countries.
2. Elimination of NTBs in the major industrialized countries (excluding agriculture and textiles and clothing).
3. Elimination of agricultural NTBs in the major industrialized countries, modeled as ad valorem tariff equivalents.
4. Elimination of NTBs on textiles and clothing in the major industrialized countries.
5. Elimination of all tariffs and NTBs in the major industrialized countries, with agricultural NTBs modeled as tariff equivalents.

Since the individual scenarios differ somewhat in terms of the assumptions made in implementing the Model, we shall discuss the results of each of them separately. The results are presented side by side in Section III, and an effort is made to highlight the main differences among them.

1. Elimination of Post-Tokyo Round Tariffs in the Major Industrialized Countries

In this scenario, we eliminated the post-Tokyo Round (1987) nominal tariffs for the eighteen major industrialized countries in the Model. Existing NTBs are assumed to remain intact as represented by the NTB trade coverage ratios discussed above. All countries are assumed to have flexible exchange rates. The overall results are summarized in Tables 6-1A and B. The principal findings are as follows:

1. Based on 1976 levels, exports will rise by around $30 billion for all the countries listed, which is about a 4.5 percent increase. U.S. exports rise by $4 billion and imports by $4.3 billion.
2. We have already noted that aggregate expenditure has been endogenized to prevent any change in total employment from occurring. As an indication of labor-market dislocation and aggregate structural adjustment, we have calculated the "Gross Change in Employment" in Tables 6-1A and B. This is the sum of all positive sectoral employment changes for a country and is also shown as a percentage of each country's 1976 labor force. The former figure represents the total number of workers in each country who would have to change jobs if post-Tokyo Round tariffs were eliminated. It includes those who might have to move only between the export and home sectors of their industries. For the United States, the gross change in employment is 141,000 workers, which is 0.16 percent of the 1976 U.S. labor force. The total for the European Economic Community is 819,000 workers, which is 0.81 percent of 1976 employment. For individual EEC-member countries, the percentages range from 0.56 for the United Kingdom to 1.72 for Belgium-Luxembourg. The total for Japan is 125,000 workers, which is 0.24 percent of the 1976 labor force.

By assuming that the existing tariffs are removed all at once, we are abstracting, as mentioned earlier, from the process of adjustment that will occur through time. In this connection, it is important to note that it is a common practice to implement trade liberalization gradually over a period of years. Thus, the Tokyo Round tariff reductions were phased in over a period of seven years, from 1980 to 1987. The case for gradualism can be made on a variety of grounds. First, there may be distortions in the economy that impede labor and capital from making socially correct calculations concerning the sectors in which they can earn maximum returns. Second, the government may wish to mitigate the economic losses that factor owners may experience in protected industries. Finally, if resources in the protected industries become unemployed as the result of

Table 6-1A. Summary of Effects on the Major Industrialized Countries Due to Elimination of Post-Tokyo Round Tariffs in Industrialized Countries

	Value of Change In Exports		Value of Change In Imports		Gross Change In Employment[a]		% Change in Terms of Trade	% Change in Eff. Ex. Rate[b]	% Change in Prices[c]
	$ Mill.	%	$ Mill.	%	000 Wkr	%			
Australia	2031.8	14.1	2052.4	17.4	66.0	1.14	0.01	-0.9	-0.9
Austria	1444.2	15.9	1412.2	12.3	94.2	3.20	-0.15	0.7	-3.1
Canada	1854.4	4.6	1857.7	4.8	53.9	0.56	-0.02	0.5	-0.7
European Community									
Belgium-Luxembourg	1384.3	4.0	1354.6	3.9	66.7	1.72	-0.08	1.6	-2.8
Denmark	555.2	5.8	556.9	4.5	37.6	1.56	0.24	0.3	-2.0
France	3092.4	5.2	3157.1	4.9	144.3	0.69	0.17	-0.6	-0.8
Germany	4558.1	4.2	4603.1	5.2	237.4	0.97	-0.12	-0.4	-1.5
Ireland	176.3	4.8	179.9	4.3	12.6	1.23	0.20	0.9	-2.0
Italy	1632.1	4.1	1633.0	3.8	123.2	0.65	0.07	-0.2	-0.8
Netherlands	1740.1	4.0	1796.1	4.6	60.2	1.32	0.05	1.0	-2.2
United Kingdom	2813.2	5.7	2718.5	4.9	137.1	0.56	-0.08	-0.8	-0.6
Total EC	15951.7	4.6	15999.2	4.7	819.0	0.81	0.01	-0.3	-1.2
Finland	487.5	7.2	475.3	6.4	37.3	1.74	-0.12	1.0	-1.8
Japan	1775.6	2.5	1862.9	2.9	125.4	0.24	0.05	-0.2	-0.4
New Zealand	456.0	15.6	454.2	13.9	24.2	2.01	0.02	-0.3	-1.3
Norway	414.4	4.9	379.6	3.4	16.2	0.91	-0.15	0.0	-0.9
Sweden	739.8	3.8	723.7	3.8	32.2	0.79	-0.10	0.4	-1.1
Switzerland	470.9	3.0	449.3	3.0	17.7	0.63	-0.19	0.1	-0.7
United States	3988.9	3.3	4261.6	3.3	141.3	0.16	0.29	-0.6	-0.1
Total Industrialized	29615.2	4.5	29928.1	4.6	1427.4	0.53	0.12	-0.3	-0.6

a. Refers to sum of changes in the home and export sectors within industries.
b. Positive = appreciation.
c. Index of import and home prices.

Table 6-1B. Summary of Effects on the Major Developing Countries Due to Elimination of Post-Tokyo Round Tariffs in Industrialized Countries

	Value of Change In Exports		Value of Change In Imports		Gross Change In Employment[a]		% Change in Terms of Trade	% Change in Eff. Ex. Rate[b]	% Change in Prices[c]
	$ Mill.	%	$ Mill.	%	000 Wkr	%			
Argentina	-33.4	-0.8	20.8	0.7	20.9	0.20	1.14	0.7	-0.1
Brazil	-73.9	-0.7	0.2	0.0	39.2	0.10	0.85	0.6	-0.1
Chile	-4.4	-0.2	-14.2	-1.1	5.6	0.20	-0.89	-0.3	0.1
Colombia	-12.7	-0.7	13.9	0.8	11.7	0.15	1.28	1.5	-0.2
Greece	-4.5	-0.2	-20.9	-0.3	6.5	0.16	0.27	0.1	-0.0
Hong Kong	-1.9	-0.0	1.2	0.0	8.3	0.63	0.23	1.2	-0.3
India	-29.3	-0.5	-28.9	-0.5	140.0	0.06	-0.06	0.6	-0.0
Israel	-1.2	-0.0	-6.7	-0.2	2.0	0.18	0.26	0.5	-0.0
South Korea	-24.8	-0.3	4.0	0.0	20.2	0.16	0.37	0.8	-0.1
Mexico	-31.3	-0.6	-17.2	-0.3	27.1	0.16	0.37	0.6	-0.1
Portugal	-0.4	-0.0	-23.7	-0.5	7.5	0.24	-0.10	0.2	0.0
Singapore	-6.4	-0.1	-19.0	-0.2	2.8	0.32	0.03	0.3	0.0
Spain	-23.7	-0.2	-44.2	-0.3	16.0	0.13	0.37	0.3	-0.0
Taiwan	-16.6	-0.2	7.2	0.1	17.9	0.32	0.18	0.8	-0.0
Turkey	-8.9	-0.4	-10.2	-0.2	10.7	0.07	0.72	0.1	-0.0
Yugoslavia	-7.0	-0.1	-5.5	-0.1	5.6	0.12	0.27	0.3	-0.0
Total LDCs	-280.7	-0.3	-143.3	-0.1	341.9	0.09	0.47	0.5	-0.1
All Countries	29334.5	4.0	29784.8	3.9	1769.3	0.28	0.17	-0.2	-0.6

a. Refers to sum of changes in the home and export sectors within industries.
b. Positive = appreciation.
c. Index of import and home prices.

liberalization, it may be desirable to liberalize gradually to minimize the loss of output.

If, in this light, the post-Tokyo Round tariff reductions were to be phased in over a period of several years, the aggregate results suggest that the adjustment of employment might not add materially to normal labor-market turnover within and among industries. Any serious disruptions in labor markets would therefore be less likely to occur. This would also be the case to the extent that adjustment took place in the context of a growing world. However, as will be noted, our disaggregated results by sector do not fully support such a conclusion, because there are numerous sectors in which the *relative* changes in employment are sufficiently large to suggest that there could indeed be difficulties in adjustment.

As for major developing countries, the gross employment changes recorded in Table 6-1B are all comparatively small.

3. The terms of trade of the United States show a small improvement of 0.29 percent, and there are comparably small improvements and declines for the other industrialized countries. Some of the changes for the developing countries are larger, in excess of 1 percent for Argentina and Colombia. It is noteworthy from the mixed signs for the industrialized countries that these countries as a group have not succeeded in uniformly improving their own terms of trade via their tariffs. However, with few exceptions, the tariffs of the industrialized countries can be seen to have worsened the terms of trade of less-developed countries.
4. The U.S. dollar will depreciate on an effective basis (by 0.6 percent), as will the French franc (0.6 percent), the German mark (0.4 percent), the Italian lira (0.2 percent), the British pound (0.8 percent), and the Japanese yen (0.2 percent). The remaining industrial-country currencies will appreciate, with the changes most notable for Belgium-Luxembourg (1.6 percent), Ireland (0.9 percent), and the Netherlands (1 percent). Except for Chile, the currencies of all the developing countries appreciate, which is the principal reason their exports are shown to decline.
5. Import prices fall, contributing to a small 0.1 percent drop in consumer prices in the United States. Price declines for most other industrialized countries are significantly greater, ranging from around 0.4 percent to more than 3 percent. Prices also fall, though by a relatively small amount, in most of the developing countries.

The country results in Tables 6-1A and B mask much industry detail that our Model is well able to calculate. These detailed results, which are not shown here, indicate that there are net percentage increases as well as reductions across the twenty-two tradeable and seven nontradeable sectors. In the United States, for example, the increases are concentrated in agriculture, machinery, transport equipment, chemicals, and paper products, and the declines in wearing apparel and textiles, leather products and footwear, miscellaneous manufactures, rubber products, nonmetallic mineral products, and certain other tradeable sectors. The nontradeable sectors, except for mining and quarrying and construction, show net declines in employment. This result is prevalent in most of the countries in the Model, as it was for an earlier analysis done for the Tokyo Round in Deardorff and Stern (1986a). It can be explained by the general substitution toward tradeable goods and away from nontradeables due to the reduction in the relative prices of tradeable goods that would result from the elimination of tariffs.

In discussing the overall gross-employment results in Tables 6-1A and B, we noted that there were several cases in which these changes represented sizable percentages of total 1976 employment. The United States is on the low side. Indeed, some of the positive and negative percentage changes in other countries are sufficiently large that they suggest sectors in which labor adjustment might present difficulties. This is particularly the case if there are factor-market distortions that hinder labor mobility and if there is a mismatch in labor skills between the industries that would expand and contract in response to tariff elimination so that unemployment may occur. Again, if tariff elimination was staged over a period of years, the difficulties would be lessened, but they might not be fully resolved in certain individual sectors. In contrast, large percentage changes in net employment are not so prevalent for the developing countries, reflecting the fact that those countries in general will be less materially affected by tariff elimination in the industrialized countries.

The employment results we have discussed so far provide a good indication of the most important and difficult structural adjustments that changes in trade can entail, but they are not the only ones. Other factors of production are affected by trade as well, and are subject to adjustment problems of their own. To provide a more complete indication of adjustment problems that may impact entire industries, we show in Table 6-2 the rankings of sectors in terms of percentage changes in per-unit value added that according to our

Table 6-2. Rankings Of Sectors According to Percentage Changes in Value Added in the Major Industrialized Countries and Brazil Due to Elimination of Post-Tokyo Round Tariffs in Industrialized Countries

Industry Name	ISIC Code	ALA	ATA	BLX	CND	DEN	FIN	FR	GFR	IRE	IT
Traded Goods:											
Agr., for. & fish.	1	3	27	7	3	4	27	3	26	7	28
Food, bev. & tob.	310	7	17	14	11	9	7	9	16	10	12
Textiles	321	4	2	2	24	5	3	4	2	3	10
Wearing apparel	322	22	1	5	27	6	1	2	23	15	2
Leather products	323	1	5	18	5	8	4	6	9	11	5
Footwear	324	18	4	15	12	12	2	5	29	20	1
Wood products	331	23	3	27	9	15	17	27	21	25	15
Furniture & fixt.	332	20	24	4	14	1	6	23	5	19	4
Paper & paper prod.	341	17	8	9	7	26	18	21	28	27	20
Printing & publ.	342	10	13	16	18	18	16	16	20	16	18
Chemicals	35A	6	10	3	28	13	8	28	3	8	29
Petrol. & rel. prod.	35B	8	14	29	29	29	12	13	24	29	25
Rubber products	355	28	25	13	15	28	29	8	10	12	6
Nonmetal min. prod.	36A	21	22	23	23	16	19	24	15	5	11
Glass & glass prod.	362	25	16	11	26	17	25	15	12	6	14
Iron & steel	371	9	11	8	10	19	20	12	8	26	16
Nonferrous metals	372	2	9	28	2	14	24	25	14	2	26
Metal products	381	24	20	24	25	10	23	11	11	9	7
Nonelec. machinery	382	15	7	10	6	7	15	1	6	4	9
Elec. machinery	383	27	12	12	20	11	9	10	7	14	13
Transport equip.	384	29	29	1	1	3	5	7	1	28	3
Misc. manufact.	38A	26	6	6	4	2	28	18	4	1	8
Nontraded Goods:											
Mining & quarrying	2	5	26	17	8	27	26	14	13	13	22
Elec., gas & water	4	14	23	22	19	24	21	26	19	23	19
Construction	5	11	18	21	13	21	11	19	25	17	23
Wh. & ret. trade	6	16	21	26	17	23	13	22	18	22	27
Transp., stor. & comm.	7	12	19	19	16	22	14	20	17	18	17
Fin., ins. & real est.	8	19	28	25	21	25	22	29	27	24	24
Comm., soc. & pers. serv.	9	13	15	20	22	20	10	17	22	21	21

Table 6-2. *Continued*

	ISIC Code	JPN	NL	NZ	NOR	SWD	SWZ	UK	US	BRZ
Traded Goods:										
Agr., for. & fish.	1	29	2	2	6	11	20	16	1	1
Food, bev. & tob.	310	6	10	7	19	21	9	26	11	11
Textiles	321	13	1	3	3	4	7	15	24	25
Wearing apparel	322	26	5	9	5	2	3	22	25	6
Leather products	323	24	7	1	2	7	19	4	26	29
Footwear	324	14	8	10	4	1	6	29	23	2
Wood products	331	5	29	11	18	17	27	28	8	21
Furniture & fixt.	332	18	18	12	11	8	28	5	12	9
Paper & paper prod.	341	10	15	8	8	12	15	27	7	20
Printing & publ.	342	17	14	14	25	20	12	18	14	19
Chemicals	35A	8	3	23	10	23	1	7	4	17
Petrol. & rel. prod.	35B	28	19	5	17	16	10	19	10	14
Rubber products	355	4	13	25	27	29	21	3	27	24
Nonmetal min. prod.	36A	15	27	24	24	26	26	9	28	15
Glass & glass prod.	362	12	6	19	29	25	22	8	19	13
Iron & steel	371	11	26	18	12	22	17	12	18	26
Nonferrous metals	372	27	25	4	7	13	18	13	22	28
Metal products	381	7	17	28	15	9	5	6	9	5
Nonelec. machinery	382	9	12	21	13	10	8	2	6	23
Elec. machinery	383	2	9	27	14	6	4	11	3	3
Transport equip.	384	1	11	29	1	3	29	14	2	4
Misc. manufact.	38A	3	4	26	16	5	2	1	29	22
Nontraded Goods:										
Mining & quarrying	2	25	28	6	9	28	24	10	5	27
Elec., gas & water	4	16	23	20	26	24	23	20	20	18
Construction	5	23	16	15	20	15	13	24	13	7
Wh. & ret. trade	6	20	22	17	23	19	16	23	17	16
Transp., stor. & comm.	7	19	20	16	22	18	14	17	16	12
Fin., Ins. & real est.	8	22	24	22	28	27	25	25	21	10
Comm., soc. & pers. serv.	9	21	21	13	21	14	11	21	15	8

Model will result from tariff elimination. These represent the incentives for factors of production to move among sectors and are reported here only in the form of ordinal rankings.

For the United States, the industries with the largest percentage increases in per-unit value added are agriculture, transport equipment, electrical machinery, chemicals, and mining and quarrying, while the smallest percentage increases (or greatest declines) are in miscellaneous manufactures, nonmetallic mineral products, leather products, rubber products, and wearing apparel. The rankings for other countries can be similarly discerned from Table 6-2. The results thus permit identification of the sectors likely to experience the greatest incentives to expand or contract as industrialized country tariffs are eliminated.

2. Elimination of NTBs in the Major Industrialized Countries (Excluding Agriculture, Textiles, and Clothing)

Having focused thus far on the effects of eliminating tariffs in the major industrialized and developing countries, we turn next to an analysis of the effects of eliminating existing NTBs in the industrialized countries. We first consider all NTBs except for those applying to agriculture (ISIC 1), textiles (ISIC 321), and clothing (ISIC 322), which are the focus of the following scenarios. As mentioned in the Appendix, we have constructed sets of "high" and "low" NTB ad valorem equivalents, the latter based on an adjustment for the percentage of trade covered by NTBs. In what follows, we report the results based on the "low" estimates. All other NTBs are assumed unchanged, as are all nominal tariffs in this scenario.

In all of our NTB elimination scenarios, we decided to exclude the petroleum sector (ISIC 35B), even though the NTB trade coverage indexes indicated the presence of some type of barrier. Our reasoning was that petroleum imports are monitored or controlled for a variety of reasons, perhaps most importantly national defense. Because, in our view, the underlying motivations involving petroleum do not reflect the usual protectionist considerations, it seemed reasonable to treat the petroleum sector as a special case.

We should also note that we decided to model the existing nontariff restrictions affecting imports of automobiles from Japan and textiles and clothing from the developing countries from the export side in terms of an export tax rather than as an ad valorem equivalent duty on imports. The reason is that our Model does not distinguish imports by country of origin, and therefore we are unable to represent from the demand side the bilateral characteristics of the current arrangements that restrict imports of automobiles and textiles and clothing. We thus converted the import ad valorem equivalent estimates to export tax equivalents for ISIC sectors 321 (textiles), 322 (clothing), and 384 (transport equipment). For purposes of this second scenario, an export tax equivalent of 11.4 percent for ISIC 384 was applied only to Japan.

The results for this scenario involving the elimination of NTBs (excluding ISIC 1, 321, and 322) are summarized in Tables 6-3A and B. The principal findings are as follows:

1. Exports increase in total by $10.7 billion, which is 1.4 percent above the 1976 level. The largest increases are for France, the United States, Japan, West Germany, and Italy. The exports of the developing countries increase only slightly.
2. The gross change in employment is largest for Japan, followed by France, the United States, Italy, and West Germany.
3. Japan's terms of trade decline by 0.53 percent. The terms of trade of the smaller industrialized countries improve, as do the terms of trade of developing countries, except Hong Kong.
4. Japan's currency appreciates by 0.6 percent. Belgium has an even larger appreciation of 1.3 percent, which may reflect its position especially as a net exporter of iron and steel products (ISIC 371).
5. Prices fall by comparatively small percentages in all the industrialized countries. The largest decline is in the case of Belgium, and this may be attributed primarily to the size of its currency appreciation and the relatively substantial importance of tradeable goods.

The positive sectoral net percentage changes in employment, which are not shown here, are most pronounced for iron and steel products especially in Belgium-Luxembourg and West Germany; leather and footwear, metal products, and nonelectric machinery in France; leather and footwear, nonferrous metals, and machinery in Italy; textiles, leather and footwear, and miscellaneous manufactures in Switzerland; and leather, agriculture, textiles, chemicals, nonelectric machinery, and miscellaneous manufactures in the United States. Since we modeled Japan as removing the export tax on its transport-equipment sector, the result is a substantial net percentage increase in employment in this sector.

Table 6-3A. Summary of Effects on the Major Industrialized Countries Due to Elimination of Nontariff Barriers in Other than Agriculture and Textiles in Industrialized Countries

	Value of Change In Exports		Value of Change In Imports		Gross Change In Employment[a]		% Change in Terms of Trade	% Change in Eff. Ex. Rate[b]	% Change in Prices[c]
	$ Mill.	%	$ Mill.	%	000 Wkr	%			
Australia	241.0	1.7	311.1	2.6	14.1	0.24	0.45	0.0	-0.1
Austria	95.4	1.0	91.8	0.8	11.7	0.40	0.03	-0.0	-0.2
Canada	90.3	0.2	113.9	0.3	15.2	0.16	0.06	0.0	-0.0
European Community									
Belgium-Luxembourg	614.9	1.8	606.8	1.7	49.9	1.29	-0.02	1.3	-1.6
Denmark	109.7	1.1	135.7	1.1	12.8	0.53	0.35	1.0	-0.7
France	1854.3	3.1	1775.8	2.8	86.2	0.41	-0.10	-0.3	-0.5
Germany	1223.0	1.1	985.5	1.1	73.9	0.30	-0.29	0.0	-0.4
Ireland	21.8	0.6	38.9	0.9	3.9	0.38	0.51	0.8	-0.3
Italy	967.7	2.5	871.5	2.0	78.1	0.41	-0.21	-0.4	-0.4
Netherlands	593.7	1.4	677.6	1.7	21.6	0.48	0.16	0.2	-0.5
United Kingdom	816.9	1.7	689.9	1.2	50.4	0.21	-0.20	-0.4	-0.2
Total EC	6201.9	1.8	5781.7	1.7	376.7	0.37	-0.15	-0.1	-0.5
Finland	66.8	1.0	60.8	0.8	5.3	0.25	-0.07	0.0	-0.2
Japan	1542.2	2.2	1192.9	1.8	144.5	0.27	-0.53	0.6	-0.2
New Zealand	5.2	0.2	30.1	0.9	6.2	0.52	0.88	0.5	-0.1
Norway	91.0	1.1	100.7	0.9	5.4	0.30	0.13	-0.1	-0.2
Sweden	135.6	0.7	92.4	0.5	10.9	0.27	-0.23	-0.4	-0.1
Switzerland	280.7	1.8	281.0	1.9	13.1	0.47	-0.02	-0.1	-0.5
United States	1836.4	1.5	1673.1	1.3	76.6	0.09	-0.12	-0.4	-0.0
Total Industrialized	10586.6	1.6	9729.7	1.5	679.8	0.25	-0.16	-0.1	-0.2

a. Refers to sum of changes in the home and export sectors within industries.
b. Positive = appreciation.
c. Index of import and home prices.

Table 6-3B. Summary of Effects on the Major Developing Countries Due to Elimination of Nontariff Barriers in Other than Agriculture and Textiles in Industrialized Countries

	Value of Change In Exports		Value of Change In Imports		Gross Change In Employment[a]		% Change in Terms of Trade	% Change in Eff. Ex. Rate[b]	% Change in Prices[c]
	$ Mill.	%	$ Mill.	%	000 Wkr	%			
Argentina	0.3	0.0	24.9	0.8	11.4	0.11	0.51	0.4	-0.1
Brazil	17.8	0.2	55.1	0.4	30.0	0.07	0.42	0.3	-0.1
Chile	-1.3	-0.1	5.0	0.4	1.7	0.06	0.26	0.1	-0.1
Colombia	0.1	0.0	7.5	0.4	3.2	0.04	0.36	0.3	-0.0
Greece	4.0	0.1	17.2	0.3	3.7	0.09	0.50	0.0	-0.0
Hong Kong	0.9	0.0	-15.2	-0.2	1.6	0.12	-0.12	-0.2	0.0
India	1.0	0.0	10.8	0.2	85.1	0.04	0.15	0.3	-0.0
Israel	5.3	0.2	2.1	0.1	0.9	0.08	0.07	0.1	-0.0
South Korea	2.8	0.0	6.3	0.1	7.3	0.06	0.05	-0.0	-0.0
Mexico	7.5	0.1	24.6	0.4	8.6	0.05	0.34	0.3	-0.0
Portugal	6.4	0.3	0.7	0.0	2.6	0.08	0.15	-0.0	0.0
Singapore	5.3	0.1	-2.4	-0.0	1.3	0.15	0.00	-0.1	0.0
Spain	30.1	0.3	3.1	0.0	10.4	0.08	0.02	0.0	-0.0
Taiwan	-4.3	-0.0	14.5	0.2	10.7	0.19	0.18	0.3	-0.1
Turkey	7.5	0.4	8.1	0.2	2.9	0.02	0.29	-0.1	-0.0
Yugoslavia	10.2	0.2	5.5	0.1	3.4	0.07	0.01	-0.1	0.0
Total LDCs	93.6	0.1	167.6	0.2	184.9	0.05	0.25	0.2	-0.0
All Countries	10680.1	1.4	9897.2	1.3	864.7	0.14	-0.10	-0.1	-0.2

a. Refers to sum of changes in the home and export sectors within industries.
b. Positive = appreciation.
c. Index of import and home prices.

Japan experiences notable net percentage declines in iron and steel, textiles, and miscellaneous manufactures. The net percentage changes in employment are fairly large in a number of sectors in the industrialized countries and suggest possible short-run adjustment difficulties unless the barriers are eliminated in stages. The largest net percentage changes in employment in the developing countries are concentrated in leather and footwear in this scenario.

3. Elimination of Agricultural NTBs in the Major Industrialized Countries, Modeled as Ad Valorem Equivalents

In this scenario, we eliminated the agricultural (ISIC 1) NTB ad valorem equivalents maintained in the industrialized countries. These NTBs are based on the estimated Producer Subsidy Equivalents (PSEs) calculated in OECD (1987). Most of the PSEs reflect the use of domestic market-price-support policies that raise prices to producers and consumers equally. Since these domestic policies would have to be facilitated by some sort of trade barrier, we chose for this scenario to model them all as ad valorem equivalents of NTBs. The estimates used for this purpose are listed in Table 6-4. As with the NTBs on industrial products, we adjusted them for the percentage of trade covered. In carrying out this scenario, all other NTBs on industrial products as well as nominal tariffs are assumed unchanged.

The summary results are contained in Tables 6-5A and B. The principal findings are as follows:

1. In terms of total trade, imports expand by $2.3 billion for the industrialized countries, with the largest increases for Japan ($1.4 billion), the Netherlands ($583.4 million), Switzerland ($215.6 million), and Italy ($208.9 million). Exports expand by $3.3 billion, with the largest increase for Japan ($2.1 billion). The changes in the trade of the developing countries are comparatively small.
2. Japan has the largest gross change in employment among the industrialized countries, followed by the United States, Italy, West Germany, the Netherlands, and France. There are large absolute gross employment changes in India and Brazil. The relative changes are under 1 percent of the 1976 labor force in all the countries listed.

Table 6-4. Estimated Producer Subsidy Equivalents (PSEs) in the Agricultural Sector (ISIC 1) in the Major Industrialized Countries (%)[a]

Industrialized Countries	Estimated Producer Subsidy Equivalents
Australia	1.7
Austria	14.1
Canada	3.8
European Community	
Belgium-Luxembourg	23.9
Denmark	12.2
France	14.1
Germany	4.7
Ireland	10.6
Italy	17.1
Netherlands	22.2
United Kingdom	14.9
Finland	17.7
Japan	36.1
New Zealand	1.3
Norway	21.6
Sweden	1.8
Switzerland	38.7
United States	0.2

a. The PSE estimates in OECD (1987) have been adjusted downward based upon the NTB trade coverage ratios for ISIC 1. For details, see Deardorff and Stern (1987, Appendix B).

Table 6-5A. Summary of Effects on the Major Industrialized Countries
Due to Elimination of Nontariff Barriers in Agriculture in Industrialized Countries

	Value of Change In Exports		Value of Change In Imports		Gross Change In Employment[a]		% Change in Terms of Trade	% Change in Eff. Ex. Rate[b]	% Change in Prices[c]
	$ Mill.	%	$ Mill.	%	000 Wkr	%			
Australia	-141.0	-1.0	-8.8	-0.1	11.2	0.19	0.93	0.4	-0.0
Austria	47.6	0.5	19.8	0.2	6.2	0.21	-0.28	-0.1	-0.1
Canada	-218.2	-0.5	-33.5	-0.1	14.7	0.15	0.46	0.0	-0.0
European Community									
Belgium-Luxembourg	237.6	0.7	134.8	0.4	29.5	0.76	-0.29	0.0	-0.8
Denmark	-5.9	-0.1	18.7	0.2	9.3	0.39	0.31	0.3	-0.3
France	194.1	0.3	156.2	0.2	37.5	0.18	-0.05	-0.1	-0.1
Germany	278.8	0.3	-380.4	-0.4	48.5	0.20	-0.70	-0.4	0.1
Ireland	-9.7	-0.3	-9.4	-0.2	8.2	0.80	0.04	0.5	-0.5
Italy	406.8	1.0	208.9	0.5	54.2	0.29	-0.46	-0.4	-0.2
Netherlands	565.1	1.3	583.4	1.5	43.3	0.95	0.00	1.1	-1.0
United Kingdom	485.4	1.0	152.4	0.3	28.9	0.12	-0.62	-0.4	-0.1
Total EC	2152.0	0.6	864.7	0.3	259.4	0.26	-0.39	-0.2	-0.2
Finland	64.2	0.9	38.2	0.5	5.8	0.27	-0.37	-0.2	-0.2
Japan	2081.8	2.9	1439.7	2.2	246.3	0.47	-0.97	-0.9	-0.4
New Zealand	-9.0	-0.3	-11.8	-0.4	2.4	0.20	-0.10	-0.1	0.0
Norway	42.6	0.5	54.6	0.5	5.1	0.28	0.17	0.0	-0.3
Sweden	-2.2	-0.0	-63.3	-0.3	7.1	0.17	-0.31	-0.1	0.1
Switzerland	296.4	1.9	215.6	1.5	21.9	0.78	-0.53	-0.2	-0.7
United States	-976.4	-0.8	-237.6	-0.2	117.7	0.13	0.64	0.1	0.0
Total Industrialized	3337.8	0.5	2277.4	0.3	697.8	0.26	0.02	-0.1	-0.1

a. Refers to sum of changes in the home and export sectors within industries.
b. Positive = appreciation.
c. Index of import and home prices.

Table 6-5B. Summary of Effects on the Major Industrialized Countries
Due to Elimination of Nontariff Barriers in Agriculture in Industrialized Countries

	Value of Change In Exports		Value of Change In Imports		Gross Change In Employment[a]		% Change in Terms of Trade	% Change in Eff. Ex. Rate[b]	% Change in Prices[c]
	$ Mill.	%	$ Mill.	%	000 Wkr	%			
Argentina	-65.4	-1.6	53.6	1.8	39.5	0.38	2.85	1.4	-0.2
Brazil	-163.1	-1.5	74.7	0.5	108.5	0.27	2.27	1.2	-0.2
Chile	-7.3	-0.4	-9.9	-0.8	10.3	0.37	-0.46	0.2	-0.0
Colombia	-30.6	-1.6	56.9	3.3	36.5	0.46	4.60	3.6	-0.6
Greece	-18.3	-0.6	12.9	0.2	9.2	0.23	1.14	0.8	-0.1
Hong Kong	7.4	0.1	-65.6	-0.7	3.8	0.29	-0.85	-0.4	0.3
India	-55.2	-1.0	-71.7	-1.3	293.0	0.13	-0.40	1.1	-0.1
Israel	-9.7	-0.4	-13.9	-0.3	4.1	0.36	0.13	0.6	0.0
South Korea	-35.3	-0.4	-29.9	-0.3	32.3	0.26	0.07	0.7	-0.0
Mexico	-51.8	-1.0	12.6	0.2	62.1	0.36	1.25	0.7	-0.3
Portugal	-8.3	-0.4	-41.9	-1.0	9.1	0.29	-0.77	0.1	0.2
Singapore	-8.2	-0.1	-18.3	-0.2	3.7	0.42	-0.09	-0.2	0.4
Spain	-53.8	-0.6	-69.1	-0.4	29.1	0.23	0.29	0.4	-0.0
Taiwan	-25.6	-0.3	-61.7	-0.8	28.1	0.50	-0.48	0.3	0.1
Turkey	-21.4	-1.0	46.2	0.9	25.8	0.18	3.01	1.2	-0.2
Yugoslavia	-13.3	-0.2	-6.7	-0.1	5.7	0.12	0.19	0.3	0.1
Total LDCs	-560.0	-0.6	-131.8	-0.1	700.8	0.19	1.14	0.9	-0.1
All Countries	2777.8	0.4	2145.6	0.3	1398.6	0.22	0.18	0.0	-0.1

a. Refers to sum of changes in the home and export sectors within industries.
b. Positive = appreciation.
c. Index of import and home prices.

3. Australia, Canada, and the United States experience improved terms of trade approaching 1 percent, while most other industrialized countries show a worsening of their terms of trade. Some of the developing countries, especially Argentina, Brazil, Colombia, and Turkey, show relatively large terms-of-trade improvements.
4. Certain industrialized countries experience currency appreciation, which in turn serves to dampen the increase in exports and to increase imports. Currency depreciation also occurs, however, especially in Japan, and the effects on trade are the opposite of those just noted. With the exceptions of Hong Kong and Singapore, the currencies of the developing countries appreciate, resulting in a dampening effect on their exports. Several developing countries also experience reductions in imports, which can be attributed to their response to the higher world prices of agricultural and related products associated with the removal of the NTBs.
5. Prices decline by small percentages in most of the industrialized countries. There is a mixture of relatively small percentage price decreases and increases among the developing countries.

The sectoral results, which are not shown here, are interesting insofar as they indicate a net increase in employment in agriculture (ISIC 1) in ten of the industrialized countries, with the largest increases in the Netherlands (7.5 percent) and the United States (3.6 percent). Switzerland shows a net decline of agricultural employment of 6.7 percent, and Japan, a net decline of 2.9 percent. There are also net percentage increases in employment in food and kindred products (ISIC 310) in a substantial number of cases. What is further noteworthy are the opposite effects on employment in other sectors, including nontradeables. In essence, when the agricultural sector expands or contracts in response to the removal of the NTBs and the associated changes in relative prices, there will tend to be opposite effects on other sectors. This phenomenon can be observed in the developing countries as well. The sizable percentage effects in a number of countries, both positive and negative, suggest the possibility of significant intersectoral adjustment problems in case the agricultural NTBs were to be eliminated all at once.

As already indicated, this scenario deals with the assumed removal of nontariff restrictions on agricultural imports. While it reveals that there would be significant impacts on employment in the agricultural and food sectors as well as in the manufacturing and nontradeable sectors, the results reflect the existing patterns of production, trade, and employment that have been shaped by domestic incentive programs.

4. Elimination of NTBs on Textiles and Clothing in the Major Industrialized Countries

We have already mentioned that imports are not distinguished in our Model according to country of origin. This makes it difficult to analyze bilateral import policies such as the Multifibre Arrangement, which restricts the quantities of textiles and clothing that developing countries can export to individual industrialized countries. Therefore, what we elected to do was to model the MFA restrictions as an export tax on textiles (ISIC 321) and clothing (ISIC 322) in the developing countries represented in the Model. For this purpose, we constructed weighted averages of the ad valorem equivalents of restrictions on imports of clothing by the industrialized countries from Hong Kong, South Korea, and Taiwan. We used these weighted averages to represent export taxes for the three countries as follows: Hong Kong (20.8 percent), South Korea (10.7 percent), and Taiwan (11.6 percent). The same rate was applied to textiles. For the remaining developing countries, we used the average (11.1 percent) of the rates calculated for South Korea and Taiwan. It was assumed that there were no NTBs affecting imports of textiles and clothing from the industrialized countries. All other NTBs and tariffs were assumed unchanged and all exchange rates were flexible.

The summary results are listed in Tables 6-6A and B. The principal findings are as follows:

1. There are only minor changes in the total trade of the industrialized countries, while the total trade of the developing countries increases by more than $900 million. Removing the export tax on textiles and clothing tends to lower their world price. Imports of these goods rise in the industrialized countries, resulting in a depreciation of their currencies, with the further effect of reducing their imports overall. Exports of the industrialized countries tend to fall because of the decline in world prices. The increase in exports of the developing countries causes their currencies to appreciate, which in turn increases their imports. The result, therefore, is that both

Table 6-6A. Summary of Effects on the Major Industrialized Countries Due to Elimination of Nontariff Barriers in Textiles in Industrialized Countries

	Value of Change In Exports		Value of Change In Imports		Gross Change In Employment[a]		% Change in Terms of Trade	% Change in Eff. Ex. Rate[b]	% Change in Prices[c]
	$ Mill.	%	$ Mill.	%	000 Wkr	%			
Australia	-7.3	-0.1	-3.3	-0.0	1.3	0.02	0.02	-0.5	0.0
Austria	-9.0	-0.1	-9.5	-0.1	4.7	0.16	-0.00	-0.2	0.1
Canada	5.2	0.0	13.3	0.0	1.5	0.02	0.02	-0.1	0.0
European Community									
Belgium-Luxembourg	3.7	0.0	2.5	0.0	2.9	0.07	-0.00	-0.1	0.0
Denmark	-0.7	-0.0	1.2	0.0	0.8	0.03	0.02	-0.1	0.0
France	-21.2	-0.0	-22.5	-0.0	10.9	0.05	-0.00	-0.1	0.0
Germany	16.6	0.0	30.2	0.0	8.0	0.03	0.01	-0.2	0.0
Ireland	-1.0	-0.0	-0.4	-0.0	0.5	0.05	0.02	-0.1	0.0
Italy	1.7	0.0	-15.7	-0.0	11.7	0.06	-0.04	-0.2	0.0
Netherlands	-9.3	-0.0	2.4	0.0	1.7	0.04	0.03	-0.1	0.0
United Kingdom	13.0	0.0	10.2	0.0	7.2	0.03	-0.00	-0.3	0.0
Total EC	2.8	0.0	7.8	0.0	43.7	0.04	0.00	-0.2	0.0
Finland	-7.1	-0.1	-9.8	-0.1	4.5	0.21	-0.04	-0.2	0.1
Japan	5.5	0.0	0.6	0.0	12.2	0.02	-0.01	-0.9	0.0
New Zealand	-3.9	-0.1	-4.2	-0.1	0.7	0.06	-0.01	-0.4	0.0
Norway	-0.4	-0.0	1.1	0.0	0.6	0.03	0.02	-0.1	0.0
Sweden	-6.3	-0.0	-3.6	-0.0	2.2	0.05	0.01	-0.2	0.0
Switzerland	-9.6	-0.1	-6.4	-0.0	2.3	0.08	0.02	-0.3	0.0
United States	-2.9	-0.0	28.3	0.0	14.9	0.02	0.03	-0.6	0.0
Total Industrialized	-33.0	-0.0	14.3	0.0	88.8	0.03	0.01	-0.4	0.0

a. Refers to sum of changes in the home and export sectors within industries.
b. Positive = appreciation.
c. Index of import and home prices.

Table 6-6B. Summary of Effects on the Major Developing Countries
Due to Elimination of Nontariff Barriers in Textiles in Industrialized Countries

	Value of Change In Exports		Value of Change In Imports		Gross Change In Employment[a]		% Change in Terms of Trade	% Change in Eff. Ex. Rate[b]	% Change in Prices[c]
	$ Mill.	%	$ Mill.	%	000 Wkr	%			
Argentina	0.7	0.0	3.6	0.1	122.9	1.18	0.06	1.0	-0.8
Brazil	24.7	0.2	28.3	0.2	23.2	0.06	0.04	0.1	-0.0
Chile	0.5	0.0	0.6	0.1	1.9	0.07	-0.01	-0.1	-0.0
Colombia	14.0	0.7	15.2	0.9	23.8	0.30	0.06	0.9	-0.2
Greece	42.5	1.5	40.0	0.7	26.0	0.65	-0.05	1.1	-0.4
Hong Kong	314.2	4.3	292.0	3.3	166.0	12.53	-0.30	16.4	-8.6
India	69.6	1.2	66.2	1.2	394.0	0.18	-0.06	1.1	-0.2
Israel	16.3	0.6	15.1	0.4	6.7	0.59	-0.01	0.5	-0.3
South Korea	141.7	1.7	128.3	1.5	132.2	1.05	-0.16	2.1	-0.8
Mexico	25.3	0.5	25.1	0.4	53.1	0.31	0.00	0.6	-0.2
Portugal	35.5	1.8	32.7	0.8	47.9	1.55	-0.10	1.9	-1.0
Singapore	0.4	0.0	-1.2	-0.0	13.5	1.55	-0.01	-0.2	-1.0
Spain	29.8	0.3	27.1	0.2	27.2	0.22	0.00	0.2	-0.1
Taiwan	138.8	1.6	128.7	1.7	73.8	1.30	-0.12	1.5	-0.8
Turkey	54.5	2.6	53.3	1.1	38.3	0.26	-0.02	1.3	-0.3
Yugoslavia	47.9	0.9	45.0	0.6	29.2	0.60	-0.04	0.9	-0.4
Total LDCs	956.4	1.1	900.2	0.8	1179.7	0.33	-0.01	0.9	-0.4
All Countries	923.4	0.1	914.6	0.1	1268.5	0.20	0.01	-0.3	-0.0

a. Refers to sum of changes in the home and export sectors within industries.
b. Positive = appreciation.
c. Index of import and home prices.

exports and imports increase for the developing countries, while there are negligible changes in the trade of the industrialized countries.

2. The gross absolute employment changes are the largest in India, Hong Kong, South Korea, Argentina, and Taiwan, and there are substantial percentage changes as well.
3. The terms of trade decline to a small extent for most of the developing countries and change only marginally for the industrialized countries.
4. We have already noted that the currencies of the industrialized countries depreciate, while the currencies of the developing countries appreciate.
5. Prices tend to rise in the industrialized countries because of the currency appreciation.

The net percentage employment changes in textiles and clothing, which are not reported here, are fairly substantial in a number of the industrialized countries. There are sizable net percentage increases in employment in textiles and clothing in several of the developing countries and net declines in employment in many other sectors. Considerable intersectoral adjustment problems might well occur in the developing countries, especially if the restrictions on their textile and clothing exports were eliminated all at once.

5. Elimination of all Tariffs and NTBs in the Major Industrialized Countries, with Agricultural NTBs Modeled as Tariff Equivalents

In this scenario, we combined complete removal of tariffs with removal of NTBs by the industrialized countries. The summary results are contained in Tables 6-7A and B. The results of this combined scenario reflect the combination of the component scenarios. With this in mind, the principal findings are as follows:

1. Based on 1976 levels, exports will rise by more than $33 billion, which is a 4.6 percent increase. U.S. exports rise by $3.6 billion and imports by $4.2 billion. The comparatively small changes in the trade of the developing countries reflect especially the responses to the appreciation of their currencies that would be experienced in the context of this broad liberalization.

2. The gross change in employment for the United States is 241,000 workers, which is 0.28 percent of the 1976 U.S. labor force. The results for the other industrialized countries range from less than 1 percent to 2.6 percent of 1976 employment, and, for the developing countries, from 0.3 percent to 12.3 percent.
3. The terms of trade improve for the United States, Australia, Canada, Denmark, Ireland, the Netherlands, New Zealand, and Norway, and they decline for the other industrialized countries. The terms of trade improve between 3 and 5 percent for Argentina, Brazil, Chile, and Turkey, and there are lesser improvements and declines for the remaining developing countries.
4. The U.S. dollar will depreciate by 1.3 percent. The Japanese yen also depreciates by 1.3 percent, and there are depreciations for several other industrialized countries. The currencies of the smaller industrialized countries appreciate. The currencies of the developing countries appreciate for the most part, ranging from 0.8 percent for Spain to 15.8 percent for Hong Kong.
5. Imports, and therefore consumer prices, fall by 0.1 percent in the United States. The declines are more substantial in the other industrialized countries, ranging from 0.6 percent in Canada to 4.1 percent in Belgium-Luxembourg.

The sectoral results, which are not reported here, indicate that the United States will have positive net employment changes in agriculture especially and to a lesser extent in leather products, paper, chemicals, petroleum products, electric machinery, and mining and quarrying. There are net declines in the remaining U.S. industries. The details for the other industrialized countries and developing countries indicate that substantial labor-market adjustments might result from liberalization in a number of sectors. The sectoral rankings of the percentage changes in value added that would occur with the elimination of tariffs and NTBs broadly parallel the employment results.

We have assumed in this scenario that the developing countries do not change their tariffs, which is an option that has been available to them in previous GATT negotiations. The same is true for developing-country NTBs. This option of not liberalizing may be less applicable in the Uruguay Round, however, as the major developing countries have come under increasing pressure to assume full obligations under the GATT and to reduce their trade barriers. If tariff elimination by the developing countries were to be undertaken at the same time that the industrialized countries

Table 6-7A. Summary of Effects on the Major Industrialized Countries
Due to Elimination of Tariff and Nontariff Barriers in all Industries in all Industrialized Countries

	Value of Change In Exports		Value of Change In Imports		Gross Change In Employment[a]		% Change in Terms of Trade	% Change in Eff. Ex. Rate[b]	% Change in Prices[c]
	$ Mill.	%	$ Mill.	%	000 Wkr	%			
Australia	1293.2	9.0	1498.3	12.7	59.4	1.02	1.32	-0.5	-0.8
Austria	849.7	9.3	813.7	7.1	50.7	1.72	-0.19	-0.0	-2.1
Canada	1328.1	3.3	1506.3	3.9	60.9	0.64	0.43	0.4	-0.6
European Community									
Belgium-Luxembourg	1677.8	4.8	1574.9	4.5	100.0	2.59	-0.29	2.2	-4.1
Denmark	463.5	4.8	529.7	4.3	38.5	1.60	0.96	1.7	-2.5
France	4158.8	7.0	4061.4	6.3	197.9	0.95	-0.08	-1.0	-1.2
Germany	4485.0	4.1	3726.8	4.2	266.9	1.09	-0.95	-0.6	-1.4
Ireland	125.8	3.4	153.2	3.7	14.9	1.46	0.89	2.2	-2.1
Italy	2602.7	6.6	2324.6	5.4	203.9	1.08	-0.59	-1.3	-1.2
Netherlands	2294.8	5.3	2483.1	6.3	86.6	1.91	0.32	2.2	-3.1
United Kingdom	3160.2	6.4	2697.9	4.8	155.4	0.64	-0.76	-1.6	-0.7
Total EC	18968.5	5.5	17551.6	5.1	1064.1	1.06	-0.48	-0.6	-1.5
Finland	399.6	5.9	359.0	4.9	19.3	0.90	-0.52	-0.3	-1.2
Japan	4898.6	6.8	3957.0	6.1	343.5	0.65	-1.46	-1.3	-0.8
New Zealand	269.8	9.2	300.0	9.2	21.6	1.79	1.11	0.1	-1.1
Norway	427.1	5.0	434.0	3.9	15.7	0.88	0.23	-0.3	-1.1
Sweden	576.0	2.9	463.4	2.4	33.6	0.82	-0.59	-0.5	-0.7
Switzerland	810.3	5.1	762.8	5.2	35.0	1.24	-0.38	-0.4	-1.7
United States	3562.4	3.0	4195.0	3.3	241.3	0.28	0.60	-1.3	-0.1
Total Industrialized	33383.2	5.1	31841.2	4.9	1945.1	0.72	-0.08	-0.9	-0.8

a. Refers to sum of changes in the home and export sectors within industries.
b. Positive = appreciation.
c. Index of import and home prices.

Table 6-7B. Summary of Effects on the Major Developing Countries
Due to Elimination of Tariff and Nontariff Barriers in all Industries in all Industrialized Countries

	Value of Change In Exports		Value of Change In Imports		Gross Change In Employment[a]		% Change in Terms of Trade	% Change in Eff. Ex. Rate[b]	% Change in Prices[c]
	$ Mill.	%	$ Mill.	%	000 Wkr	%			
Argentina	-70.5	-1.7	88.1	2.9	111.2	1.07	3.63	3.1	-1.0
Brazil	-130.8	-1.2	148.5	1.1	126.7	0.31	2.85	1.8	-0.3
Chile	-8.9	-0.4	-11.1	-0.9	13.9	0.50	-0.68	-0.1	-0.1
Colombia	-17.5	-0.9	77.4	4.5	42.0	0.53	4.92	5.0	-0.8
Greece	27.5	0.9	66.2	1.1	29.9	0.75	1.75	1.8	-0.5
Hong Kong	319.3	4.4	194.4	2.2	163.1	12.31	-1.34	15.8	-8.3
India	8.2	0.1	1.7	0.0	514.4	0.23	-0.27	2.6	-0.3
Israel	15.8	0.6	5.2	0.1	9.3	0.83	0.39	1.4	-0.4
South Korea	102.2	1.2	103.3	1.2	127.5	1.02	0.05	3.0	-0.8
Mexico	-26.9	-0.5	55.9	0.9	106.7	0.62	1.68	1.8	-0.5
Portugal	36.2	1.9	-13.8	-0.3	45.8	1.48	-0.61	1.9	-0.8
Singapore	-4.8	-0.1	-32.4	-0.4	14.6	1.67	-0.08	-0.1	-0.6
Spain	8.5	0.1	-48.2	-0.3	55.9	0.45	0.50	0.8	-0.2
Taiwan	103.0	1.2	100.0	1.3	80.4	1.42	-0.19	2.7	-0.9
Turkey	40.0	1.9	90.8	1.8	54.4	0.37	3.07	2.0	-0.5
Yugoslavia	47.6	0.9	43.3	0.6	29.6	0.61	0.24	1.1	-0.3
Total LDCs	448.8	0.5	869.4	0.8	1525.3	0.42	1.46	2.1	-0.6
All Countries	33832.0	4.6	32710.6	4.3	3470.3	0.55	0.14	-0.5	-0.7

a. Refers to sum of changes in the home and export sectors within industries.
b. Positive = appreciation.
c. Index of import and home prices.

removed their tariffs and NTBs, we would witness a considerable expansion of trade overall, which would be reinforced presumably if developing-country NTBs were also eliminated. The precise impacts across sectors would depend on differences in the levels of existing barriers and on the response of exchange rates to the assumed liberalization. Our results for the various scenarios involving the removal of tariffs and NTBs suggest the possibility of considerable dislocations in labor markets in many countries, and that it might be desirable accordingly to phase in the liberalization over an extended period to mitigate any adjustment costs that might occur.

III. COMPARISONS OF ALTERNATIVE LIBERALIZATION SCENARIOS

To provide an overall perspective on the results, we have prepared a series of tables reporting the results of all five scenarios side by side. These include tables for each country listing the net percentage changes in employment by sector, and tables for each sector listing the net percentage changes in employment by country. The reason for focusing on the net percentage changes in employment is that they provide some indication of the intersectoral labor-market adjustment problems that might be experienced due to trade liberalization. Only the results for the U.S. are reported here.

The results indicate that the United States would experience a net percentage increase in agricultural employment in every scenario presented in Table 6-8. There are positive and negative signs for the other sectors across all the scenarios.

The results in scenario 5 are of interest insofar as they may help in identifying the positive and negative employment effects for the United States that might be associated with the removal of existing tariffs and NTBs by the industrialized countries only. The sectors that would experience net increases in employment include agriculture, leather products, paper products, chemicals, petroleum products, machinery, and mining and quarrying. There would be net reductions in employment in clothing, footwear, printing and publishing, rubber products, nonmetallic mineral products, glass products, iron and steel, metal products, transport equipment, and miscellaneous manufactures.

Comparable results exist for the other countries included in the Michigan Model, but space constraints do not permit us to discuss them. There are differences in employment experiences in these

Table 6-8. Net Percentage Changes in Employment in the United States Due to Each of Five Scenarios for Elimination of Tariffs and/or NTBs

	ISIC CODE	DC Tariffs	DC NTBs excl. Agric. & Text.	DC NTBs Agric. Only, Tar. Eq.	DC NTBs Text. Only	DC Tar. + NTBs all Sect., Ag T-Eq
Traded Goods:						
Agr., for. & fish.	1	1.51	0.54	3.63	0.10	4.71
Food, bev. & tob.	310	0.06	0.23	-1.05	0.01	-0.52
Textiles	321	-0.64	0.54	-1.15	-0.45	-1.20
Wearing apparel	322	-1.32	0.11	-0.23	-0.80	-0.90
Leather products	323	-1.25	2.22	-1.84	0.85	0.56
Footwear	324	-0.78	-1.34	-0.13	0.05	-3.20
Wood products	331	0.10	0.22	-0.54	0.04	-0.16
Furniture & fixt.	332	0.02	0.03	-0.15	0.03	-0.03
Paper & paper prod.	341	0.41	0.24	-0.40	0.01	0.21
Printing & publ.	342	0.00	-0.29	-0.10	0.01	-0.36
Chemicals	35A	0.46	0.54	-0.37	0.00	0.70
Petrol. & rel. prod.	35B	0.50	1.44	-0.03	0.07	2.04
Rubber products	355	-0.59	0.24	-0.42	0.04	-0.77
Nonmetal min. prod.	36A	-0.65	0.13	-0.20	0.02	-0.66
Glass & glass prod.	362	-0.10	0.20	-0.44	0.01	-0.33
Iron & steel	371	-0.15	-1.20	-0.40	0.03	-1.77
Nonferrous metals	372	-0.24	0.46	-0.37	0.05	-0.18
Metal products	381	0.15	-0.04	-0.25	0.03	-0.14
Nonelec. machinery	382	0.34	-0.00	-0.35	0.03	0.09
Elec. machinery	383	0.57	0.39	-0.26	0.04	0.76
Transport equip.	384	0.48	-0.71	-0.19	0.02	-0.94
Misc. manufact.	38A	-0.71	0.47	-0.55	0.15	-0.56
Total Traded		0.22	0.14	0.17	-0.02	0.42
Nontraded Goods:						
Mining & quarrying	2	0.30	0.92	-0.18	0.06	1.14
Elec., gas & water	4	-0.12	-0.12	-0.17	0.01	-0.35
Construction	5	0.00	-0.04	-0.01	0.01	-0.02
Wh. & ret. trade	6	-0.09	-0.06	-0.09	0.01	-0.20
Transp., stor. & comm.	7	-0.04	-0.03	-0.11	0.01	-0.15
Fin., ins., & real est.	8	-0.10	-0.06	-0.07	0.01	-0.17
Comm., soc. & pers. serv.	9	-0.08	-0.06	-0.02	0.01	-0.13
Total Nontraded		-0.07	-0.05	-0.05	0.01	-0.14
Total All Industries		0.00	0.00	0.00	0.00	0.00

other countries as well, depending on the scope of liberalization that is considered.

IV. SUGGESTIONS FOR FURTHER RESEARCH

The scenarios we have analyzed using the Michigan Model by no means exhaust the universe of multilateral trade liberalization options. There is certainly a great deal more that could be done. While the Model has of necessity to rely on certain simplifying assumptions and is not well suited to analyze bilateral and preferential policies, it nonetheless can provide insight into the sectors in individual countries that will expand or contract in response to different liberalization measures that might be considered in the Uruguay Round negotiations. Among our most striking findings were the size and ramifications of changes in employment in agriculture in the United States and other countries, the role that the exchange rate can play in a general equilibrium modeling context, and the possible tradeoffs between different scenarios. These are certainly issues that deserve further study.

Perhaps the biggest problem that exists is the availability of data. In particular, there is a need for more accurate and current information, especially on NTBs for both the industrialized and developing countries. The NTB estimates we have used are subject to an undetermined margin of error because the studies from which the estimates have been obtained vary considerably in terms of their methodology, level of aggregation of trade coverage, and time period. While we are currently working to improve these estimates, progress is slow because many existing NTBs do not lend themselves readily to precise measurement. Further, there is a need for information on the numerous domestic taxes and subsidies that may affect trade. Accordingly, the results we present here should be considered highly tentative pending more comprehensive data. Finally, it would be useful to assess the costs of adjustment for labor and capital as the result of liberalization and to determine what the optimal timing of the liberalization might be.

APPENDIX: SIMPLIFIED DESCRIPTION OF THE MICHIGAN MODEL

Since the theoretical structure and equations of the Michigan Model are described in detail in Deardorff and Stern (1986b), we present here accordingly an overview of the model and call attention to its most important features.

STRUCTURE OF THE MICHIGAN MODEL

The Model is best thought of as composed of two parts: the country system and the world system. The country system contains separate blocks of equations for each country. The world system contains a single set of equations for the world as a whole. The country blocks are used first to determine each country's supplies and demands for goods and currencies on world markets, as functions of exogenous variables, such as tariffs, and of world prices and exchange rates. These functions for each country are then combined to provide the input to the world system, which permits world prices and exchange rates to be determined. These variables are finally entered back into the separate country blocks to obtain values for other country-specific variables.

It is important to note that the aggregate behavior of the Model depends crucially on what is assumed about aggregate expenditure. Since our objective is to concentrate on microeconomic and intersectoral issues, we wanted a neutral characterization of macroeconomic policy such that aggregates would remain largely unaffected when allowing for some policy change. At various times, we have either treated aggregate nominal expenditure as essentially exogenous, or, alternatively, we have let aggregate expenditure vary endogenously so as to maintain aggregate employment unchanged.[2] It is this latter assumption that underlies all of the experiments that are described below.

In designing the Michigan Model, the objective was to take into account as many as possible of the interconnections among industries and countries at the microeconomic level. This enables us to examine a variety of economic issues that most other existing models cannot address, either because they are too highly

2. In both cases, while we do not require equilibrium in individual labor markets, we also do not attempt to model disequilibrium explicitly in terms of which side of the market is rationed and how that rationing may give rise to changes in "effective" supply and demand in other markets.

aggregated, or because they are specified only in partial-equilibrium terms. By the same token, however, the Michigan Model is far too large to be able to say anything concrete without further specification of its parameters. Thus, to implement the Model, we need a realistic selection of countries and industries using, as far as possible, actual data to generate the parameters.

DATA AND PARAMETERS

The version of the Model used in this paper includes twenty-two tradeable and seven nontradeable industries in thirty-four countries, plus an aggregate sector representing the rest of the world. We have been using a base of 1976 data on trade, production, and employment for all thirty-four countries, plus tariffs and constructed measures of NTBs for the eighteen major industrialized countries.[3] The countries in the Model are listed in Tables 6A-1A and B, together with their assumed exchange regimes, input-output coverage, the average post-Tokyo Round (1987) tariff levels, and the average percentage of trade covered by NTBs. The industries are listed in Tables 6A-2A and B, with the assumed elasticities of capital-labor substitution, import-home good substitution, and U.S. import demand, as well as the post-Tokyo Round average tariff levels and trade coverage of NTBs.

Trade, Production, and Employment

The import and export data are adapted from United Nations trade tapes, with concordances that relate the Standard International Trade Classification (SITC) to our International Standard Industrial Classification (ISIC) industry categories. Information on the gross value of production and employment by ISIC sector is directly calculated or estimated from United Nations, *Yearbook of Industrial Statistics*, from Organization for Economic Cooperation and Development (OECD) publications on national accounts and labor statistics, and from various national statistical sources.

3. We are currently updating the database to 1980 and making a number of improvements in the input-output coverage for individual countries.

Tariffs

Ad valorem tariff data for the major industrialized countries are from the Office of the U.S. Trade Representative (USTR), based on information compiled in machine-readable form by the Secretariat of the GATT. The post-Tokyo Round ad valorem tariff rates are available on a line-item basis according to the detailed Brussels Tariff Nomenclature (BTN), together with import data. The BTN classification has been concorded to SITC, and own-country imports are used in calculating the tariff rates. We then concord from SITC to ISIC and aggregate to our ISIC categories used in the Model. The resulting tariff rates are thus own-country, import-weighted averages by ISIC sector.

Tariff data for the major developing countries are not readily available in systematic and comprehensive form. We have therefore made an effort to compile such data from a variety of sources and to estimate the rates for particular sectors and countries when the information was incomplete.

Nontariff Barriers

NTBs in the Model are represented in two forms: as coverage indexes and as tariff equivalents. The coverage indexes serve to reflect the role of existing NTBs when other barriers are removed. The tariff equivalents, on the other hand, permit analysis of the removal of the NTBs themselves.

The coverage indexes are meant to measure the extent to which imports are subject to nontariff restrictions (for example, quotas and health regulations). A value of 100 percent indicates that all trade in a given sector/country is covered by NTBs; zero denotes that no NTBs are present. The calculations are based on data in Murray and Walter (1978), who recorded the value of 1973 imports for a given country and SITC commodity category that was subject to some type of NTB, as identified in underlying documents prepared by the U.S. Department of State and UNCTAD. We in turn aggregated their results and concorded them with our ISIC classification. The indexes were updated to take into account more recent restrictions on such products as footwear, iron and steel, and television receivers. The indexes for textiles (ISIC 321) and wearing apparel (ISIC 322) are based on the proportion of each country's imports in these sectors from all of the world's nonindustrialized countries. The resulting indexes, which are summarized in the last columns

Table 6A-1A. Industrialized Countries of the Model, their Assumed Exchange Regimes, and the Source and Levels of Input-Output, Tariff, and NTB Data for Each

Country Name	Country Abbrev.	Flexible (F), Pegged (P), or Licensed (L), and Country Pegged To:				Input-Output Table		Post-Tokyo Round Average Tariff Level (%)	Assumed Average Coverage by NTBs (%)
		F	P	L	Pegged to:				
Australia	ALA		x		Basket	USA	1972	14.8	12.2
Austria	ATA	x				USA	1972	11.3	6.7
Canada	CND	x				CAN	1976	4.6	11.7
European Community									
Belgium-Luxembourg	BLX	x				BEL	1970	5.4	4.8
Denmark	DEN	x				DEN	1970	6.4	3.0
France	FR	x				FR	1970	4.9	30.1
Germany	GFR	x				GFR	1970	5.7	17.1
Ireland	IRE	x				IRE	1969	6.6	5.7
Italy	IT	x				IT	1970	4.4	13.3
Netherlands	NL	x				NL	1970	5.7	6.0
United Kingdom	UK	x				UK	1970	4.9	5.3
Finland	FIN		x		Basket	USA	1972	6.2	4.0
Japan	JPN	x				JPN	1975	6.2	56.9
New Zealand	NZ			x	Basket	USA	1972	13.8	13.6
Norway	NOR		x		Basket	USA	1972	4.5	7.4
Sweden	SWD		x		Basket	USA	1972	3.9	3.8
Switzerland	SWZ		x		GFR	USA	1972	3.5	13.2
United States	US	x				USA	1972	3.3	22.3

Table 6A-1B. Developing Countries of the Model, their Assumed Exchange Regimes, and the Source and Levels of Input-Output, Tariff, and NTB Data for Each

Country Name	Country Abbrev.	Flexible (F), Pegged (P), or Licensed (L), and Country Pegged To: F	P	L	Pegged to:	Input-Output Table		Post-Tokyo Round Average Tariff Level (%)	Assumed Average Coverage by NTBs (%)
Argentina	ARG			x	Basket	BRZ	1970	-	-
Brazil	BRZ			x	Basket	BRZ	1970	-	-
Chile	CHL			x	Basket	BRZ	1970	-	-
Colombia	COL			x	Basket	BRZ	1970	-	-
Greece	GRC			x	Basket	BRZ	1970	-	-
Hong Kong	HK	x				BRZ	1970	-	-
India	IND			x	Basket	BRZ	1970	-	-
Israel	ISR	x				ISR	1977	-	-
South Korea	SK			x	Basket	BRZ	1970	-	-
Mexico	MEX	x				BRZ	1970	-	-
Portugal	POR			x	Basket	BRZ	1970	-	-
Singapore	SNG		x		Basket	BRZ	1970	-	-
Spain	SP			x	Basket	BZR	1970	-	-
Taiwan	TWN			x	Basket	BRZ	1970	-	-
Turkey	TRK			x	Basket	BRZ	1970	-	-
Yugoslavia	YUG	x				BRZ	1970	-	-

Table 6A-2A. Industries of the Model, their Assumed Elasticities of Substitution and Demand, and Tariff and NTB Data for Each

(Traded Goods)

Industry Name	ISIC Code	Elasticity of Capital-Labor Substitution	Elasticity of Import-Home-Good Substitution	U.S. Import Demand Elasticity	Post-Tokyo Round Average Tariff Level (%)	Assumed Average Coverage by NTBs (%)
Agr., for. & fish.	1	0.787	1.139	1.130	6.9	18.4
Food, bev. & tob.	310	1.746	1.133	1.130	11.0	23.4
Textiles	321	0.963	1.147	1.140	8.5	29.1
Wearing apparel	322	1.191	4.269	3.920	17.5	46.5
Leather products	323	1.230	1.810	1.580	3.0	1.1
Footwear	324	1.436	2.825	2.390	12.0	37.1
Wood products	331	0.852	1.757	1.690	1.9	0.0
Furniture & fixt.	332	1.122	3.096	3.000	6.9	0.0
Paper & paper prod.	341	1.626	1.585	1.550	4.3	0.6
Printing & publ.	342	0.810	3.013	3.000	1.5	10.4
Chemicals	35A	1.098	2.612	2.530	6.4	4.1
Petrol. & rel. prod.	35B	10.011	2.359	1.960	1.4	47.8
Rubber products	355	1.647	5.707	5.260	4.1	3.1
Nonmetal min. prod.	36A	1.246	2.784	2.700	4.0	8.4
Glass & glass prod.	362	1.267	1.628	1.600	8.0	0.0
Iron & steel	371	1.382	1.446	1.420	4.3	8.2
Nonferrous metals	372	1.350	1.430	1.380	1.7	6.9
Metal products	381	0.943	3.674	3.590	6.2	2.5
Nonelec. machinery	382	0.677	1.022	1.020	4.7	1.9
Elec. machinery	383	0.521	2.110	2.000	7.1	7.1
Transport equip.	384	0.344	3.585	3.280	5.9	10.4
Misc. manufact.	38A	1.272	1.984	1.780	4.8	2.7

Table 6A-2B. Industries of the Model, their Assumed Elasticities of Substitution and Demand, and Tariff and NTB Data for Each

(Nontraded Goods)

Industry Name	ISIC Code	Elasticity of Capital-Labor Substitution	Elasticity of Import-Home-Good Substitution	U.S. Import Demand Elasticity	Post-Tokyo Round Average Tariff Level (%)	Assumed Average Coverage by NTBs (%)
Mining & quarrying	2	1.541	-	-	-	-
Elec., gas,& water	4	2.266	-	-	-	-
Construction	5	1.105	-	-	-	-
Wh. & ret. trade	6	2.266	-	-	-	-
Transp., stor. & comm.	7	1.457	-	-	-	-
Fin., ins. & real est.	8	1.657	-	-	-	-
Comm., soc. & pers. serv.	9	1.087	-	-	-	-

of Tables 6A-1A and B and 6A-2A and B, thus represent the percentage of trade subject to NTBs of all kinds as of the late 1970s.[4] These indexes are used in the basic version of the Model to generate endogenous implicit tariff variables that serve to limit the responsiveness of trade to liberalization measures on the assumption that the NTBs remain in place.

The representation of NTBs in terms of the fractions of trade coverage does not enable us to capture the economic effects that would be experienced if the NTBs themselves were reduced or removed. It is necessary for this purpose to have direct estimates of the price or quantity effects associated with particular NTBs by sector. While such estimates are very difficult to obtain for a variety of reasons discussed at length in Deardorff and Stern (1985), we have nevertheless made an effort to construct ad valorem tariff equivalents of existing NTBs by sector for the major industrialized countries and for a subset of the developing countries included in the Model.

The procedures that we followed in constructing these estimates and the sources utilized are given in Deardorff and Stern (1987, Appendix B). Briefly, we reviewed the relevant sources and extracted from them the NTB ad valorem equivalents that had been calculated.[5] However, there are problems in using these ad valorem equivalents directly inasmuch as the sources varied widely with respect to methodology, year, and the level of aggregation of the trade coverage. For this reason, we decided to construct "high" and "low" estimates of the ad valorem equivalents. The high estimates were based on the assumptions that the available ad valorem equivalents reflected restrictions that were applicable to the entire sector and implemented on a global basis. Since it appeared to us, however, that many of the NTBs did not apply to an entire sector, and that they were often bilateral rather than global in character, we adjusted the "high" ad valorem equivalents by multiplying them by NTB percentage trade coverage indexes of the type mentioned above. For this purpose, we used the detailed sectoral indexes that we had already calculated for use in the Model together with more recent indexes calculated from Nogués, Olechowski, and Winters (1985) to estimate the ad valorem equivalents used in scenarios 2-5.

4. We are currently updating the NTB coverage indexes using more recent information compiled by the UNCTAD Secretariat and made available by the World Bank.

5. Our information on NTBs is not exhaustive. For example, antidumping and countervailing duties and procedures, which may be used to inhibit trade, are not included.

As already noted, we have data on trade, production, and employment for the major developing countries covered in the Model, and we also have constructed preliminary estimates of their nominal tariffs by sector. We have made some limited progress in compiling estimates of the ad valorem equivalents of NTBs for a subset of the developing countries in the Model. But given the tentative nature and incomplete coverage of these NTB estimates, we do not report them here. Thus, in what follows we do not attempt to analyze directly the effects of removing NTBs for the developing countries as a group.

Exchange Rates

In the basic version of the Michigan Model, the exchange regimes of most developing countries are characterized in terms of a system of import licensing with exchange-rate pegging, as reported in Tables 6A-1A and B. The purpose was to capture elements of the existing NTBs in these countries. To analyze the potential effects of liberalization in what follows, however, we assume that all of the industrialized and developing countries in the Model operate under a regime of flexible exchange rates. This assumption can be justified simply on the grounds that trade liberalization is not meaningful under conditions of import licensing.

Input-Output Tables

Our input-output coverage currently includes the 1972 input-output table for the United States, the 1976 table for Canada, the 1975 table for Japan, and the 1970 national tables for each of the industrialized EEC-member countries. The U.S. table is applied to the remaining industrialized countries. We use the 1977 table for Israel and the 1970 table for Brazil. The Brazilian table is applied to the remaining developing countries. Each of the national tables used is of necessity concorded to our ISIC classification.

Coefficients and Elasticities

In general, the coefficients of explanatory variables that appear in the Model are calculated from our data on production, trade, and employment by sector in each country, from the input-output matrices, and from relevant published estimates of demand and substitution elasticities. The import-demand elasticities used in the Model are based on the "best guesstimates" of U.S. import-demand elasticities calculated by Stern, Francis, and Schumacher (1976).[6] Using the import-demand elasticities together with data on trade, we calculate the implied elasticities of substitution in demand between imports and home-produced goods in each country. These elasticities of substitution for the United States are listed in Tables 6A-2A and B, together with the U.S. import-demand elasticities from which they were calculated. The implicit import-demand elasticities in other countries are derivable from the common elasticities of substitution and differ across countries due to their differences in shares of trade. We use elasticities of substitution between capital and labor in each sector, based on Zarembka and Chernicoff (1971). These were estimated from U.S. data, but were assumed in our Model to apply for all countries.[7]

SOLUTION PROCEDURE

Given appropriate data and parameter estimates for the countries and sectors noted, solution of the Model is, in principle, straightforward. By differentiating the equations of the Model, we obtain a system of linear equations relating changes in all of the variables of the system. The coefficients in each of these linear equations are evaluated using the data and elasticity information collected. All that remains is to solve the system. Because the system is linear, it can in principle be solved by any of a variety of means.

In our solution procedure, we have devised several Fortran subroutines that process large, partitioned matrices in which many of the partitioned blocks contain only zeros, and which avoid costly but meaningless computations involving these zeros. We use a Fortran programming technique known as dynamic dimensioning to avoid wasting computer-memory space on these empty blocks, even as the contents of all blocks change during the course of the solution. We apply these techniques first to each of the thirty-four countries separately to solve for their net exports in terms of world

6. These are currently being updated using more recent information.

7. Use of these elasticities is subject to the limitation that they are valid, at most, only for the range of prices for which they were estimated. This should not be a problem for the results reported here, however, for which individual prices changed in most cases on average by only a few percent.

prices, exchange rates, and exogenous variables. We then use the world system equations to complete the solution.

REPORTING OF RESULTS

The Model solution yields percentage changes in all of the endogenous variables. While these could be reported directly, we commonly refrain from doing so because of the detail involved. More typically, we multiply the percentage changes by the data values to express the results in terms of absolute values. We also calculate percentage changes relative to the base year data, which, as mentioned, refer to 1976.

There is a problem in using realistic data for any given year, because the data will reflect the economic conditions for that year, including the effects of policies of all kinds. We make allowance conceptually in the Model for a variety of domestic and external policies, but our primary data relate mainly to trade barriers. We have done some analysis of the effects of domestic taxes and subsidies using the Model, but we have been hampered by lack of information. Thus, in interpreting the results of the experiments that follow, with the exception of our experiment involving the removal of subsidies in agriculture in the industrialized countries, the role and importance of domestic taxes and subsidies are not taken into account.

COMPARISON WITH OTHER MODELS

In addition to the Michigan Model, there are several other empirical trade models in existence. These various models, which are reviewed in Shoven and Whalley (1984), differ greatly in terms of their industry, country coverage, the extent to which they incorporate general-equilibrium interactions, and the closeness with which they adhere to the theoretical paradigm of smoothly functioning, perfectly competitive markets. In many of these respects, the assumptions of the Michigan Model lie somewhere in the middle of the range of assumptions made by other models. The Michigan Model is, for example, neither the most nor the least disaggregated, nor the most nor the least "pure" in its assumptions of competition. If the Michigan Model is unusual in any dimension, it is in the large number of countries that it covers and in its efforts to incorporate aspects of trade policy such as NTBs.

In recent years, empirical trade models have evolved in two main directions. On the one hand, Whalley (1984) and a number of others have continued the development of full Walrasian general-equilibrium models, which are characterized computationally by their use of an algorithm to solve first for a benchmark equilibrium of the system and then for a new equilibrium in the presence of the disturbance being analyzed.

On the other hand, there are models that have taken the same approach as the Michigan Model—that is, the equations of the model are first differentiated and then only the resulting linear system is solved computationally. This second approach is actually older, having been pioneered by Johansen (1960), and while it could easily be used to analyze a complete Walrasian system, it has more typically been applied to models in which some elements of disequilibrium are assumed. Though less accurate than the benchmark-equilibrium approach that has been used for Walrasian models, the Johansen approach has the advantage of permitting greater computational detail. As a result, the Michigan Model and others like it tend to include a greater variety of policy parameters and other sometimes ad hoc institutional details than can be encompassed in models where a full equilibrium solution is to be obtained.

Another source of difference among models is the timeframe that they attempt to represent. Because the models are typically static, their time dimension cannot be explicit, but it is nonetheless implicit in the assumptions that are made about what is and is not variable. In full equilibrium models such as Whalley's, for example, it is assumed that both capital and labor are variable, and thus these models implicitly are directed at the fairly long run. In the Michigan Model, in contrast, capital is assumed to be fixed and labor is the only variable factor of production. Together with other of our assumptions, such as the fixity of money wages, this means that the Michigan Model is directed more at the short run.

One final direction in modeling activity should also be mentioned. The Michigan Model, despite its allowance for disequilibrium in labor markets, holds otherwise to the assumption of perfect competition in all markets. There has been growing interest in recent years among trade theorists in recasting trade theory to allow for imperfect competition. So far, this interest has carried over to empirical trade models in one notable instance—Harris and Cox (1984). Harris allows both economies of scale and forms of nonprice-taking behavior on the part of firms in models that otherwise follow the full equilibrium approach of Whalley.

While Harris' work is valuable in its effort to incorporate the reality of imperfect competition, there is as yet no consensus that his particular assumptions represent the best road one can take in this direction.

Compared to other models, the Michigan Model perhaps may appear to be less pure theoretically, less sophisticated in its computational procedures, and less comprehensive in terms of efforts to incorporate undoubtedly important but still controversial representations of imperfect competition. Granting all of this, it should be stressed that the Michigan Model has been designed primarily as a practical tool of analysis for trade policy. With that in mind, the Michigan Model is to be viewed as encompassing many important features of trade policy not included in other trade models, as well as a variety of general-equilibrium interactions among markets that are especially pertinent in the short run.

REFERENCES

Deardorff, Alan V., and Robert M. Stern. 1985. *Methods of Measurement of Nontariff Barriers.* United Nations Conference on Trade and Development, UNCTAD/ST/MD/28, Geneva.

——. 1986a. "Neighborhood Effects of Developing Country Protection." *Journal of Development Economics* 21.

——. 1986b. *The Michigan Model of World Production and Trade: Theory and Applications.* Cambridge: MIT Press.

——. 1987. "A Computational Analysis of Alternative Scenarios for Multilateral Trade Liberalization." In process.

Harris, Richard G., and David Cox. 1984. *Trade, Industrial Policy, and Canadian Manufacturing.* Toronto: Ontario Economic Council.

Johansen, Leif. 1960. *A Multi-Sectoral Study of Economic Growth.* Amsterdam: North-Holland.

Murray, Tracy, and Ingo Walter. 1978. "Special and Differential Liberalization of Quantitative Restrictions on Imports from Developing Countries." *Trade Policies Toward Developing Countries: The Multilateral Trade Negotiations.* Ed. L. Perez. Washington, DC: Agency for International Development.

Nogués, Julio J., Andrzej Olechowski, and L. Alan Winters. 1985. "The Extent of Non-Tariff Barriers to Industrial Countries' Imports." World Bank Development Research Department, Report No. DRD115 (January): 43.

OECD. 1987. *National Policies and Agricultural Trade,* II-1 - II-25. Paris.

Shoven, John B., and John Whalley. 1984. "Applied General Equilibrium Models of Taxation and International Trade: An Introduction and Survey." *Journal of Economic Literature* 22.

Stern, Robert M., Jonathan Francis, and Bruce F. Schumacher. 1976. *Price Elasticities in International Trade.* London: Macmillan.

Whalley, John. 1984. *Trade Liberalization Among Major World Trading Areas.* Cambridge: MIT Press.

Zarembka, Paul, and Helen Chernicoff. 1971. "Further Results on the Empirical Relevance of the CES Production Function." *Review of Economics and Statistics* 53.

III FOREIGN DIRECT INVESTMENT IN THE UNITED STATES

Foreign direct investment has been an important subject in economics for nearly two decades. What is striking about the two papers in this section is that they examine foreign direct investment in the United States, whereas most previous studies have considered the foreign activities of U.S. multinationals. This, of course, reflects the very recent trend toward an increased presence of foreign firms in the United States that was documented in the Introduction.

Rachel McCulloch provides a basic picture of the extent and role of Japanese investment in the United States. She offers a measurement of how Japanese investment in the U.S. has evolved over time, along with explanations for the observed shifts. In particular, McCulloch addresses the issue of whether the United States should encourage or discourage Japanese investors. While these questions have recently received considerable attention in the popular press, there has been a remarkable scarcity of studies providing a systematic analysis.

Richard E. Caves empirically examines the short-run sensitivity of foreign direct investment in the United States to exchange-rate fluctuations. His paper is important because it provides insight into both the way in which multinational corporations behave and the process by which the balance of payments adjust. Caves offers the first empirical evidence suggesting that the existence of multinational enterprises has actually had a stabilizing effect on exchange-rate volatility. Most importantly, he finds that, just as previous authors in this volume have concluded for product markets, the market for corporate control in the United States is evolving from a domestic to a global level. Thus, the internationalization of U.S. markets applies to ownership issues as well as goods and services.

7 JAPANESE INVESTMENT IN THE UNITED STATES

Rachel McCulloch

The necessary counterpart of Japan's record surpluses on current account since 1981 has been the unprecedented outpouring of Japanese capital into world financial markets. In just a few years, Japan has emerged as a creditor on a vast scale, the earnings generated by its assets abroad reinforcing the nation's already persistent tendency toward current-account surplus. Both the volume of Japan's foreign holdings and the nature of the new investments are clear signals of Japan's increased integration into the global economy and of its enlarged influence on economic activity beyond its borders.

Likewise, the necessary counterpart of record U.S. deficits on current account has been a massive inflow of capital from abroad, including the redirection toward the domestic market of lending by U.S. financial institutions. From a net creditor position of $141 billion at the end of 1981, the United States moved into net debtor status less than four years later. As with trade, the nation's global imbalance on capital account has been reflected disproportionately in its bilateral relationship with Japan. Formerly marginal participants in U.S. financial markets, Japanese investors are now

This research was supported by the Ford Foundation.

believed to exercise major influence on day-to-day movements in U.S. asset prices.

Perhaps the most startling capital-market development for the United States is its recent emergence as the world's leading host to inward direct investment. Along with record purchases of U.S. securities, individual and institutional investors across the globe have bought up U.S. farm land, department stores, luxury hotels, and condominiums. Foreign manufacturing firms have expanded their U.S. distribution and service facilities and added to local production capacity. Foreign banks and insurance companies have opened branch offices in New York, Los Angeles, and even Lexington, Kentucky. These direct investments imply an increasing role of foreign firms in shaping economic activity within the United States. Foreign investors with U.S. operations have also become a visible influence in the political sphere, lobbying actively at both the local and the national level.

While Japanese companies are by no means the only source of new inward investments, their role has become significant overall (nearly 12 percent of total foreign assets in the United States at the end of 1986) and large in some specific sectors (automobiles) and regions (Hawaii, California). But, it is less the size than the assumed role of these investments in the intense commercial rivalry between Japan and the United States that accords them special significance in the eyes of the U.S. business community, organized labor, and government.

What accounts for the rapid increase in Japanese investments in the United States? How is the flood of capital from Japan linked to U.S. trade problems? Should the United States welcome Japanese investors, or are there reasons to limit the sale of U.S. assets? This paper reviews forces underlying the recent surge in foreign investment in the United States and assesses some implications for the nation's economy, with particular reference to investments from Japan. Section I analyzes the forces underlying the nation's emergence in the 1980s as a net importer of foreign capital. Section II looks at the importance of Japanese investors relative to total foreign investment in the United States. Section III focuses on the most controversial component of capital inflows from abroad—direct investments allowing foreign firms control over economic activity within U.S. borders. And Section IV offers some concluding comments.

I. HOW THE UNITED STATES BECAME A CAPITAL IMPORTER

Have the nation's recent trade deficits provided potential foreign investors with the means to acquire U.S. assets? Or has the desire of foreign investors to purchase U.S. assets made the trade deficits inevitable? The large net inflow of foreign capital into the United States and the nation's large deficit on current account are simply two measures of the same macroeconomic relationship: the excess of domestic expenditure over production. A deficit on current account must be financed by an equal volume of net foreign borrowing. Economists disagree, however, on the extent to which one of these phenomena can be labeled the "cause" of the other.

Under one interpretation, the successful export drives of Japan and other U.S. trading partners came first, generating large new pools of funds to be invested. This view leaves unexplained why the new funds were "recycled" so differently from the petrodollars of the 1970s. In the case of the petrodollars, U.S. financial institutions became the intermediaries through which the OPEC surpluses found their way to interested borrowers around the world (and mainly outside the United States).

A second interpretation, championed by then-Treasury Secretary Donald Regan, is that changed conditions in capital markets worldwide produced a massive movement of funds into U.S. financial markets, driving up the market-determined value of the dollar. The movement of funds constituted a "transfer" of current purchasing power to the United States. The nation's current-account deficit was required to grow enough to effect the transfer; to produce the required deficit, the dollar needed to reach new heights. In this view, the U.S. current-account deficit was the inevitable result of the great attractiveness of U.S. assets.

But why did dollar assets suddenly become so attractive? A variant on the Regan interpretation is that global capital-market developments were indeed the proximate cause of the movement of funds to the United States, but that those developments were the product of important changes in macroeconomic and regulatory policies in the major countries. In the United States, the greatly increased federal budget deficit was the major factor; by reducing total national saving (public plus private) relative to production, the deficit increased U.S. demand for funds from abroad.

At the same time, for reasons both related and unrelated to U.S. macroeconomic policies, the United States also became a relatively more attractive borrower. Financial and industrial deregulation, enhanced fiscal incentives for capital formation, and a credible commitment to reducing the rate of inflation were positive factors directly linked to post-1980 economic policies in the United States. Actual and anticipated increases in U.S. trade barriers provided incentives for inward direct foreign investments. This was true particularly for Japanese firms; Japanese exports were the overwhelming target of U.S. selective protection. The United States also repealed the withholding tax on earnings from U.S. assets held by foreigners.

Abroad, the Japanese liberalized restrictions on capital outflows. Although this liberalization was part of a longer-term policy trend in Japan, the United States instigated an acceleration of its pace as one element of the dollar-yen accord engineered by Treasury Secretary Regan in 1984. Capital flight and debt crises of the developing nations and "Eurosclerosis" were other factors contributing to the vast flow of funds into U.S. capital markets.

Given these influences on the supply of funds, the sharp increase in U.S. capital inflows reflected both one-time adjustments of international portfolios and ongoing effects on the placement of new additions to those portfolios. Thus, even without a reduction in the U.S. government deficit, the implied rate of capital inflows and the associated value of the dollar would have been expected to fall over time as stock adjustments to new conditions were completed (see McCulloch and Richardson 1986). In practice, however, this effect was offset in part by rising foreign official purchases of U.S. assets as private demand abroad waned. Official holdings of reserves (mainly dollar assets) by Japan, West Germany, and the United Kingdom soared in 1986 and 1987.

Another implication of considering supply as well as demand factors is that compliance by Japan and West Germany in expanding domestic demand would aid the United States in reducing its external imbalance by reducing the supply of new foreign funds to the U.S. capital market. But if the United States does not simultaneously reduce its demand for such funds through curtailed private or public spending, the price is likely to be higher interest rates in the United States.[1] In 1986, net capital inflows amounted to about one-fourth of total U.S. private investment. While the country's foreign borrowing is often painted as a debt-financed consumption binge, a rapid reduction in net inflows from

1. This was the outcome predicted in 1981 when the likely size of future U.S. budget deficits began to be appreciated. However, the unanticipated supply of funds from abroad allowed the United States to expand total domestic absorption.

abroad would probably have its largest impact on capital formation rather than consumer spending.

Foreign Investment and Internationalization

The shift of the United States toward capital-account surplus, that is, net capital inflows, appears to be the result of mainly macroeconomic factors. However, the soaring U.S. trade deficit and capital-account surplus have masked a second development of at least equal importance: the increased integration of the United States into world markets.

This trend—toward internationalization of the U.S. economy—can be measured in a number of ways. The most obvious is that U.S. markets for goods and services are far more open than in the past. Almost every manufacturing industry has experienced a dramatic rise in the ratio of imports to domestic production—perhaps no surprise at a time when the nation is running a trade deficit of record proportions. Less well known is that almost every U.S. manufacturing industry has also experienced a rise, albeit not as dramatic, in its exports. The same is true for agriculture, for the extractive industries, and for many of the service activities that now dominate U.S. employment.

Even more striking than the increased flow of goods across U.S. borders is the growth in the volume and variety of asset transactions with other nations. The increased trade in financial assets reflects several independent developments. The United States and most other industrial nations have greatly reduced legal barriers to both inward and outward financial flows, part of a more general trend toward deregulation of financial markets. The recycling of petrodollar surpluses in the 1970s contributed to the growth of institutions capable of handling huge international capital flows.

Revolutionary changes in global communications have facilitated the integration of national financial markets into a single worldwide network of lenders and borrowers. Together with expanded options for international communication, reduced costs of transporting goods and people have promoted a shift by many firms from national to global management of innovation, production, and distribution.

The much-publicized move of the United States into net-debtor status has tended to overshadow the fact that U.S. assets abroad have continued to grow, though not at the same pace as foreign assets in the United States. The recent changes in the international investment position of the United States should be interpreted as reflecting two separate developments: macroeconomic forces producing a (presumably temporary) excess of domestic spending over production, and technological and regulatory forces producing a (presumably permanent) integration of national asset markets into a single global market. Even when the United States returns to its customary role of net capital exporter, foreign investors are likely to maintain and even increase their role in U.S. asset markets.[2]

An Investment Backlash?

Like the OPEC investments of the 1980s, the recent inflows of capital from abroad have aroused strong passions. In February 1988, United States trade representative Clayton Yeutter privately warned foreign officials that rising foreign investment was creating a backlash in the business community. One example noted by Yeutter was an editorial by Malcolm Forbes, owner of *Forbes* magazine, in which he wrote that "it's one thing for Japanese and Germans and others to buy U.S. Government bonds to finance our huge trade imbalances with them . . . but it's a whole and totally impermissible other thing for them to use their vast billions of dollars to buy great chunks of America's big businesses or to take over the high-tech, medical or other strategic, vital U.S. concerns" (Tolchin 1988). Both Forbes and financier Felix Rohatyn advocated federal restrictions on foreign purchases of U.S. assets.

Less dramatic but nonetheless controversial was an amendment to the House version of the 1988 Omnibus Trade Bill sponsored by Rep. John Bryant of Texas. Under the Bryant amendment, private foreign owners of U.S. assets would have been required to disclose ownership and financial information similar to that now required of all publicly held companies. While the requirements appear mild, they would have imposed stronger reporting requirements on private foreign investors than apply to private U.S. investors, thus putting the latter at a competitive advantage (Altany 1988).[3]

Advocates of the Bryant amendment claimed that the current lack of such disclosure requirements prevents even federal agencies

2. The stock-market meltdown of October 1987 clearly dealt a blow to the progressive internationalization of asset markets, but was only a temporary reversal in the move toward internationally diversified portfolios and integrated markets.

3. The Act as passed did give the president new powers to block investments on national security grounds.

from obtaining complete information on the extent of foreign ownership in the United States. Favorite examples include the extensive U.S. holdings of Ferdinand Marcos and the attempted acquisition of four Silicon Valley banks by the Soviet Union (Tolchin 1987). Opponents, including officials of the Reagan administration and lobbyists for foreign companies, stressed the potential for discouraging foreign investments that are beneficial to the country. But like anticipated trade barriers, anticipated limits on inward investments may actually add to the current flow of foreign funds into the United States.

II. WHO INVESTS IN THE UNITED STATES

Despite the extensive press and television coverage of Japanese automobile and electronics plants, the "typical" foreign investment in the United States is not a direct investment, that is, does not involve foreign control over U.S. production, nor is the typical foreign investor Japanese. While direct foreign investments have risen substantially in recent years, they have only maintained, on average, their share in total capital inflows. At the peak of new direct investment activity in 1981, such investments constituted less than 30 percent of total capital inflows from abroad. In 1985 and 1986, direct investments were only 14 and 12 percent of total foreign investments, respectively (see Table 7-1).[4]

Moreover, even among direct investments, the typical foreign investment in the United States is not Japanese, nor is the typical Japanese investment in manufacturing. While Japanese investments have indeed grown in relative importance, that

4. Statistics used in this paper are mainly those collected by the Bureau of Economic Analysis of the U.S. Department of Commerce. These data are compiled on the basis of individual firm responses to mandatory U.S. reporting requirements. Alternative data on inward direct investments are now collected and published by Commerce's Office of Trade and Investment Analysis. The latter data are compiled in part from public secondary sources, including business press accounts; dollar values in a given year are the projected foreign equity at completion of any investment begun in that year. Because they draw from different sources and use different definitions, the two series are not directly comparable. Both series confirm a major increase in the level of direct investment in the United States, as well as an increase in the relative role of Japan in the total. However, the apparent role of Japanese investors is larger in the second series. The difference may reflect greater press diligence in reporting Japanese investments, as well as greater use of domestic financing by Japanese investors than by their European counterparts. Data on Japanese investments in the United States are also published by the Japanese Ministry of Finance, but these do not allow a comparison of Japanese activity with that of other important source countries.

Table 7-1. Foreign Investment in the United States, 1960-1986[a]
(Billions of U.S. Dollars)

Year	Total Inflow	Total DFI	DFI as % of Total	Japanese DFI	% of DFI from Japan
1960	2.3	0.3	13.7	na	na
1970	6.4	1.5	23.0	0.0	3.6
1972	21.5	0.9	4.4	0.0	2.0
1974	22.5	4.8	21.2	0.2	4.4
1976	42.7	4.3	10.2	0.6	13.5
1978	65.4	7.9	12.1	1.0	12.5
1980	84.7	13.7	16.1	0.7	5.3
1981	78.2	22.0	28.1	2.8	12.6
1982	109.7	10.4	9.5	1.7	16.8
1983	96.9	11.9	12.3	1.7	13.8
1984	108.2	25.4	23.4	4.4	17.2
1985	127.1	17.9	14.0	3.1	17.3
1986	213.3	25.1	12.0	4.1	16.4

a. Percentages are calculated from unrounded flow data. Data for 1986 are preliminary.

Sources: Survey of Current Business, June 1987 and earlier issues (for 1972-1986); *Business Statistics 1984* (1960 and 1970).

growth has been from a negligible base. In part, this reflects the role of Japanese policies limiting capital outflows. Those restrictions have been liberalized gradually, facilitating the rapid expansion of Japanese investments abroad.

By the end of 1986, total Japanese assets in the United States were $156.5 billion, still less than 12 percent of total foreign assets (see Tables 7-2 and 7-3). Of these, direct investments constituted less than one-fifth, while Japanese investors accounted for less than 2 percent of total foreign holdings of U.S. corporate stocks.[5] Even in 1986, Japanese firms still accounted for less than one-fifth of total

5. Writing in September 1987, the Feldsteins (1987) hypothesized that Japanese equity investments may have contributed to the "extraordinary bull market of 1987." However, the size of their stake at the end of 1986 suggests that Japanese investors were not a major factor in either the rise of U.S. equity prices nor in their subsequent collapse.

Table 7-2. Japanese Assets in the United States, 1984-1986[a]
(Billions of U.S. Dollars)

	1984	1985	1986
Total Japanese Assets in U.S. of which:	67.6	102.8	156.5
Direct Investment	16.0	19.3	23.4
Corporate and other non-U.S. Treasury Bonds	2.9	8.6	19.7
Corporate Stocks	1.3	1.9	5.6
U.S. Liabilities to Unaffiliated Japanese Reported by Nonbank Concerns	2.5	4.7	3.0
Total Foreign Assets in U.S.	893.8	1061.3	1331.5

a. Data for 1986 are preliminary.

Source: Survey of Current Business, June 1986 and June 1987.

Table 7-3. Japanese Assets in the United States, 1984-1986[a]
(Percent of Total Foreign Assets in the United States)

	1984	1985	1986
Total Japanese Assets in U.S. of which:	7.6	9.7	11.8
Direct Investment	9.7	10.5	11.2
Corporate and other non-U.S. Treasury Bonds	8.9	10.4	13.9
Corporate Stocks	1.3	1.5	1.8
U.S. Liabilities to Unaffiliated Japanese Reported by Nonbank Concerns	7.9	15.9	11.4

a. Percentages are calculated from unrounded flow data. In each case, Japanese assets in the United States are compared to total foreign assets in the same category. Data for 1986 are preliminary.

Source: Survey of Current Business, June 1986 and June 1987.

new direct investment inflows into the United States; Japan was third, after the United Kingdom and Netherlands, in the size of its U.S. direct investment stake in the United States at the end of 1986 (Table 7-4).[6]

While the American press appears preoccupied with "transplant" Japanese-owned manufacturing operations, the major part of Japanese direct investment has gone into the U.S. service sector rather than into manufacturing. In no year since 1974 has Japanese direct investment in U.S. manufacturing enterprises constituted even one-fifth of total Japanese direct investment in the United States nor of total foreign direct investment in U.S. manufacturing (Table 7-5). However, by 1987, the United States was by far the largest host country for Japanese direct investment (Table 7-6), accounting for about one-third of Japan's global position.

The category of wholesale trade alone accounts for about two-thirds of total Japanese direct investment in the United States (Tables 7-4 and 7-5). Wholesale trade investments include the distribution networks that facilitate sale in the United States of goods produced in Japan. Such investments, much larger for Japan than for other major direct investors, are linked directly to the spectacular rise in U.S. imports from Japan. They may also facilitate a future surge of exports from U.S. manufacturing subsidiaries of Japanese companies.

A second area of Japanese activity in the service sector, banking, has received much more attention in the U.S. press than wholesale trade. As Table 7-7 indicates, Japanese banks have indeed increased their U.S. presence in recent years. However, they have not been alone in doing so. Measured in terms of the number of foreign-owned U.S. agencies, branches, and subsidiaries, Japan's share actually fell from 28 percent in November 1972 to 15 percent in June 1987, even though the number of such investments by Japan had risen from 28 to 98 over that period.

III. DIRECT INVESTMENT IN THE UNITED STATES

Although the recent cries of alarm suggest otherwise, U.S. net borrowing abroad is itself nothing new. The United States was a

6. The data in Table 7-5 show that the British stake at the end of 1986 was more than twice that of the Japanese. Moreover, these data are based on historical costs and thus tend to understate the real value of British holdings in the United States. Other major source countries for U.S. direct investments have been Germany and Canada.

Table 7-4. Foreign Direct Investment Position in the United States, 1986
By Industry and Country[a]
(Billions of U.S. Dollars)

	Total	U.K.	Netherlands	Japan
All Industries	209.3	51.4	42.9	23.4
Mining	4.7	0.3	0.3	na
Petroleum	29.6	11.6	na	0.0
Manufacturing	68.1	15.0	14.7	3.0
Food & Kindred Products	11.9	2.9	4.9	0.2
Chemicals & Allied Products	23.0	5.4	4.6	0.3
Primary & Fabricated Metals	7.8	0.8	0.4	0.6
Machinery	10.0	1.7	2.0	0.9
Other Manufacturing	15.4	4.1	2.8	1.1
Wholesale Trade	31.9	4.7	2.5	13.0
Retail Trade	9.8	3.3	2.5	0.3
Banking	12.4	2.2	1.7	2.7
Finance, Except Banking	4.9	1.7	1.9	0.5
Insurance	13.6	5.0	2.5	na
Real Estate	21.2	5.0	2.6	1.2
Other Industries	13.2	2.6	na	1.2

a. Details may not add to totals due to rounding.

Source: Survey of Current Business, August 1987, p. 90.

borrower and net debtor for most of the period between the nation's founding and World War I. What is new, however, is the emergence of the United States as the major host country for inward direct foreign investments by multinational corporations based in other countries. From 1961 through 1967, less than 3 percent of the world's flow of new direct investment came to the United States. That fraction rose gradually during the 1970s and peaked in 1981, when the United States attracted nearly one-half of total direct investment inflows worldwide and two-thirds of total inflows going to developed countries (Lipsey 1988). In subsequent years, the absolute size of direct investment flows has continued to rise, although their importance in total capital inflows has dropped.

This influx of direct investments represents a dramatic shift from the established pattern of the earlier postwar period. Until the 1970s, direct foreign investment globally was so dominated by the outward thrusts of U.S. firms that the multinational firms doing the investing were portrayed as a peculiarly American phenomenon. Now direct foreign investment appears to be one more area in which other industrial nations, and particularly Japan, are catching up to the United States. After years of relative stability, the ratio of inward to outward direct investments rose from less than one-quarter in 1977 to more than three-quarters by 1985 (Lipsey 1988) and nearly 90 percent by 1986. But it is worth emphasizing that even in 1986, when net U.S. borrowing in international markets totalled $117 billion, U.S. multinationals continued to invest more abroad than foreign firms were investing in the United States.

The Shoe on the Other Foot

As the foreign presence grows, U.S. policy concerns shift accordingly. Policymakers in the United States once focused primarily on the effects of direct investments abroad by U.S.-based corporations and particularly the implications of such investments for employment at home. The key question was whether U.S. investments abroad were "defensive," that is, necessary to secure markets that would otherwise be lost to foreign rivals. The issue was complicated by the product-cycle character of most U.S. direct investments abroad; the industries and firms with above-average propensities to invest abroad were also those with above-average propensities to export.

Today, the presumed loss of U.S. jobs associated with establishment of foreign subsidiaries remains an important policy concern, but attention has moved to issues raised by inward direct investment—issues that are novel from the U.S. perspective but widely discussed during the postwar period in other major host countries, industrialized and developing. The fundamental concern is the extent to which the investing firm, rather than the host country, derives the lion's share of economic benefits from controlled local production.

The distinguishing feature of direct foreign investment is an ownership stake sufficient to permit a local management role for

Table 7-5. Japanese Direct Investment in U.S. Manufacturing[a]
(Billions of U.S. Dollars)

Year	(1) Japanese DFI in U.S.	(2) Japanese DFI in U.S. Manufacturing	(3) Total DFI in U.S. Manufacturing	(2) as % of (3)	(2) as % of (1)
1974	0.2	0.2	2.2	9.5	101.4
1976	0.6	-0.0	1.2	-1.7	-3.6
1978	1.0	0.1	3.2	4.3	13.7
1980	0.7	0.1	4.3	3.3	19.3
1981	2.8	0.3	4.8	6.8	11.6
1982	1.7	0.3	2.2	15.0	18.6
1983	1.7	0.0	3.5	0.3	0.5
1984	4.4	0.6	4.0	15.1	13.8
1985	3.4	0.3	8.0	3.7	8.7
1986	4.1	0.3	8.8	3.5	7.4

a. Percentages are calculated from unrounded flow data.

Source: Survey of Current Business, August 1987 and earlier issues.

Table 7-6. Japanese Direct Investment by Country, FY1982-FY1986[a]
(Billions of U.S. Dollars)

	FY 1982	FY 1983	FY 1984	FY 1985	FY 1986	Cumulative March 1987
Total worldwide	7.7	8.1	10.2	12.2	22.3	106.0
United States	2.7	2.6	3.4	5.4	10.2	37.4
Canada	0.2	0.1	0.2	0.1	0.3	2.0
Latin America	1.5	1.9	2.3	2.6	4.7	20.4
Asia	1.4	1.8	1.6	1.4	2.3	21.8
Middle East	0.1	0.2	0.3	0.0	0.0	3.0
Europe	0.9	1.0	1.9	1.9	3.5	15.5
Africa	0.5	0.4	0.3	0.2	0.3	3.7
Oceania	0.4	0.2	0.2	0.5	1.0	5.2

a. Data based on reporting by Japanese companies to the Ministry of Finance. Real estate transactions are not included.

Source: Japan Economic Institute Report 5A, "Offshore Production: Boon or Bane for the Japanese Economy?" February 5, 1988.

the investor.[7] Although in dollar terms direct investment inflows from abroad remain small relative to the nation's total foreign borrowings, this measure may understate their potential economic, political, and social impact. By definition, such investments represent the extension of foreign firms' managerial control into the United States economy, just as U.S. direct investments abroad have allowed American firms to control significant parts of the domestic economies of other nations.[8] The new pattern is controversial in the United States for many of the same reasons that the former one has been controversial in host nations abroad, though in relative terms the foreign stake in the United States is still far below that of other host countries. Just as the massive foreign investments of the United States aroused concern and animosity in Europe, Canada, and many developing nations in past decades, the current size and continuing growth of foreign—and especially Japanese—investment flows have become a focus of concern in the United States.

It should be emphasized that the growth in U.S. trade and the growth in direct foreign investment have been linked developments. Transactions between multinational firms and their foreign subsidiaries have accounted for a major share of the overall rise in the volume of U.S. trade.[9] Coordinated by a single global management, trade in intermediate inputs as well as completed goods allows international comparative advantage to operate not only at the level of individual products but also in determining the location of different steps in the production of a single product.

At the end of 1986, about 15 percent of all direct foreign investments in the United States—and nearly two-thirds of all Japanese direct investments—were in the wholesale trade sector (see Table 7-4). The main task of such investments is to promote the

7. Statistically, the line is drawn at 10 percent of equity, although most U.S. direct investments abroad and many foreign direct investments in the United States are wholly-owned subsidiaries of the parent. Other asset purchases, of private or government bonds or smaller blocks of stocks, for example, are termed portfolio investment.

8. The size of the ownership stake does not indicate the total size of the controlled activity. A fall in measured direct investment could, in principle, be accompanied by an increase in the extent of controlled activity. Alternative measures of foreign influence include sales, employment, or profits of the controlled enterprise.

9. In 1983, U.S. multinational corporations accounted for more than three-quarters of U.S. exports and almost one-half of U.S. imports. However, these shares have been declining from their peaks in the 1970s (the comparable percentages for 1977 were 84 and 58), while the U.S. trade role of foreign multinational firms appears to have grown over the same period. See Barker (1986).

Table 7-7. Japanese Banks in the United States
(Number of Agencies, Branches, and Subsidiaries)

	All Foreign Banks	Japanese Banks	Japan's Share (%)
November 1972	101	28	27.8
May 1978	269	59	21.9
December 1979	345	63	18.3
June 1981	384	69	18.0
May 1982	466	71	15.2
June 1983	537	75	14.0
June 1984	562	75	13.3
March 1986	623	84	13.5
June 1987	658	98	14.9

Source: Japan Economic Institute Report 3A, "Japanese Banks in the United States," January 22, 1988.

parent's imports to or exports from the United States. But even when local production by a manufacturing subsidiary replaces finished goods previously imported, as has occurred in autos and electronics, the resulting fall in imports of finished goods is typically offset by an associated increase in imports of components.[10]

Why Firms Invest in the United States

To understand why foreign firms have been increasing their ownership stakes in the U.S. economy, it is useful to review the basic conditions required for profitable direct foreign investment. These conditions provide a context for identifying specific changes

10. This has been alleged in recent years about Japanese investments in the United States, but it is also a long-standing complaint of less-developed host countries. These nations invite foreign investments with the hope of reducing chronic balance-of-payments difficulties, but the usual experience is that induced imports of machinery and components tend to offset any direct reduction in imports or rise in exports of the product itself. This is, of course, consistent with the notion that the sources of aggregate international imbalances are fundamentally macroeconomic. See McCulloch and Richardson (1986).

in the global environment that may underlie the recent surge in establishment of U.S. subsidiaries by firms abroad.

In one sense, the central puzzle concerning direct foreign investment is why it takes place at all, given the significant competitive disadvantages faced by a firm entering a foreign market. To make the strategy viable, the investing firm must possess an "advantage" in terms of product, process, or management sufficient to outweigh its obvious disadvantages relative to actual or potential domestic competitors in the host country. The existence of additional hurdles and risks facing a foreign entrant suggest that foreign subsidiaries should on average yield higher profits than domestic operations in the same industry. These conditions imply that direct investments will be concentrated in markets that do not conform to the paradigm of perfect competition—markets characterized by incomplete information, barriers to entry, or other "imperfections."[11]

But a rent-generating competitive advantage is still only a necessary condition for the viability of direct foreign investment. Since the firm's competitive advantage could in some circumstances be better exploited by exporting from the home country, an additional requirement for setting up foreign operations is a locational advantage. This could reflect the usual considerations of production and transport costs, as well as advantages arising from national policy at home and abroad, for example, taxation, regulation, and barriers to trade. In the absence of a significant locational advantage, the potential investor is likely to choose exporting over the more costly and risky option of establishing a local subsidiary.

Like the competitive advantage, the locational advantage is necessary but not sufficient. Even given a locational advantage, there must be an organizational advantage of direct foreign investment over alternative strategies, such as licensing or other long-term contractual arrangements with firms in the host country. In the language of industrial organization, there must be an *internalization* advantage—an advantage to substituting internal modes of resource coordination within a single firm for an external market-based arrangement between independent firms.

11. The key idea that direct foreign investment requires a significant departure from conditions of perfect competition was advanced by Hymer (1960) and expanded by Kindleberger (1969), Caves, and many others. See Caves (1982, chap. 2) for a comprehensive survey of the literature.

In other words, there must be an advantage of integrated global management.[12]

Internalization and Internationalization

Direct foreign investment *is* precisely a firm's internalization of economic activity across a national boundary—internationalization of management. The underlying motives are essentially the same ones that promote expansion of a firm's activities within a single domestic market, but with a larger anticipated benefit required to offset the larger costs of international expansion.

This perspective is supported by the empirical finding that firms investing abroad are on average larger in their *domestic* operations than other firms in the same industry. Multinational firms based in small countries are also typically smaller than their counterparts from large countries. Both observations are consistent with the hypothesis that firms should exhaust the gains from domestic internalization before going abroad.

Since the investments abroad of U.S. multinationals dominated the global picture for several decades after World War II, most of the empirical research has focused on these. Studies of direct foreign investments by U.S. manufacturing firms have verified that investment activity is clustered in the industries where research and development (R&D) and advertising expenditures are important. Such expenditures presumably create the competitive advantage necessary for a U.S. firm to operate profitably in a foreign environment. Competitive advantages interact with potential gains from internalization. For example, high-technology firms tend to exploit their newest technologies via subsidiaries, while older products and processes are licensed to independent foreign producers.

Evidence on locational advantage is less compelling, except for resource-based industries. Predictable factors such as availability of suitable labor at lower cost, a large and protected domestic market, favorable tax or regulatory treatment, and stable political environment all appear to have some influence on location decisions. However, other locational considerations cannot be separated from the benefits of a single global management

12. The three "necessary conditions" are elaborated by Dunning (1981 and earlier papers). Dunning uses this classification to explain the distribution of investment by home and host country and industry. See Rugman (1980) for a detailed analysis of direct investment as international internalization.

structure, that is, internalization. Some direct foreign investment is primarily for the purpose of enhancing local sales of goods imported from a firm's production facilities elsewhere, as with distribution and service facilities.[13] Local operations can also enhance exports by the parent to the host market by providing the parent with up-to-date market information when conditions are changing rapidly, thus keeping the parent in close touch with market trends. In a concentrated industry, the establishment of local production capacity may be central to the investing firm's competitive strategy (see, for example, Graham 1978). The subsidiary represents the firm's precommitment to a substantial presence in the local market.

Other advantages of multinational activity are associated with being multinational rather than with any specific host location. A global production network permits the firm to diversify risk and, more generally, increases its options when conditions are volatile (see, for example, Kogut 1983). The risk-handling motive may be relevant in explaining investments in the post-Bretton Woods era of volatile exchange rates but also the classic direct foreign investments in extractive industries. Enhanced opportunities for tax avoidance are another widely cited benefit of multinational operations.

Exchange Rates and Direct Investment

Recent accounts of the rapid build-up of direct investment in the United States usually cite the low international value of the dollar as an important causal influence. However, the flow data in Table 7-1 give little indication of such a link between the international value of the dollar and new direct investments in the United States. And acquisitions of U.S. assets by Canadian firms have kept pace with those of their European and Japanese counterparts, despite the absence of any push from realignment of exchange rates.

Other things equal, a lower dollar makes U.S. products a better buy in world markets. Should the same hold for assets? If a U.S. asset is seen as a claim to a future stream of dollar-denominated profits, and if profits will be converted back into the domestic currency of the investor at the same exchange rate, the level of the

13. The U.S. investments by Japanese firms are a case in point. While this kind of complementary relationship between exporting and direct investment was suggested by Bergsten, Horst, and Moran (1978) for manufacturing investments, it may be even more important in the case of service industries such as banking and insurance.

exchange rate does not affect the present discounted value of the investment. Thus, dollar undervaluation (or overvaluation) is relevant only to the extent that one motive for the investment is speculation on future movements in exchange rates. For direct investments, where the planning horizon usually extends over years or even decades, exchange-rate fluctuations are unlikely to affect the decision *whether* to invest but may well affect the *timing* of planned investments.

Another relevant consideration is that a weak dollar makes the United States more attractive as a *production* site. By lowering U.S. production costs relative to those in Europe or Japan, a fall in the dollar might shift locational preference for direct investors toward the United States. Even so, advantages of internalization would be required to make direct investment a profitable response to the new currency values. In the absence of such advantages, foreign firms would be unable to compete with U.S. firms in exploiting the locational advantage of lower production costs.

A more basic problem with attributing investment flows to exchange-rate levels is that the post-Bretton Woods regime of generalized floating has been characterized by large swings in key rates, from apparent undervaluation to apparent overvaluation and back again.[14] Thus, the motive for increased U.S. investments may lie less in the specific level of the exchange rate around the time of the investment than in the high probability of future large movements. Here, internalization does play a key role, allowing increased costs in one location to be offset by reduced costs elsewhere and permitting some flexibility in shifting marginal production between locations on different sides of a major rate alignment.

The Role of Protection

No other incentive for direct foreign investment has received as much attention as import barriers. As a common-sense proposition, it seems almost self-evident that tariffs or quotas will stimulate direct investments in the protected markets, and recent developments in the U.S. auto and electronics industries offer visible support for the proposition. Yet statistical analyses of Canadian and U.S. data have failed to confirm a systematic

14. As long as rates are determined mainly by market forces, in one sense under- or overvaluation cannot occur. These descriptions usually refer to a deviation of market-determined rates from rates calculated using relative price levels (purchasing power parity).

relationship between direct investment and protection. The likely reason for the weak empirical findings is that protection by itself confers only a locational advantage. Whether that locational advantage leads to inward investment or simply alters conditions of domestic entry and exit depends on other industry characteristics. In the absence of a firm-specific competitive advantage best exploited through internalization, domestic producers will be better able than subsidiaries of foreign companies to capture the benefits of local production.

Important though they are in their own right, autos and electronics may thus be exceptions to the general rule. In these industries, technological and managerial know-how are firm-specific advantages that allow foreign producers (notably Japanese) to compete effectively with established domestic firms.[15] In contrast, the highly protected U.S. apparel and footwear industries have seen far less direct investment from abroad. For these low-technology industries, firm-specific advantages are apparently too small to offset the greater costs incurred by foreign investors.

Evidence at the country rather than the industry level also casts doubt on the hypothesis that protection is a strong magnet for inward direct investments. Among the less-developed countries, open, export-oriented economies have been more successful than nations pursuing import-substitution strategies in attracting new investments. For U.S. outward investments, Canada, the United Kingdom, and Germany, all with relatively liberal trade regimes, have been the most important host countries.

A more subtle link between protection and direct investment is posited by Bhagwati (1985) with the concept of *quid pro quo* foreign investment—investment made to defuse protectionist pressure rather than to circumvent actual current or anticipated protection. On this interpretation, Japanese investments in the automobile industry were intended at least in part to avoid future increases in protection (for example, local-content requirements), rather than to circumvent existing import restrictions. Presumably such investments would lessen the perceived need for protection and also shift the domestic political balance toward a more liberal trade stance.

But an alternative "strategic" interpretation is suggested by the oligopolistic structure of the auto industry and the high degree of

15. Eads (1987) attributes the cost advantage of Japanese auto plants in the United States over the indigenous Big Three primarily to superior organizational and managerial practices. He notes that the new plants pay nearly the same wages as the Big Three and do not typically rely on newer or more capital-intensive technologies for their higher labor productivity.

publicity surrounding Japanese entry into U.S. production. Japanese firms may wish to demonstrate to their U.S. rivals that Washington cannot protect them from yielding part of their customary shares in the U.S. market. The new Japanese entrants could actually benefit from future increases in protection if their competitive advantage translates into lower costs in U.S. production while trade barriers prevent the Big Three from putting their own nameplates on captive imports from Japan or elsewhere.

Foreign Investment and U.S. Labor

For host countries worldwide, the most important anticipated benefit from foreign investment is the creation of new jobs. In this, the United States has been no different. Holding out the prospect of hundreds or even thousands of new jobs, U.S. state and local officials have mounted formidable campaigns to lure foreign plants, usually offering sizable financial incentives to supplement the region's other attractions.[16] Yet, as with the presumed job losses associated with outward investments of U.S. multinationals, the overall effects of inward investments on domestic employment are far from clear.

First, while there are obviously "new jobs" created by new subsidiaries, to some extent these new jobs will be offset by employment losses elsewhere. In the most optimistic scenario, local production will simply substitute for goods previously imported, so that at least for the industry, the effect on total employment should be positive.[17] But local production by foreign affiliates may also cut into the market share of domestic competitors, so that the new jobs are matched by layoffs elsewhere in the same industry. If the affiliates use more imported inputs than their domestic counterparts, production and employment may be reduced accordingly in the supplier industries. A second concern is about the types of jobs created. Will foreign multinationals use U.S. labor for routine assembly operations, keeping the "good jobs" at home? Reich and Mankin (1986) interpret

16. These benefits include tax breaks, cheap loans, worker training, and free infrastructure. According to a Kentucky legislative study, the state committed incentives worth $125 million, or about $42,000 per job, to attract Toyota's new plant (Lore 1987). Other sources place the value of the incentives even higher.

17. In early 1987, the president of Ford Motor Company called for further reductions in auto imports from Japan to compensate for increased production by Japanese plants in the United States.

Japanese joint ventures in the United States as "part of a continuing, implicit Japanese strategy to keep the higher paying, higher value-added jobs in Japan and to gain the project engineering and production process skills that underlie competitive success."

While the Japanese presence in U.S. manufacturing is still too new to offer much systematic evidence on this issue, most analysts agree that U.S. operations abroad have benefited U.S. managers and skilled workers at the expense of less-skilled U.S. production workers. A related concern expressed by other host countries is that foreign affiliates allow little opportunity for local workers to rise into management ranks. But Leonard (1987), in comparing characteristics of domestic and foreign-controlled U.S. firms in the same industry, finds little evidence to support this fear. Rather, he concludes that "foreign ownership does not greatly affect the operations of domestic industry."

A third issue is the impact on U.S. labor-management relations. Much attention has focused on differences between the roles of U.S. and Japanese unions and between U.S. and Japanese management practices more generally. As Table 7-8 indicates, the total number of U.S. workers employed in foreign affiliates by the end of 1985 was still very small (less than 3 percent of total U.S. employment and only about 7 percent of manufacturing employment). Japanese manufacturing employment in turn accounted for less than 5 percent of all affiliate employment in manufacturing and less than 1 percent of total manufacturing employment. These figures suggest that any effects on overall U.S. practice are likely to occur mainly through example.

However, the high degree of concentration of Japanese investments both by region and by sector implies the potential for greater degree of direct impact on U.S. practice in selected industries, such as autos. The strongest evidence so far of such an impact is for Great Britain rather than the United States. A 1988 strike by workers at Ford (Britain's largest auto producer) centered on Ford's desire to introduce Japanese-style organizational practices patterned on those used in Nissan's British operations.[18]

U.S. Competitiveness and Inward Direct Investment

The close link between direct foreign investment and the investing firm's competitive advantage suggests that the rise in inward

18. *Business Week*, February 29, 1988.

Table 7-8. Employment of Nonbank U.S. Affiliates, 1985
By Country of Ultimate Beneficial Owner
(Thousands of Employees)

	All Industries	Manufacturing	Wholesale Trade
All countries	2,854	1,439	296
United Kingdom	628	314	41
Canada	528	286	22
Germany	407	251	51
Netherlands	213	92	5
Switzerland	199	115	13
Japan	209	72	92

Source: Survey of Current Business, May 1987, p. 46.

foreign investments in the United States, as well as the slowing of U.S. direct investments abroad, reflects the industrial catch-up of other nations to the United States. Where the competitive advantages were once controlled almost exclusively by U.S. companies, new rivals have emerged in Europe, Japan, and even some of the developing countries. As with the successful U.S. multinationals of earlier decades, these firms have exploited their competitive advantages first through exports and later through direct investment in the market countries.

Like other host countries over the years, the United States is reevaluating the potential gains and losses from allowing free entry to foreign subsidiaries. As already noted, there is the concern that the foreign investors, and particularly the Japanese, will "colonize" the United States, keeping the good jobs—and the profits—at home, and that foreign-controlled employment will grow mainly at the expense of other U.S. jobs.

A related worry is that the active competition among states and localities will allow foreign investors to extract the lion's share of any economic benefits through lucrative concession packages. Existing domestic firms in the same industry may find themselves disadvantaged—without similar tax breaks and perhaps even with higher taxes to pay for the concessions offered to new entrants.

Moreover, established firms usually have an older workforce and thus higher wage and benefit costs even with the same pay scale.[19]

A final issue, unique to the United States as the world leader in science and technology, is that foreign producers may use their U.S. subsidiaries and especially joint ventures as listening posts to gain better access to new scientific and technological information. The proposed acquisition of Fairchild Instrument by Fujitsu in early 1987 was opposed on these grounds, among others—even though Fairchild was already owned by a different foreign (but non-Japanese, and therefore less threatening?) company.[20]

IV. CONCLUDING REMARKS

The previous sections examine the extent of Japanese investment activity in relation to overall foreign investment in the United States and review evidence on its motivation and sectoral impact. Analysis based on the data available in early 1988 provides little support for the alarmist view that has become increasingly fashionable in the United States. In particular:

1. The "typical" foreign investment in the United States is not a direct investment, nor is the typical foreign investor Japanese.
2. In direct investment, Japan is a distant third, behind the United Kingdom and the Netherlands, in the size of its U.S. stake. Japanese investments have been concentrated in wholesale trade rather than manufacturing.
3. The increased flow of direct investment into the United States predates the emergence of the nation's large net borrowings from abroad.

19. For example, Donald Peterson, chairman of Ford Motor Company, claims that the new Japanese auto plants in the United States have a labor-cost advantage of $6 per hour due to a younger, healthier workforce (Bussey 1987). However, older workers have lower absentee rates and fewer on-the-job injuries. As previously noted, George Eads, the chief economist for General Motors, sees differences in organization and management, rather than worker age, as the key factor accounting for the cost advantage of the Japanese-owned U.S. plants (Eads 1987).

20. Perhaps at issue was the ability of Fairchild to participate in the U.S.-funded Sematech research venture aimed at restoring the international competitiveness of U.S. semiconductor firms. The director of a corporate-funded research program at Stanford's Center for Integrated Systems told me that Japanese-controlled companies would not be allowed to join the program. Phillips, a Dutch electronics company, was a founding member. On Japanese access to U.S. technology, see Dreyfuss (1987).

4. U.S. firms continue to increase their direct investments abroad, although at a slower pace than in earlier decades.

Like the 1970s furor over OPEC investments, the public outcry about the increased role of the Japanese appears to ignore the relatively modest size of total foreign holdings and of the Japanese share in most investment categories. The focus on investors who are "different" suggests that racism may play some role in shaping public attitudes, or perhaps merely that being different makes Asian investors more conspicuous than their British, Dutch, German, or Canadian counterparts.

Overall, recent changes in the international investment position of the United States have reflected three distinct developments. The first is the temporary constellation of macroeconomic forces leading to net U.S. capital inflows. The second is the emergence of important new players in international financial markets: first OPEC, more recently Japan, and soon the newly industrializing countries of Asia. The third is the increased integration of world capital markets. While public attention has focused on the first and second, the implications of the third are likely to be more profound. As the 1980s have dramatically demonstrated, integrated financial markets change the options available to national policymakers. Given the new constraints on national action, countries will be forced to choose between accepting a greater degree of policy consistency (however achieved) or foregoing some of the efficiency benefits from market integration.

REFERENCES

Altany, David R. 1988. "Disclosure Debate." *Industry Week,* January 4.

Barker, Betty L. 1986. "U.S. Merchandise Trade Associated With U.S. Multinational Companies." *Survey of Current Business* (May): 55-72.

Bergsten, J. Fred, Thomas Horst, and Theodore H. Moran. 1978. *American Multinationals and American Interests.* Washington, DC: The Brookings Institution.

Bhagwati, Jagdish. 1985. *Investing Abroad.* Esmee Fairbairn Lecture, University of Lancaster, November 27.

Bussey, John. 1987. "An Older Workforce Burdens Big Producers in the Basic Industries." *Wall Street Journal,* March 5.

Caves, Richard E. 1982. *Multinational Enterprise and Economic Analysis.* Cambridge, MA: Cambridge University Press.

Dreyfuss, Joel. 1987. "How Japan Picks America's Brains." *Fortune,* December 21.

Dunning, John H. 1981. "Explaining the International Direct Investment Position of Countries: Towards a Dynamic or Developmental Approach." *Weltwirtschaftliches Archiv* 117: 30-64.

Eads, George C. 1987. "The Impact of Recent Exchange Rate Changes, the International Trade Regime, and Technology on the Pattern of Future Competition in Motor Vehicles." Paper prepared for a symposium on Technological Competition in the 21st Century, Duisberg, West Germany, August 3-7.

Feldstein, Martin and Kathleen. 1987. "Fear of Foreigners." *Boston Globe,* September 8.

Graham, Edward M. 1978. "Transatlantic Investment by Multinational Firms: A Rivalistic Phenomenon?" *Journal of Post Keynesian Economics* 1 (Fall).

Hymer, Stephen. 1960. *The International Operations of National Firms.* Doctoral dissertation, MIT.

Kindleberger, Charles P. 1969. *American Business Abroad: Six Lectures on Direct Investment.* New Haven: Yale University Press.

Kogut, Bruce. 1983. "Foreign Direct Investment as a Sequential Process." *The Multinational Corporation in the 1980s.* Ed. Charles P. Kindleberger and David B. Audretsch. Cambridge: MIT Press.

Leonard, Jonathan S. 1987. "Working for Foreign Masters: Wages and Employment in Foreign Direct Investment in the U.S." University of California at Berkeley and National Bureau of Economic Research, September.

Lipsey, Robert E. 1988. "Changing Patterns of International Investment by and in the United States." *The United States in the World Economy*. Ed. Martin Feldstein. Chicago: University of Chicago Press.

Lore, Dave. 1987. "Japanese Auto Investments: Great Today But What About Tomorrow?" *midAmerican Outlook* (Spring): 2-4.

McCulloch, Rachel, and J. David Richardson. 1986. "U.S. Trade and the Dollar: Evaluating Current Policy Options." *Current U.S. Trade Policy: Analysis, Agenda, and Administration.* Ed. Robert E. Baldwin and J. David Richardson. Cambridge: National Bureau of Economic Research.

Reich, Robert B., and Eric D. Mankin. 1986. "Joint Ventures with Japan Give Away Our Future." *Harvard Business Review* (March/April): 78-86.

Rugman, Alan M. 1980. "Internalization as a General Theory of Foreign Direct Investment: A Re-Appraisal of the Literature." *Weltwirtschaftliches Archiv* 116: 365-79.

Tolchin, Martin. 1988. "Foreigners' Investing: A Warning." *New York Times,* February 22.

Tolchin, Martin and Susan. 1987. "Foreign Money, U.S. Fears." *New York Times Magazine,* December 13.

U.S. Department of Commerce. *Survey of Current Business,* various issues.

U.S. Department of Commerce. 1987. *Foreign Direct Investment in the United States: 1986 Transactions.* Washington, DC: International Trade Administration. September.

Vernon, Raymond. 1971. *Sovereignty at Bay.* New York: Basic Books.

8 EXCHANGE-RATE MOVEMENTS AND FOREIGN DIRECT INVESTMENT IN THE UNITED STATES

Richard E. Caves

I. INTRODUCTION

Research on foreign direct investment has paid rather little attention to its sensitivity to short-run movements of exchange rates, either nominal or real. However, casual evidence suggests that the large swings of real exchange rates seen in the 1970s and 1980s have given rise to correspondingly large fluctuations in the flows of direct investment—certainly investment in the United States by foreign sources.

This behavior holds interest for what it tells us about both the adjustment process in the balance of payments and the behavior of multinational corporations. The wide swings in exchange rates have given cause for concern about the effectiveness of the current system of managed floating exchange rates among the major industrial countries or blocs. Although we generally do not expect

Research support by the Division of Research, Harvard Business School, is gratefully acknowledged. Heng-fu Zou provided research assistance, and Marni Hoyle and Barry Feldman aided in organizing the data base. I am grateful for suggestions by many participants at the Tenth Annual Middlebury Conference on Economic Issues, in particular Richard Baldwin, Rachel McCulloch, Thomas Pugel, and Mark Roberts.

long-term capital flows to serve as short-run stabilizers of exchange-rate movements, foreign direct investment may have assumed this role to an important degree.

The sensitivity of direct investment to exchange rates sheds light on the behavior of multinational companies and their transactions in the U.S. market for corporate control. About three-fourths of U.S. assets obtained by foreign investors are now acquired by purchase of existing business units. Foreign enterprises have become important players in the market for corporate control, in which operating authority over business units and free-standing companies changes hands. Shifts in foreign firms' demands or reservation prices for participating in this market can clearly affect the going prices of established business units, as well as their subsequent market behavior and economic performance.

In this paper, we focus on the short-run sensitivity of foreign investment in the United States to the exchange rate and other appropriate determinants. Statistical tests of the exchange rate's effect on foreign investment have suffered from a lack of suitable natural experiments. The Bretton Woods period of pegged exchange rates provided little useful variance.[1] The collapse of that system, soon followed by the 1973 energy crisis and a sharp recession in the industrial countries, put off into the latter 1970s a time when we could hope to observe a stable pattern of responses by companies to short-run influences on their transnational investment decisions. Given the lead time required for foreign-investment decisions, we still have few observations in the time-series dimension to indicate the working of their determinants. We seek to get around that problem in this paper by using the leverage provided by inflows to the United States from different countries of origin. We utilize up to fifteen source countries as the basis for a panel data set, which offers hope that some useful evidence on time-series behavior can be extracted from series that reach only from 1977 to 1985.

Some descriptive evidence helps to motivate the inquiry. The United States long stood as a major gross and net exporter of foreign investment, but the relatively faster growth of national income and productivity in other industrial countries has been accompanied by proportional gains in the prevalence of

1. It did, however, display a relation of direct investment to exchange rates consistent with the pattern apparently present nowadays, with substantial outflows moving from the United States (overvalued dollar) to the European countries that sustained undervalued exchange rates (Makin 1974).

multinational firms based in other countries.[2] The balance-of-payments data on inflows of foreign direct investment to the United States show an increase from an average of $1.2 billion in 1971-1974 to $22.0 billion in 1984-1986. The net-equity position of foreign investors in the United States rose from $13.3 billion in 1970 to $27.7 billion in 1975, and $83.0 billion in 1980.

Especially revealing are the data published since 1979 by the Bureau of Economic Analysis (BEA) on U.S. business enterprises acquired or established by foreign investors, shown in Table 8-1. These fluctuate greatly from year to year, with peaks occurring in 1981 and 1986. The U.S. dollar exchange rate is also shown as a reminder of the size of its swings and for the rough suggestion it offers of the association with new foreign investments. The table distinguishes between enterprises newly established by foreign parents and ongoing businesses whose control has shifted to foreign parties. For the whole period, acquisitions of control over existing businesses make up 78.2 percent of the total, and they evidently fluctuate much more from year to year than start-ups of new businesses—partly but not entirely because of the occasional occurrence of very large acquisitions.[3]

The figures in Table 8-1 should be distinguished, incidentally, from inflows recorded in the balance of payments, because they represent the total assets of U.S. business units (divisions or companies) acquired or established and not just the net increase in foreigners' equity. Part of the purchase price is often borrowed from an independent domestic or foreign lender; if that part is an international capital flow, it represents portfolio rather than direct investment. For example, in 1979, 46 percent of the total acquisition cost actually came from within the United States, 9 percent internally generated by existing U.S. affiliates of foreign enterprises, and the remaining 37 percent borrowed from U.S.

2. This statement is consistent with our microeconomic evidence on the genesis of multinational companies. They arise where internationally decentralized production activities are efficiently coordinated by administrative rather than by market links. New multinationals tend to emerge when a national company acquires some skill, competence, technology, or other intangible asset that can be efficiently used in diverse locations but not readily rented or traded at arm's length. Bouts of rapid economic growth in a nation tend to be correlated with the copious emergence of such successes among its businesses and, accordingly, with an efflux of multinationals based in the fast-growing country (Rowthorn and Hymer [1971], provided evidence of the pattern).

3. The BEA reports the concentration of each year's large transactions. In 1986, for example, 46 investments of $100 million or more accounted for only 8 percent of the total number but 75 percent of total outlay (Herr 1987).

parties. Of the 54 percent from foreign sources, 39 was supplied by the parent enterprises (direct investment) and 15 percent by foreign lenders (portfolio investment). Another distinction between Table 8-1's data and balance-of-payments flows is that the latter include increased foreign equity in previously established enterprises. The plowback of funds by established subsidiaries and the placement of new investments may differ considerably in their sensitivity to short-run influences such as the exchange rate and the movement of securities prices. Accordingly, we shall distinguish between inflows of foreign investment on a balance-of-payments basis and business assets newly passing into foreign control.[4]

II. THEORETICAL BACKGROUND

One reason why the effect of exchange rates on foreign investment has attracted little interest is no doubt the lack of much compelling theory on the subject. Indeed, in a long-run or comparative-statics context, the effect of exchange rates on direct investment is either nonexistent or indeterminate. We review these traditional approaches briefly, then turn to the context of short-run dynamics, where we obtain the framework for the empirical investigation that follows.

Traditional Approaches

The exchange rate is in essence a monetary phenomenon, and any model that embraces monetary neutrality will reject any influence of the exchange rate on real resource allocation in the long run. Foreign direct investment entails the firm's decision where to locate production facilities to undertake some activity at minimum cost. The exchange rate will affect this choice if and only if its level or movement enters into the profit-seeking calculations that determine this locational choice. Thus, if the exchange rate is

4. The fungibility of sources for financing the acquisition of foreign business assets may help explain the strong substitution relation between U.S. outflows of direct and portfolio investment found by Ruffin and Russekh (1986). Jun (1988, chap. 3) estimated a "true" measure of foreign direct investment in the United States that is defined as the total value of assets acquired plus increases of investment in already foreign-controlled businesses, which will exceed either the balance-of-payments measure or the measure based on acquired business assets. In 1979, he found these were respectively 62 and 79 percent of the "true" measure; for 1980, the fractions were 79 and 57 percent, respectively.

Table 8-1. Value of U.S. Business Assets Established or Acquired by Foreign Investors, 1979-1986
(Billions of Dollars)

Year	Newly Established	Obtained by Acquisition	Total	Acquisitions % of Total	Exchange Rate
1979	$2.2	$13.2	$15.3	86	79.1
1980	3.2	9.0	12.2	74	80.1
1981	5.1	18.2	23.2	78	83.9
1982	4.3	6.6	10.8	61	94.5
1983	3.2	4.8	8.1	59	98.0
1984	3.4	11.8	15.2	78	103.6
1985	3.0	20.1	23.1	87	106.7
1986	6.0	25.5	31.5	81	87.6

Source: *Survey of Current Business*, various issues 1981-1987. Index of effective exchange rate (price of U.S. dollar, 1970 = 100) is OECD *Economic Outlook*, no. 42 (December 1987), p. 195.

modelled as the instrument that preserves purchasing-power parity between national price levels, it does not bias foreign-investment decisions but rather *averts* any distortion to them that might arise from disturbances to national price levels.[5] It is natural to conclude that exchange rates in long-run equilibrium have no influence on foreign direct investment.

If we shift the focus to long-run partial equilibrium and allow exchange-rate changes to correspond to real shifts between countries in money cost levels, then foreign investment becomes sensitive to the exchange rate, but in a way that varies with the configuration of the foreign investor's activities. This line of investigation was first developed in the 1970s as economists sought to understand the ramifications of the new regime of managed floating exchange rates (Stevens 1977; Kohlhagen 1977) and to distinguish between effects of exchange rates on portfolio investment and on allocations by multinational companies (Prachowney 1972; Logue and Willett 1977).

5. Recent research in the pure theory of international trade has shown how foreign direct investment can be incorporated into real general equilibrium, in the assumed absence of any monetary influences (Helpman 1984). Our concern here is with monetary influences on whatever equilibrium is determined by real factors.

Assume that the price levels in the United States and in the foreign country are given, and that some unspecified disturbance lowers the price of the U.S. dollar. Actual or potential multinational companies based in the foreign country expect the dollar depreciation to be permanent. It thus reduces both the cost of production in the United States and the value of profits obtained in the U.S. market upon conversion back to foreign currency. Whether and in what direction the exchange-rate change affects the firm's foreign-investment decision then depends on the configuration of its international production and trade activities:

1. Assume that the firm's U.S. subsidiary obtains all of its real inputs in the United States, except for its (financial) equity capital, and sells all of its output in U.S. markets. Assume that relative prices in U.S. dollars are unaffected (in equilibrium) by the exchange-rate change. Then the foreign-currency value of all revenues earned and costs incurred in the U.S. market change in the same proportion, and the foreign firm's expected (home-currency) rate of return on any investment in the United States is unchanged. Flows of foreign investment should be unaffected by the dollar depreciation.
2. Change the conditions of the preceding case to make the firm's investment in the United States a forward vertical integration, requiring the use of an input supplied from the source country, its production costs constant in terms of the source country's price level. (The source-supplied input might be either a capital or an intermediate good.) Then a dollar devaluation raises the firm's unit costs (in dollars) of producing in the United States, while the quantity of its output demanded at any dollar price remains unchanged. The profitability of foreign investment falls, and the firm reduces its investment in the United States.
3. Assume that the firm produces in the United States in order to supply some market external to the United States, where money prices and costs are unaffected by the dollar depreciation. The United States might serve the foreign multinational as a "platform" for supplying world markets, or it might provide an input used in the parent's source-country activities (that is, represent a backward vertical integration for the foreign firm). Then the (derived) demand for the output of the U.S. subsidiary is unchanged in foreign currency, while the dollar's depreciation lowers the foreign-currency value of its costs. The profitability of U.S. production increases, as does foreign investment.

In short, these cases show that the effect of an exchange-rate change on foreign investment depends on the particular configuration of the foreign investor's activities. No prediction emerges for the sign of the overall response of the source country's multinationals, unless we can aggregate over the various firms classified by their structural situations. Thus, this line of theory concerning exchange-rate effects yields indeterminate results, while the line that assigns the exchange rate the task of maintaining purchasing-power parity predicts no relationship at all.

Effect of Expectations

While the preceding theory fails to support the casual impression that foreign investment is sensitive to exchange rates in the manner of "stabilizing speculation," the fault may well lie with the theory rather than the impression. Recent research, notably Cushman (1985), has shifted from an approach based on (long-run) comparative statics to one that emphasizes short-run actions based on expectations about how current market conditions diverge from those that will prevail in the future. While the predicted behavior of multinational companies continues to depend on the configurations of their activities, this approach comes closer to predicting that aggregate flows of direct investment will behave as casual impressions suggest.[6]

In Cushman's analysis, exchange-rate expectations introduce the foreign-investment inducement of capital gains on resources committed to a national market whose currency is expected to appreciate, or withdrawn from one where depreciation is anticipated. In his model, this effect is due to physical capital that can be sourced in either country, in anticipation of later production. But the spirit of the model applies to any resources that the multinational firm can commit to a market at times when the purchase terms appear favorable—notably including the purchase of in-place physical and intangible capital. We can develop cases parallel to those listed above, treating the assumed situation as a dollar depreciation that is expected by foreign companies subsequently to incur some reversal:

6. The main focus of Cushman's (1985) research is on the effect of uncertainty rather than mean expectations, but his models serve to cover the risk-neutral case as well. While we express skepticism below concerning his approach to multinational firms' responses to uncertainty, we rely heavily on both his theoretical results and empirical research strategy.

1. When the foreign firm's decision involves whether to serve the U.S. market from source-country or U.S. production facilities, and the dollar is expected to recover from a current depreciation, the foreign multinational expands its capital in the U.S. to obtain the expected capital gain. The result differs from the case of a permanent depreciation, which effects no net change in the profitability of supplying the U.S. market from a U.S. plant.
2. The foreign multinational that supplies an input to its U.S. production facility (that is, is vertically integrated forward) is still deterred by a dollar depreciation because of the current squeeze on its margins. However, an expected reversal of the exchange-rate depreciation cuts against this incentive to withdraw capital by supplying a contrary incentive to invest for capital gains.
3. The firm producing in the U.S. to supply external markets still has an incentive to move production to the U.S. market on the occasion of a dollar depreciation, but the incentive is mitigated by the reduction or elimination of the cost advantage brought about by any appreciation expected to occur subsequently.

When these cases are consolidated, they still yield no unambiguous prediction about the effect of a dollar depreciation that is subject to an expected reversal. However, the balance of expected situations is tilted toward the prediction of an inflow. The second and third cases can in this regard be read as mutually offsetting—outflows and inflows respectively predicted for them previously are now qualified. But the first case, which formerly predicted no effect, now predicts an inflow. The relatively small reliance of most foreign multinationals on the United States as a platform for supplying overseas markets tends to deprive the third case of empirical relevance. And the flexibility of the make-or-buy decision for many foreign firms that export components used by their U.S. subsidiaries means that situations matching the second case tend to transform them into situations matching the first case under the stimulus of dollar depreciation.

III. THE STATISTICAL MODEL

With this background in hand, we proceed to test the sensitivity of new foreign investments in the United States to the exchange rate and other variables, using data on inflows from (a maximum of) fifteen countries over the period 1978-1986. The fifteen countries can be divided into a group of seven major investors (Canada, France, West Germany, Japan, Netherlands, Switzerland, and United Kingdom) and eight lesser ones (Australia, Austria, Belgium, Denmark, Italy, Norway, Spain, and Sweden). To gain degrees of freedom, we sought to include the maximum number of reasonably regular foreign investors in the United States. Table 8-2 shows for each of these countries the estimated mean annual constant-dollar value of business assets acquired during 1978-1986 and the coefficient of variation of the annual flows. The relative year-to-year variability of inflows for the smaller foreign investors is quite high, and so our expected ability to explain their investment flows is attenuated.

The time period was strongly influenced by the availability of data sources, but also by the considerable increase in flows of direct investment to the United States during the 1970s. The reasons for this upswing support interesting speculations, but they invoke long-run influences with little kinship for the short-run factors that concern us here. In selecting the period 1978-1986, we make the assumption that the major step-up of interest in the United States as a target for foreign investment had largely run its course by 1977,[7] giving way to a period in which annual changes depend largely on short-run shifts in their determinants.

Dependent Variables

Inflows of foreign investment can be measured in various ways, and the choice must be matched to the hypotheses at hand. Balance-of-payments flows directly measure the increase in the book equity of foreign persons in U.S. businesses or assets deemed to be under foreign control. These flows consist of reinvested earnings of already established subsidiaries and newly placed equity from foreign sources. It is now widely accepted that internally generated funds typically have a lower shadow price for further investment in a business than do funds secured from the financial market, and research on the operation of multinational companies affirms the heavy reliance of established subsidiaries on plowed-back earnings.[8]

7. Our dependent variable and regressors actually come available for 1977, but the need to express most regressors as indexes (1977=100) made 1978 effectively the first year of the analysis.

8. The research literature does agree that investments by ongoing subsidiaries are influenced by global opportunity costs of funds to their parents, but it does not reject the implied rule that established subsidiaries enjoy some priority in using their internally generated funds. See sources cited by Caves (1982, pp. 161-168, 178).

Therefore, the short-run determinants of reinvestment in foreign subsidiaries are likely to depend more sensitively on their current profitability than on the variables that influence new inflows from abroad. We preferred to work with a measure that deemphasizes these plow-backs, and not with inflows recorded in the balance of payments.

Two data sources exist that highlight newly established or acquired business units coming under the control of foreign parents. One is by the U.S. International Trade Administration (ITA), an annual series published since 1974 on the value of business assets in the United States acquired by foreign parties; details of individual transactions are reported, including their reported values and ultimate beneficial owners. The other is an annual series published since 1977 by the U.S. Bureau of Economic Analysis on the year-end value of business assets under foreign control. Either can supply an estimate of the value (net, in the case of BEA) of business assets coming under foreign control. These assets may be financed by borrowing from either U.S. domestic or foreign sources as well as by new equity from abroad, so their total value considerably exceeds the additional foreign equity utilized to acquire them. Given the actual predominance of acquisitions of existing assets and the theoretical importance of capital gains for affecting short-run inflows, it seems appropriate to focus on acquired assets found in balance-of-payments data rather than the funds that flow to acquire them. We chose to work with the ITA data, despite important limitations, because they represent gross inflows (the sunkenness of many such investments means that shut-downs and sell-offs depend on very different factors from new investments) and for other pragmatic reasons.[9]

Exogenous Variables

We discuss the exogenous short-run influences to which these direct-investment measures should be related, then turn to the specific form of the relationship and the results. We already identified the exchange rate as the influence of central concern in

9. BEA data are obtained under mandatory reporting, while the ITA data are gathered from public sources. While that fact weighs importantly for the BEA series, we found important anomalies when we first-differenced the BEA stock figures in the form of large declines for a few countries and years that corresponded to no large sell-offs or closures that we could identify. A data appendix discusses the sources for this and other variables used in the analysis.

Table 8-2. Summary Data on Annual Changes in Values of U.S. Business Assets Controlled by Ultimate Beneficial Owners in Fifteen Foreign Countries 1978-1986

Country	Mean ($ Million)	Coefficient of Variation
Canada	$4,694.6	0.62
France	1,435.4	0.76
Germany, Federal Republic	1,524.5	0.64
Japan	2,013.1	1.44
Netherlands	2,181.8	0.99
Switzerland	1,007.4	1.06
United Kingdom	4,668.5	0.37
Australia	603.1	1.33
Austria	31.5	1.68
Belgium	212.0	1.10
Denmark	60.0	1.25
Italy	212.1	0.86
Norway	47.8	1.71
Spain	24.8	1.14
Sweden	282.9	1.00

Source: Estimated from U.S. International Trade Administration, *Foreign Direct Investment in the United States: Completed Transactions 1974-1983*, vol. I, and subsequent annual versions of this publication.

this paper. The theoretical relations explored above ascribe to the exchange rate's movement shifts in the cost (in source-country currency) of production between the source country and the United States. National price levels were assumed constant for the purpose of that exercise. Actual changes in real exchange rates, however, of course are the net result of differential changes in national price levels and the nominal exchange rate. Define:

EX_{it} = bilateral nominal exchange rate of source-country i, expressed as the price of the U.S. dollar in year t;

REX_{it} = bilateral real exchange rate of source-country i in year t. If P_{it} and P_{USt} are indexes of the price levels of countries i and the United States respectively, then $REX_{it} = EX_{it}(P_{USt}/P_{it})$.

We work with both nominal and real exchange rates, because we expect different elasticities of expectation to apply to them. The nominal and real exchange rate of the dollar during the past decade was subject to a strong cyclical movement that could to some extent be anticipated by direct investors. For example, when the U.S. government committed itself to a large and sustained budget deficit, appreciation of the dollar could be anticipated as foreign portfolios absorbed the resulting outpouring of securities; eventually, however, portfolio-balance considerations and the need to service the accumulating debt would require depreciation. The movement of national price levels may to some extent have rested on foreseeable, persistent processes, but we assume that year-to-year variations in the industrial countries resulted from short-run interactions of economic disturbances and policy choices that were hard to predict. Therefore, we focus on the formation of expectations about the nominal exchange rate; we assume that any actions of foreign investors on the basis of price-level expectations were too unsystematic to be captured in our model.

Exchange-rate expectations can be modelled in many ways, and the investigator's choice must ride merely on an informed guess about the information available to and used by foreign investors. We employ three options. One assumes that on average they correctly anticipated the future exchange rate as the one prevailing in the next year.[10] The others hypothesize more naive processes, in which the current year's change in the exchange rate is expected either to be partially reversed or continued in the following year:

$EXP1_{it} = EX_{it+1}$, the nominal exchange rate that actually prevailed in the succeeding year;

$EXP2_{it} = (EX_{it-1} + EX_{it})/2$, which assumes that half of this year's change in the exchange rate will be reversed next year;

$EXP3_{it} = EX_{it} + (EX_{it} - EX_{it-1})$, which assumes that this year's change in the exchange rate will be repeated next year.

These hypotheses are no more than plausible guesses, and their relative statistical performance could suggest other formulations.

While the direction of the exchange rate's influence is formally indeterminate, we argued that a strong case can be made for a short-run dollar depreciation encouraging foreign investment in the United States, and hence a negative coefficient for *EX* or *REX*.

10. An analytically preferable assumption would be that investors anticipated a sequence of exchange rates stretching into the future and acted on the basis of a discounted series and not just the next year's value. Working with a short time series with a recent termination, we unfortunately cannot test this.

The same logic of short-run arbitrage implies a positive coefficient for *EXP1* or *EXP2*, or a negative coefficient for *EXP3* (depending on which hypothesis about expectations proves correct). Cushman obtained a significant negative coefficient for the real exchange rate's effect on U.S. direct investment abroad. His analysis of expectations in effect confirmed an extrapolative hypothesis like *EXP3*, but it should be noted that exchange rates were pegged during half of his period of observation (1963-1978);[11] inflation rates probably supplied most of the variation in his expectations variable during the final years of Bretton Woods and possibly during the succeeding oil-crisis years as well.

Observers' descriptions of direct-investment inflows to the United States during 1977-1985 repeatedly assigned a negative influence to *EX*, but influences of expectations were also noted. For example, the dollar's decline in 1985 from its 1980-1985 high was held to have ambiguous effects, because further declines were anticipated (Shea 1986). The dollar's depreciation was thought to promote investment in 1980 (Belli 1981), and rapid appreciation of the dollar that began in 1980 was mentioned as a substantial deterrent for investment in 1982 (Belli 1983). Also, negative influences of short-run changes in particular countries' bilateral rates are stressed (Herr 1987). Finally, Ray (1988) recently reported that dollar depreciation significantly increased direct-investment inflows to the United States during the same period as our study—from all overseas sources and individual major sources except for Japan.

The exchange rate's effect on a company's investment decision depends, we saw, on its international configuration of activities—notably whether U.S. facilities are to serve the U.S. or overseas markets. At this macroeconomic level of analysis, no close control is feasible for investors' planned configurations. However, we did include as an indicator of a country's short-run comparative advantage the variable:

TB_{it} = exports minus imports, the difference divided by the sum of exports plus imports, for country *i* in year *t*.

11. Kohlhagen (1977), working with data from the 1960s, found that direct investment funds flowed in anticipation that disequilibrium pegged exchange rates would be changed, with a reflux following the change. One would expect the one-way expectations generated by suppressed disequilibria under pegged exchange rates to have more readily detectable effects than the less distinct disequilibria that occur in the present-day policy regime.

TB_{USt} describes the situation for the United States, while $TBDIF_t$ is the difference between this ratio for the source country and for the United States. If an improvement in the U.S. trade balance indicates a shift of advantage toward a U.S. production location *not* observable from the exchange rate itself, TB_{USt} would take a positive coefficient, or $TBDIF_t$ would take a negative one.

Because the acquisition of existing companies or businesses has become such a prominent mode of direct investment, movements of securities prices exert a potentially important influence independent of real exchange rates. We have assumed that the prices of new plant and equipment are tied to the movements of national price levels (incorporated in *REX*), but differential movements of securities prices could affect flows of direct investment as bargains attract foreign firms to the market for corporate control or high prices deter them.[12] Relatively stable U.S. share prices and abundant sell-offs of divisions by U.S. enterprises were thought to promote direct investment in 1984 and 1985 (Belli 1985; Shea 1986). We utilized the share-price indexes reported in IMF *International Financial Statistics* to generate:

$SHARE_t$ = index of securities prices in the U.S. in year t;

$SHDIF_{it}$ = index of securities prices in country i in year t - $SHARE_t$.

It is unclear whether share prices in the source country should also be considered; that depends on whether the purchase of existing assets at home and the acquisition of business units in the United States commonly are close alternatives. If foreign investors seek out bargains in the market for corporate control, *SHARE* should exert a negative and *SHDIF* a positive influence on direct investment.[13]

Obvious short-run influences on direct investment are levels of GNP, reflecting both expected yields on real investments and supplies of corporate profits and liquidity. Direct investment is expected to increase with:

12. Using microeconomic data, Caves and Mehra (1986) found strong evidence that foreign firms investing in the United States treat acquisition and the establishment of new facilities as direct alternatives; their results did not indicate a significant role for share prices, but the data base was not well suited to isolating their effect.

13. Direct-investment inflows include substantial purchases of land and buildings, whose asset prices are not closely related to securities prices or the general price level and thus are omitted variables in our model. The inflation of real-estate prices in Japan was said to promote direct investment in 1986 (Herr 1987), but slackening appreciation of U.S. real estate was said to discourage it in 1982 (Belli 1983).

YUS_t = U.S. real gross national product in year t.

Even though direct investments represent long-run commitments of resources, short-run U.S. macroeconomic conditions can evidently affect the pace of their realization, allegedly by reducing short-run expected returns and increasing uncertainty.[14] Prosperous years are likely to increase the business liquidity and retained earnings of established foreign subsidiaries in the United States. Their abundant cash increases the direct-investment inflow when these funds are used by large multinational parents to make further acquisitions of U.S. businesses.[15] Each of these channels indicates a positive relation between *YUS* and direct investment.

While both of the obvious channels of influence predict a positive influence for *YUS*, they pull in opposite directions for:

YF_{it} = real GNP in country i in year t.

A rising value of *YF* improves the outlook for alternative investments at home, to serve the foreign firm's base national market, at the same time it generates more liquidity for investing either at home or abroad. Observers' comments on foreign investment in the United States tend to emphasize the liquidity effect (Belli 1981, 1982, 1983, 1984). Predominance of the liquidity effect implies a positive influence on the inflow of direct investment, the alternative investments effect a negative one. Cushman (1985) found U.S. real GNP to exert a negative influence on outflows of direct investment from the United States.[16]

While we assume that expected profit drives foreign-investment decisions, it is another question whether current profits reported on

14. In recessed 1982, "reasonably confident earnings forecasts—an essential ingredient in most major acquisitions—were especially difficult to make" (Belli 1983).

15. In 1979, for example, acquired businesses accounted for 45.9 percent of total U.S. business assets purchased by foreign firms, and U.S. affiliates of the acquirors supplied 20.3 percent of the total cost of the assets and, obviously, a much larger fraction of the acquirors' equity investment (International Investment Division 1981).

16. The study by Reuber and Roseman (1972) of takeovers in Canada highlighted the roles of corporate liquidity in the United States and Canada as determinants of the relative prevalence of foreign and domestic takeovers of Canadian companies. Severn (1972) concluded from micro data that a trade-off does not exist in the short run between domestic and foreign investment by multinational companies, and that domestic earnings affect the means of financing foreign capital expenditures but not the amount; however, his finding pertained to a data set and time period (1961-1966) in which business acquisitions surely played a much lesser role in direct foreign investment.

similar investments convey much information to investors. Earlier studies generally failed to find any statistical relationship (see Caves 1982, p. 35, for citations), and it was pointed out that the shake-down losses often experienced by new subsidiaries could make average profit fall just when foreign investment is increasing rapidly. Nonetheless, the straightforward expectation that an increase in the average profit of current foreign investments should enlarge the inflow induced us to include:

$PROFIT_{it}$ = net income divided by owner's equity for investments belonging to investors in country i for the year $t - 1$.

Its influence should be positive. While we have generally assumed a short planning horizon (that is, no lags for the exogenous variables), because of the importance of acquisitions of outstanding assets, we assume that any profit effects involve on average a year's lag.

Omitted Influences

The short time-series dimension of our data base sharply discourages incorporating other influences that theory and past empirical evidence suggest will be weaker than those already listed. We take no account of differential prices of new capital goods (except through national price levels) or international differences in interest rates. The internationalization of capital-goods markets and the high mobility of financial capital both support these omissions. However, the growing importance of international real-estate transactions and the prevalence of relatively local mortgage lending makes it possible that selected capital costs could remain a significant influence (cf. Belli 1981). A number of time-specific influences must be left in the error term, such as changes in U.S. tax laws that encouraged a wave of entries by acquisition at the end of 1986 (Herr 1987). The bilateral focus of the analysis intrinsically neglects variations in the opportunities that foreign firms had to invest in third countries.

One omitted variable calls for a more extended comment. A good deal of research has focused on the uncertainty associated with fluctuating exchange rates as a possible deterrent to international trade, and some but not all investigators have found a deterrent effect (see de Grauwe 1988). The micro foundations of the empirical hypothesis are not especially clear. With all else constant, and perfect hedging facilities assumed unavailable, one can hypothesize that uncertainty about exchange rates will decrease the risk-adjusted expected returns from international-trade transactions and thus reduce their volumes. However, those whose memories reach back to the Bretton Woods era will recall that governments' efforts to maintain disequilibrium pegged exchange rates led them to make frequent and diverse interventions into international transactions, and these interventions created their own risks for international traders. Therefore, the hypothesis that exchange-rate fluctuations post-Bretton Woods reduced trade due to *increased* risk over the preceding pegged-rate period rests on an empirically dubious assumption.

Be that as it may, the hypothesis that exchange-rate fluctuations depress trade by no means translates directly to a parallel prediction about foreign direct investment, for the reason that foreign investment itself may represent a portfolio strategy that reduces risk for the multinational firm and its owners (compare Itagaki 1981 and Cushman 1985). Furthermore, variations in exchange rates do not in general reduce the hedging value of multinational investments. We have some evidence that U.S. firms diversifying domestically seek out industries with intertemporal activity patterns uncorrelated with those of their base industries (Marshall, Yawitz, and Greenberg 1984), and one study found evidence of a similar pattern in the foreign countries chosen by U.S. multinationals when they invest overseas in activities that are diversified from their base industries (Hisey and Caves 1985).[17] Thus, risk aversion within the firm may well promote rather than repel foreign investment. This attraction is reinforced if risk-averse shareholders are willing to pay premia for the shares of multinational companies that offer built-in diversification across national boundaries, possibly at a lower transaction cost than the shareholder can achieve by diversifying his portfolio into foreign equities. Agmon and Lessard (1977) and Fatemi (1984) found evidence that investors pay a premium for such prediversified earnings streams offered by U.S. multinationals.

While these considerations can support a hypothesis that international risks in fact promote foreign direct investment, we nonetheless exclude the hypothesis from our own test. The reason is that our research is designed to highlight short-run influences on foreign investment in the time-series dimension. Even if

17. Such deals are especially likely to reflect risk-spreading objectives, because real economies of integration or shared facilities are likely to be absent.

international risk does promote foreign direct investment, that effect is unlikely to show up in the intertemporal variations of direct investment over the past decade.

IV. ESTIMATION PROCEDURE AND RESULTS

Details of the estimation strategy have so far been left vague except for the tactic of using a panel data to gain statistical leverage against intertemporal effects that are observable only for a short period of time. The basic form of the relation between the annual investment flow and the determining variables is the familiar stock-adjustment process, which calls for inclusion of the lagged stock of foreign-subsidiary assets as one of the regressors. For this we use:

$STOCK_{it-1}$ = value of stock of business assets in the U.S. controlled by foreign investors from country i at the end of year t - 1.

The coefficient of the lagged stock variable should take a negative sign.

The use of panel data for estimating relationships requires careful specification to regulate what sources of variance in the regressors do and do not influence the dependent variable. The relationships that concern us are those varying over time and not between countries, and so the exogenous variables in the model were converted to indexes based on 1977, with the exception of the dependent variable and the variables TB_{US} and *TBDIF*, which cannot be naturally expressed in index form, and *STOCK* and *PROFIT*, for which international variance is welcome. Intercept shifts were employed for fourteen of the fifteen countries included in the analysis to control for average differences in the scales of their foreign investments in the United States. The dependent variable was expressed in logarithms, as were all time-related regressors except the trade-balance measures TB_{US} and *TBDIF* (which can take either positive or negative signs).

We have been able to deal with some but not all of the econometric hazards attending this sort of panel data analysis. Ordinary-least-squares have been employed for the results reported below; although a full information maximum likelihood procedure has the advantage of efficiency in estimation, we have been unable to obtain satisfactory results with it. Lack of success also attended our efforts to correct for autocorrelation in the time-series dimension (because of the short series involved). Heteroskedasticity is expected to affect the estimation, and we did use White's procedure for obtaining heteroskedasticity-consistent standard errors. Finally, simultaneous-equations bias may be present, especially for the coefficients of share prices and exchange rates; we did not seek to correct for this, although we note that its bias is against the acceptance of our maintained hypotheses.

We can now examine the results appearing in Table 8-3. The signs of all coefficients are consistent with our expectations except for that of *YUS*, real U.S. GNP, which is uniformly quite insignificant. Of the other variables, the lagged stock of foreign-controlled capital *(STOCK)* takes a significant negative coefficient (one-tail test). Real income in the source country *(YF)*, for which we have no sign prediction, takes a positive coefficient significant at 1 percent (two-tail test). That is, the effect of real-income growth abroad on the liquidity of foreign investors seems to outweigh its effect on their investment opportunities at home, increasing their investment outlays abroad (indeed, with a notably high elasticity of response).

If the U.S. level of real GNP does not influence the acquisition of U.S. business assets, the movements of the exchange rate and securities prices evidently do. The current nominal exchange rate *EX* (price of U.S. dollar) takes a highly significant negative coefficient with a response elasticity (absolutely) around -2. We argued that theory leans strongly toward, but does not absolutely predict, this negative coefficient; the t-statistic leaves little doubt that direct investment behaves as a stabilizing factor in response to movement of the dollar's exchange rate. Results for the real exchange rate (equation 2) are very similar to those for the nominal rate. Therefore, in equation 3 we factored the real rate into its two components, the nominal rate and the relative movement of national price levels. The differential-inflation component is not at all significant. Whether due to its much smaller variance or a lesser tendency to bestir large international cost disparities, the relative price level appears to induce less foreign investment than do exchange-rate movements.

If direct investment seems so sensitive to the current exchange rate, is it also responsive to expected future rates? Our results at this stage are entirely negative. Equation 4 illustrates this finding for *EXP2* (regressive expectations), but the results are equally insignificant for extrapolative and rational expectations and independent of whether nominal exchange rates (as in equation 4) or real exchange rates are used. That our proxies are too simple is a sufficient explanation.

We investigated whether movements of the trade balance of the United States (absolutely, or relative to that of the source country) might wield a short-run influence on direct-investment flows not captured by the exchange rate. This hypothesis is plausible in light of the increasing amount of intrafirm trade carried out by established multinational companies and the apparently greater dependence of exchange-rate movements on disturbances to the capital account than the current account of the balance of payments. As equation 5 shows, *TBDIF* takes the expected negative sign and is significant (5 percent, one-tail test); if TB_{US} (the U.S. value alone) is substituted, its expected positive coefficient takes a t-statistic only around 1.0. This hypothesis receives only tenuous support.

The next short-run price determinant is the relative movement of securities prices, governing the cost to foreign investors of acquiring existing assets. The coefficients of *SHDIF* in Table 8-3 are positive and significant in three models, indicating that (with other factors controlled) direct investment is pulled by lower prices of business assets in the United States and pushed by higher prices in the source country. When relative price levels are included (equations 2, 3), however, it becomes insignificant. This qualified positive finding is consistent with the predominance nowadays of transactions in existing business assets among foreign investors, and it affirms the internationalization of the U.S. market for corporate control.

Finally, the lagged profit rate *(PROFIT)* consistently takes a positive coefficient but is not significant.

In the models reported in Table 8-3, we restricted each country's foreign-investment flow to exhibit the same sensitivity to each regressor. Our sparse degrees of freedom in the time-series dimension argue against the otherwise desirable course of allowing each country its own slope coefficient on key determinants. We employed a compromise procedure suggested by the data summarized in Table 8-2. Our fifteen source countries include seven with high average levels of direct investment during 1977-1985 and eight others with diverse but smaller flows. Flows of the "Big 7" differ considerably in their year-to-year regularity, as shown by the coefficients of variation in Table 8-2. We therefore selected three groups as follows:

D1 Canada, France, West Germany, and United Kingdom (high mean, low variance).

Table 8-3. Results of Estimating Model by OLS Regression

	STOCK	YUS	YF	Other Variables	R^2
1.	-1.804	-0.333	9.429	- 2.255 EX + 0.875 SHDIF + 0.053 PROFIT	0.786
	(2.98)	(0.10)	(3.31)	(5.39) (2.11) (0.96)	
2.	-2.337	-1.046	11.460	- 2.202 REX + 0.366 SHDIF + 0.037 PROFIT	0.786
	(4.04)	(0.31)	(4.13)	(5.53) (0.90) (0.69)	
3.	-2.039	-0.522	10.273	- 2.309 EX + 1.046 P_{US}/P_i + 0.646 SHDIF	
	(3.17)	(0.16)	(3.78)	(5.54) (0.89) (1.16)	
				+ 0.047 PROFIT	0.786
				(0.88)	
4.	-1.819	-0.075	9.288	- 1.988 EX - 0.324 EXP2 + 0.907 SHDIF	
	(2.93)	(0.02)	(3.20)	(1.31) (0.18) (1.95)	
				+ 0.050 PROFIT	0.785
				(0.85)	
5.	-1.956	3.976	8.763	- 2.194 EX - 2.838 TBDIF + 1.000 SHDIF	
	(3.24)	(1.00)	(3.05)	(5.35) (2.05) (2.46)	
				+ 0.047 PROFIT	0.789
				(0.83)	

Note: Each equation also includes an intercept and intercept-shift dummies for fourteen of the fifteen countries.

D2 Japan, Netherlands, and Switzerland (high mean and variance).

D3 the remaining eight countries (low mean, high variance).

We defined *Di* as a dummy variable set equal to 1 for observations on countries in the *i*th group and zero for all other observations. We then allowed the coefficient of each appropriate regressor to take a different slope for each group. The results of this exercise are summarized in Table 8-4. In equation 1, the technique is applied to U.S. real GNP *(YUS)*. This procedure yields the expected positive coefficients for *YUS* for groups *D2* and *D3*, but the coefficients are still insignificant. We thus retain the conclusion that the short-run swings in U.S. real GNP exert no confirmed influence on direct-investment flows.[18]

18. Not much should be made of this negative conclusion. Ray (1988), working with disaggregated data on direct-investment inflows from the same source, did find a significant influence for the real growth of U.S. GNP, though not for output growth in the individual recipient industries.

Equation 2 of Table 8-4 applies the technique to the nominal exchange rate *(EX)*, obtaining the result that the exchange-rate sensitivity is greatest in the smaller and (by and large) newer foreign investors in the U.S., but is also significant for the mature foreign investors (*D1*). The same conclusion is reached if the real exchange rate is substituted for the nominal rate (not shown). Our wholly negative findings concerning exchange-rate expectations were confirmed for each of these three groups of countries separately.

Equation 3 applies the technique to the share-price differential *SHDIF*. The results depend somewhat on the other variables included in the model, but *SHDIF*'s significant influence appears for groups *D2* and (in some specifications) *D3* and not *D1*. The mature and large-scale foreign investors in the United States do not seem sensitive to short-run movements of inducement variables, while the newer arrivals are. One can speculate on the factors that dull these sensitivities for the *D1* group. Canada may be a special case—an economy closely linked to the U.S., and subject to little variation in its exchange rate or relative income levels. Also, Canadian (as well as British) foreign investors are large purchasers of land and real estate, for which our model controls poorly if at all. France, Germany, and especially the United Kingdom held large stocks of business assets in the United States at the start of the period, and so their flows are heavily weighted by reinvestment decisions of established multinational companies. We argued above that these are likely to show less short-run sensitivity to the short-run inducement variables than new foreign investments. That explanation does not, however, accord very well with the prevalence of British buyers in the U.S. market for corporate control.

We would expect the influence of lagged profit on existing investments to be strongest for those countries with the most mature stocks. That is confirmed in equation 4, where *PROFIT* is significant for the *D1* group and takes a large though not significant coefficient for *D2*.

One final experiment can be mentioned briefly. The source of our dependent variable gives a breakdown of investments into several classes that can be very roughly grouped into those involving new plant construction (new plants, expansions of existing plants, joint ventures) and others mainly involving the acquisition of land or other existing assets. Some regressors (such as *SHDIF*) should apply mainly to purchases of outstanding assets, while others *(TBDIF)* should mainly influence purchases of new assets. We tried weighting selected regressors by the proportion of the asset type for which each should have an affinity. This maneuver produced small

Table 8-4. Effect of Allowing Selected Slope Coefficients to Differ Among Three Groups of Source Countries

No.	Equation	R^2
1.	$-\underset{(3.07)}{1.953}\,\text{STOCK} - \underset{(0.72)}{2.143}\,\text{YUS*D1} + \underset{(0.18)}{0.656}\,\text{YUS*D2} + \underset{(0.51)}{2.477}\,\text{YUS*D3} + \underset{(3.16)}{9.168}\,\text{YF} - \underset{(5.68)}{2.383}\,\text{EX} + \underset{(1.51)}{0.725}\,\text{SHDIF} + \underset{(1.27)}{0.08}\,\text{PROFIT}$	$R^2 = 0.786$
2.	$-\underset{(3.09)}{2.005}\,\text{STOCK} - \underset{(0.39)}{1.195}\,\text{YUS} + \underset{(3.80)}{10.584}\,\text{YF} - \underset{(2.62)}{1.620}\,\text{EX*D1} - \underset{(0.84)}{0.871}\,\text{EX*D2} - \underset{(5.19)}{2.769}\,\text{EX*D3} + \underset{(1.30)}{1.457}\,\text{INFLDIF} + \underset{(1.34)}{0.769}\,\text{SHDIF} + \underset{(0.90)}{0.047}\,\text{PROFIT}$	$R^2 = 0.786$
3.	$-\underset{(2.87)}{1.753}\,\text{STOCK} - \underset{(0.21)}{0.725}\,\text{YUS} + \underset{(3.21)}{9.519}\,\text{YF} - \underset{(5.09)}{2.237}\,\text{EX} + \underset{(0.32)}{0.277}\,\text{SHDIF*D1} + \underset{(2.60)}{2.392}\,\text{SHDIF*D2} + \underset{(1.92)}{0.842}\,\text{SHDIF*D3} + \underset{(0.88)}{0.048}\,\text{PROFIT}$	$R^2 = 0.786$
4.	$-\underset{(3.40)}{2.046}\,\text{STOCK} + \underset{(1.12)}{4.405}\,\text{YUS} + \underset{(3.25)}{9.603}\,\text{YF} - \underset{(5.36)}{2.150}\,\text{EX} + \underset{(2.17)}{0.899}\,\text{SHDIF} - \underset{(2.02)}{2.874}\,\text{TBDIF} + \underset{(2.36)}{5.952}\,\text{PROFIT*D1} + \underset{(1.07)}{4.546}\,\text{PROFIT*D2} + \underset{(0.90)}{0.051}\,\text{PROFIT*D3}$	$R^2 = 0.790$

Note: Each equation also includes an intercept and intercept-shift dummies for fourteen of the fifteen countries.

increases in the regressors' significance levels, but not enough to count as a substantial finding.

V. SUMMARY AND CONCLUSIONS

This paper has reported preliminary results on the internationalization of certain U.S. markets through the actions of foreign investors based abroad. The role of foreign competitors in major U.S. product and service markets grows more evident from day to day, and it has been demonstrated in a number of statistical studies. The close choices made by many foreign firms between exporting to the United States and establishing production facilities here have been demonstrated statistically, as well as growing increasingly evident to the casual observer. In this paper we have offered provisional evidence of two other forms of internationalization effected by these firms.

1. Given the massive disturbances to the U.S. exchange rate due (apparently) to saving behavior and public finance in the United States and abroad, theory suggests that direct investment flows will take on the short-run guise of stabilizing speculation. That hypothesis is strongly confirmed by our analysis of inflows from fifteen source countries since 1977. This finding is relevant to the debate over whether the genie of market-determined exchange rates should be somehow jammed back into the bottle: however large and/or nonfunctional one feels that exchange-rate swings have been, their amplitude would apparently have been greater had multinational enterprises not adjusted the timing of their long-run investments. While we expect that these transactions have rested on anticipated future exchange rates and not just a mechanical response to current changes, our analysis did not confirm the role of expectations.
2. The press is full of news about transactions by foreign parties in the U.S. market for corporate control, with European corporate raiders in full cry and the Japanese rapidly overcoming their inhibitions. We saw that foreign investment in the United States consists increasingly of buying up established businesses, and our statistical results confirm that foreign investment responds in the expected way to opportunities to arbitrage between the markets for such assets abroad and in the United States. This conclusion affirms one form of internationalization of the U.S. economy that has not been widely appreciated—that the rapidly thickening market for corporate control (and for business divisions traded among multi-activity firms) is on its way to becoming a global rather than a national one.

APPENDIX: SOURCES OF DATA

For reasons explained in the text, the dependent variables considered for this project were not the flows of direct investment reported in the balance of payments (*Survey of Current Business*, March issue, for the preceding year) but two data sources that indicate the business assets of U.S. affiliates of foreign companies.

The measure of the flow of assets into foreign control that we chiefly used is taken from U.S. Department of Commerce, International Trade Administration, *Foreign Direct Investment in the United States: Completed Transactions, 1974-1983* (Washington, DC: Government Printing Office, 1985), vol. I, and subsequent annual publications bearing the same title. This publication, based on published data, records the number of investments from each country and their values (when available). We made the assumption that the average value of reported transactions could be applied to transactions for which no value was reported; examination of the lists of individual investments makes it clear that this procedure by no means overstates the average values of all direct investments—values may be missing more frequently for large than for small transactions. Occasionally no transaction values were reported in a given year for a small investing country; we substituted an average for other small countries, for a similar small country, or for a comparable class of investments. Although this source goes back to 1974, we used it only from 1977 on; despite the large increase in foreign investment during the 1970s shown in the balance-of-payments data, the coverage of the ITA data appears to have increased over 1974-1977. These current-dollar flows for each country were deflated by the U.S. GNP deflator for capital expenditures.

The International Trade Administration's tabulation distinguishes seven classes of foreign investments that allow a rough breakdown into those involving the purchase of new physical capital and those involving the purchase of outstanding assets. Investments in new plants, plant expansions, and joint ventures were included in the former class; acquisitions of companies or business units and of real estate were put in the latter. The allocation of real estate represents a close call. Purchases of land and existing buildings appropriately fall into the acquired-assets category, but new construction does not; we assumed on the basis of impressionistic evidence that the former category has accounted for the majority of the total value of foreign investments in real estate.

The other source of data on acquired business assets is U.S. Department of Commerce, Bureau of Economic Analysis, *Foreign Direct Investment in the United States: Operations of U.S. Affiliates of Foreign Companies.* These data are tabulated annually (from 1977) for a population of affiliates determined by periodic benchmark surveys (most recently 1980). A reporting threshold deletes very small foreign investments. Asset data are reported on a fiscal-year basis, but the bulk of assets are accounted for by affiliates that close their fiscal years in the last quarter of the calendar year. To obtain annual flows of business assets into foreign control from this source, one must first-difference these end-of-year stock values. When we did so, we obtained some puzzling values that disagree sharply with the ITA data. The ITA data do not include sell-offs and shut-downs, of course, but we encountered some negative estimated flows from the BEA data that could not be explained by any large sell-offs that we could detect. The BEA data were therefore put aside.

Exogenous Variables

For bilateral nominal exchange rates against the U.S. dollar we used the data given in International Monetary Fund, *International Financial Statistics* (various issues). These were restated (where necessary) as a price of the U.S. dollar and indexed with 1977=100. To deflate them, we used GNP deflators for the United States and for each of the source countries.

Indexes of share prices were also taken from *International Financial Statistics* (various issues) and expressed in index form based on 1977.

Data on the merchandise trade flows of the United States and the source countries were required to calculate their trade balances. These were taken from OECD, *Main Economic Indicators* (various issues). We did not seek to deflate these data, because they were used only to calculate an index in the form (X-M)/(X+M), which is sensitive to changes in the terms of trade but not the general price level.

To obtain data on real GNPs, we utilized the convenient summary table given in OECD, *OECD Economic Outlook,* no. 41 (1987), Table R1. It provides for each country and year a rate of growth of real GNP, which is readily converted to an index (1977=100).

Profit data were obtained from the machine-readable Bureau of Economic Analysis data source, Table E-2, and divided by the value of owners' equity shown in Table B-4.

The stock-adjustment model requires a value for the lagged stock (taken at the end of the preceding year). We obtained a benchmark figure for the end of 1977 from the BEA, then simply added it to each year's deflated asset acquisitions (that is, the dependent variable). No deduction is made for sell-offs and shutdowns, so this variable is overstated, as is its statistical association with the dependent variable.

REFERENCES

Agmon, Tamir, and Donald G. Lessard. 1977. "Investor Recognition of Corporate International Diversification." *Journal of Finance* 32 (September): 1049-55.

Belli, R. David. 1981. "U.S. Business Enterprises Acquired or Established by Foreign Direct Investors in 1980." *Survey of Current Business* 61 (August): 58-72.

——. 1982. "U.S. Business Enterprises Acquired or Established by Foreign Direct Investors in 1981." *Survey of Current Business* 62 (June): 27-31.

——. 1983. "U.S. Business Enterprises Acquired or Established by Foreign Direct Investors in 1982." *Survey of Current Business* 63 (June): 27-32.

——. 1984. "U.S. Business Enterprises Acquired or Established by Foreign Direct Investors in 1983." *Survey of Current Business* 64 (May): 16-20.

——. 1985. "U.S. Business Enterprises Acquired or Established by Foreign Direct Investors in 1984." *Survey of Current Business* 65 (May): 18-23.

Caves, Richard E. 1982. *Multinational Enterprise and Economic Analysis.* Cambridge: Cambridge University Press.

Caves, Richard E., and Sanjeev Mehra. 1986. "Entry of Foreign Multinationals into U.S. Manufacturing Industries." *Competition in Global Industries.* Ed. Michael E. Porter. Boston: Harvard Business School Press, 449-81.

Cushman, David O. 1985. "Real Exchange Rate Risk, Expectations, and the Level of Direct Investment." *Review of Economics and Statistics* 67 (May): 297-308.

de Grauwe, Paul. 1988. "Exchange Rate Variability and the Slowdown in Growth of International Trade." *IMF Staff Papers* 35 (March): 63-84.

Fatemi, Ali M. 1984. "Shareholder Benefits from Corporate International Diversification." *Journal of Finance* 39 (December): 1325-44.

Helpman, Elhanan. 1984. "A Simple Theory of International Trade with Multinational Corporations." *Journal of Political Economy* 92 (June): 451-71.

Herr, Ellen M. 1987. "U.S. Business Enterprises Acquired or Established by Foreign Direct Investors in 1986." *Survey of Current Business* 67 (May): 27-35.

Hisey, Karen B., and Richard E. Caves. 1985. "Diversification Strategy and Choice of Country: Diversifying Acquisitions Abroad by U.S. Multinationals." *Journal of International Business Studies* 16 (Summer): 51-64.

International Investment Division. 1981. "U.S. Business Enterprises Acquired or Established by Foreign Direct Investors in 1979." *Survey of Current Business* 61 (January): 28-39.

Itagaki, Takao. 1981. "The Theory of the Multinational Firm Under Exchange Rate Uncertainty." *Canadian Journal of Economics* 14 (May): 276-97.

Jun, Joosung. 1986. "Taxation, Capital Mobility, and International Investment." Ph.D. dissertation, Harvard University.

Kohlhagen, Steven W. 1977. "Effects on Capital Flows: Comment." *The Effects of Exchange Rate Adjustments.* Ed. Peter B. Clark, Dennis E. Logue, and Richard J. Sweeney. Washington, DC: U.S. Government Printing Office, 194-7.

Logue, Dennis E., and Thomas D. Willett. 1977. "The Effect of Exchange-Rate Adjustment on International Investment." *The Effects of Exchange Rate Adjustments.* Ed. Peter B. Clark, Dennis E. Logue, and Richard J. Sweeney. Washington, DC: U.S. Government Printing Office, 137-50.

Makin, John H. 1974. *Capital Flows and Exchange-Rate Flexibility in the Post-Bretton Woods Era.* Essays in International Finance, No. 103. Princeton, NJ: International Finance Section, Princeton University.

Marshall, William J., Jess B. Yawitz, and Edward Greenberg. 1984. "Incentives for Diversification and the Structure of the Conglomerate Firm." *Southern Economic Journal* 51 (July): 1-23.

Prachowney, M. F. J. 1972. "Direct Investment and the Balance of Payments of the United States: A Portfolio Approach." *International Mobility and Movement of Capital.* Ed. Fritz Machlup, Walter Salant, and Lorie Tarshis. New York: Columbia University Press for National Bureau of Economic Research, 443-64.

Ray, Edward J. 1988. "The Determinants of Foreign Direct Investment in the United States: 1979-1985." Universities Research Conference on Trade Policies for International Competitiveness, National Bureau of Economic Research.

Reuber, Grant L., and Frank Roseman. 1972. "International Capital Flows and the Takeover of Domestic Companies by Foreign Firms: Canada, 1945-61." *International Mobility and Movement of Capital.* Ed. Fritz Machlup, Walter Salant, and Lorie Tarshis, 465-503. New York: Columbia University Press for National Bureau of Economic Research.

Rowthorn, Robert, with Stephen H. Hymer. 1971. *International Big Business, 1957-1967: A Study of Comparative Growth,* University of Cambridge, Department of Applied Economics, Occasional Paper No. 24. Cambridge: Cambridge University Press.

Ruffin, Roy J., and Farhad Russekh. 1986. "The Role of Foreign Direct Investment in U.S. Capital Outflows." *American Economic Review* 76 (December): 1126-30.

Severn, Alan K. 1972. "Investment and Financial Behavior of American Direct Investors in Manufacturing." *International Mobility and Movement of Capital.* Ed. Fritz Machlup, Walter Salant, and Lorie Tarshis. New York: Columbia University Press for National Bureau of Economic Research, 367-96.

Shea, Michael A. 1986. "U.S. Business Enterprises Acquired or Established by Foreign Direct Investors in 1985." *Survey of Current Business* 66 (May): 47-53.

Stevens, Guy V. G. 1977. "Effects on Capital Flows: Comment." *The Effects of Exchange Rate Adjustments.* Ed. Fritz Machlup, Walter Salant, and Lorie Tarshis. Washington, DC: U.S. Government Printing Office, 183-8.

INDEX

ABOUT THE CONTRIBUTORS

Deborah Battles is Assistant Professor of Economics at the University of Colorado, Colorado Springs.

Harry P. Bowen is Associate Professor of Economics and International Business at the Stern Graduate School of Business at New York University.

Richard E. Caves is Professor of Economics and Business Administration at Harvard University.

Alan V. Deardorff is Professor of Economics and Public Policy at the University of Michigan.

Charles P. Kindleberger is a Ford International Professor of Economics, Emeritus, Massachusetts Institute of Technology.

Albert N. Link is Professor of Economics and Director of the Industrial Technology Program at the University of North Carolina at Greensboro.

Stephen P. Magee is the Fred H. Moore Professor of Finance and Economics at the University of Texas at Austin.

Keith E. Maskus is Associate Professor of Economics at the University of Colorado, Boulder, and Director of the Carl McGuire Center for International Studies.

Rachel McCulloch is Professor of International Finance at Brandeis University. She is also a Research Associate of the National Bureau of Economic Research and a faculty member for the International Forum of the Western Behavioral Sciences Institute.

Michael H. Moffett is Assistant Professor of Finance and International Business at Oregon State University.

L. Fernando Ruiz-Mier is Professor of Economics at the University of North Carolina at Greensboro.

Robert M. Stern is Professor of Economics and Public Policy at the University of Michigan at Ann Arbor.

Leo Sveikauskas is an economist at the Division of Productivity Research of the U.S. Bureau of Labor Statistics.

Hideki Yamawaki is currently at the Wissenschaftszentrum Berlin, where he is engaged in comparative research on European, American, and Japanese market dynamics and corporate policy.

ABOUT THE EDITORS

David B. Audretsch

Since 1985, David B. Audretsch has been a research fellow at the Wissenschaftszentrum Berlin für Sozialforschung. Prior to going to Berlin, he taught economics at Middlebury College and at the University of Wisconsin, where he received his Ph.D. He has been a consultant at the U.S. Federal Trade Commission and U.S. International Trade Commission. His research focuses on the international aspects of industrial organization and technological change.

Michael P. Claudon

Michael P. Claudon is president and managing director of the Geonomics Institute, a nonprofit, nonpartisan organization dedicated to helping countries raise their standards of living by bringing together those who affect government and business policy. He has been a member of the Middlebury College economics faculty since 1970, and currently serves on the Governor's Vermont-Quebec Commission to promote economic and cultural interaction between the United States and Canada. He is the author of numerous articles and books on economics.